Introducing Course Design in English for Specific Purposes

Introducing Course Design in English for Specific Purposes is an accessible and practical introduction to the theory and practice of developing ESP courses across a range of disciplines. The book covers the development of courses from needs analysis to assessment and evaluation, and also comes with samples of authentic ESP courses provided by leading ESP practitioners from a range of subject and global contexts. Included in this book are:

- the basics of ESP course design;
- the major current theoretical perspectives on ESP course design;
- tasks, reflections and glossary to help readers consolidate their understanding;
- resources for practical ESP course development;
- examples of authentic ESP courses in areas such as business, aviation and nursing.

Introducing Course Design in English for Specific Purposes is essential reading for pre-service and in-service teachers, and students studying ESP and applied linguistics.

Lindy Woodrow is Honorary Senior Lecturer at the University of Sydney, Australia.

Routledge Introductions to English for Specific Purposes provide a comprehensive and contemporary overview of various topics within the area of English for specific purposes, written by leading academics in the field. Aimed at postgraduate students in applied linguistics, English language teaching and TESOL, as well as pre- and in-service teachers, these books outline the issues that are central to understanding and teaching English for specific purposes, and provide examples of innovative classroom tasks and techniques for teachers to draw on in their professional practice.

SERIES EDITOR: BRIAN PALTRIDGE

Brian Paltridge is Professor of TESOL at the University of Sydney. He has taught English as a second language in Australia, New Zealand and Italy and has published extensively in the areas of academic writing, discourse analysis and research methods. He is editor emeritus for the journal *English for Specific Purposes* and co-edited the *Handbook of English for Specific Purposes* (Wiley, 2013).

SERIES EDITOR: SUE STARFIELD

Sue Starfield is a Professor in the School of Education and Director of The Learning Centre at the University of New South Wales. Her research and publications include tertiary academic literacies, doctoral writing, writing for publication, identity in academic writing and ethnographic research methods. She is a former editor of the journal *English for Specific Purposes* and co-editor of the *Handbook of English for Specific Purposes* (Wiley, 2013).

For more information on this series visit www.routledge.com/series/RIESP

TITLES IN THIS SERIES

Introducing English for Academic Purposes
Maggie Charles and Diane Pecorari

Introducing Needs Analysis and English for Specific Purposes
James Dean Brown

Introducing Genre and English for Specific Purposes
Sunny Hyon

Introducing English for Specific Purposes
Laurence Anthony

Introducing Course Design in English for Specific Purposes
Lindy Woodrow

Introducing Course Design in English for Specific Purposes

Lindy Woodrow

Routledge
Taylor & Francis Group

LONDON AND NEW YORK

First published 2018
by Routledge
2 Park Square, Milton Park, Abingdon, Oxon OX14 4RN

and by Routledge
711 Third Avenue, New York, NY 10017

Routledge is an imprint of the Taylor & Francis Group, an informa business

British Library Cataloguing-in-Publication Data
A catalogue record for this book is available from the British Library

Library of Congress Cataloging-in-Publication Data
A catalog record for this book has been requested

ISBN: 978-1-138-10065-7 (hbk)
ISBN: 978-1-138-10067-1 (pbk)
ISBN: 978-1-315-14327-9 (ebk)

Typeset in Sabon
by Sunrise Setting Ltd, Brixham, UK

Contents

Figures

Tables

Acknowledgements

One of the most interesting and useful aspects of this book is the inclusion of authentic ESP courses which are not usually available. The courses included in Part 3 cover a range of types of ESP and I am sure will be very useful to ESP practitioners in the field. I am extremely grateful to these course designers who have shared their ESP courses and materials: Catherine Nickerson from Zayed University, Dubai, for her course *Language in the workplace*; Susan Bosher from St. Catherine University, St. Paul, for her course *English for cross-cultural nursing*; Jill Northcott from Edinburgh University for her course *English for lawyers;* Joan Cutting for her course *Airport English;* Brian Paltridge from the University of Sydney for his course *Writing for publication;* Maggie Charles from Oxford University for her course *Writing in your field with corpora*; and Zuocheng Zhang from the University of New England for his *Programme for business-English majors*.

I also wish to thank the following for granting me permission to reproduce text and tables. In Chapter 5, BALEAP for EAP teacher-competency statements presented in Table 5.2. In Chapter 6, Janet Jones and Helen Bonanno (2007) and the University of Sydney for Table 6.1, the MASUS assessment grid. In Chapter 10, Shelley Staples and *English for Specific Purposes* (2015) for Tables 10.1 (Generic structure of patient–nurse interactions) and 10.2 (Lexico-grammatical features of patient–nurse interactions). In Chapter 12, Thawa Bosowon, my co-author, and *RELC Journal* (2009) for Figure 12.3. In Chapter 15, S. Wozniak (2010) and *English for Specific Purposes* for the excerpt from 251–2 on needs analysis; Y. Deutch (2003) and the *Journal of English for Academic Purposes* for the excerpt from 142–4 on needs analysis; Paul Spence and Gi Zen Liu and *English for Specific Purposes* (2013) for the excerpt from 107–8 on needs analysis; and Clarice Chan (2009) and *English for Specific Purposes* for the excerpt from 132 of a checklist for evaluating materials.

My thanks go to Brian Paltridge and Sue Starfield for their unfailing support and to Helen Tredget from Routledge who was extremely helpful during the production of this book.

Abbreviations in English for specific purposes

AWL	Academic Word List
BALEAP	The British Association Lecturers in English for Academic Purposes
BASE	British Academic Spoken English Corpus
BAWE	British Academic English Written Corpus
BE	Business English
BESIG	Business English special-interest group
BEC	Business English Certificate
BELF	Business English as a lingua franca
BNC	British National Corpus
BULATS	Business Language Testing Service
CAE	Cambridge Advanced English
CALL	Computer-assisted language learning
CANCODE	Cambridge and Nottingham Corpus of Discourse in English
CARS	Creating a research space
CBI	Content-based instruction
CEFR	Common European Framework of Reference
CLIL	Content and language integrated learning
CLT	Communicative-language teaching
COCA	Corpus of Contemporary American English
CPE	Cambridge Proficiency English
DOD	Department of Defence
EAL	English as an additional language
EALP	English for academic legal purposes
EAP	English for academic purposes
EBP	English for business purposes
EFNOP	English for no obvious purpose
EGP	English for general purposes
EGAP	English for general academic purposes
EGBP	English for general business purposes
ELF	English as a lingua franca
ELP	English for legal purposes

ELT	English language teaching
EMI	English mediated instruction
EMP	English for medical purposes
EOLP	English for occupational legal purposes
EOP	English for occupational purposes
EPP	English for professional purpose
ESAP	English for specific academic purposes
ESBP	English for specific business purposes
ESCP	English for socio-cultural purposes
ESP	English for specific purposes
ESPIS	English for specific purposes special-interest section
EST	English for science and technology
EVP	English for vocational purposes
E4W	English for work
E4WP	English for the workplace
FCE	First Certificate in English
GSL	General Service List
IATEFL	International Association of Teachers of English as a Foreign Language
IEEE	Institute of Electrical and Electronics Engineers
IELTS	English Language Testing System
KET	Key English Test
KWIC	Keyword in context
LMS	Learning management system
MBA	Master of Business Administration
MT+2	Mother tongue plus two (other languages)
NA	Needs analysis
OET	Occupational English Test
PBL	Problem-based learning
PET	Preliminary English Test
SFL	Systemic functional linguistics
TBL	Task-based learning
TEEP	Test of English for Educational Purposes
TOEFL	Test of English as a Foreign Language
TOEIC	Test of English for International Communication
TOLES	Test of Legal English Skills
VOICE	Vienna–Oxford International Corpus of English
WBE	Wolverhampton Corpus of Business English

Introduction
How to use this book

This book introduces course design in English for specific purposes (ESP), which covers English for academic purposes, English for business purposes and English for occupational purposes. The book can be used by practising ESP teachers, teachers who would like to move into ESP teaching, pre-service English teachers and those who are studying ESP as part of an academic or practical TESOL course. The aim of this book is to enable readers to have a good understanding of ESP and be able to design an ESP course. This is achieved by using a mixture of theory, research, reflection, tasks and resources.

The book is structured in a way to promote learning about ESP and course design. Part 1 addresses the major issues in ESP and course design, Part 2 addresses the current theoretical perspectives informing ESP course design and Part 3 presents eight authentic ESP course outlines and sample materials.

To facilitate learning, each chapter in Parts 2 and 3 includes reflections, tasks, further reading and a chapter on resources.

Reflections address your current knowledge and thinking about the topic of the chapter. These reflections can be done individually or with a fellow student or colleague.

Tasks lead the reader to consider applications of the chapter content to teaching and learning situations.

Further reading suggestions include the central works in the area and consolidate the issues presented in each chapter.

Resources Chapter 15 presents a range of resources which can be used by ESP practitioners. These include templates useful in course design, internet and published resources and professional ESP organisations.

Building on the chapters in Parts 1 and 2, Part 3 presents examples of courses where the major issues in ESP are illustrated. Each of these courses includes sample materials, which are followed by tasks.

The appendix includes a selection of suggested articles which could be used for seminar presentations or posters. Thinking and reading about ESP courses and then presenting findings to others is an excellent way to consolidate learning.

Finally, a glossary of the major terms in ESP and course design is included.

Part 1

Essential aspects of English for specific purposes

Chapter 1

Overview of English for specific purposes (ESP)

This chapter aims to provide a foundation in the major issues in English for specific purposes (ESP) which underpin current thinking in ESP curriculum and course design. ESP theorising is informed by teaching and learning contexts, with curriculum and course design at its core. Essentially, ESP courses are focused on the needs of the learners and other stakeholders, such as employers and universities. The focus of an ESP course may be narrow or broad. The chapter presents an overview of the development of ESP and its different branches. This includes English for occupational purposes and English for socio-cultural purposes, both of which are recent areas of ESP. The chapter defines ESP and discusses the classification of ESP.

What is ESP?

ESP may be considered as an approach to course design and teaching that targets groups of learners who have a common goal or purpose in learning English. This may be an educational or occupational focus. The single most defining feature of ESP courses is that they are based on the analysis of learner needs. This important aspect of ESP course design is addressed in Chapter 2.

Dudley-Evans and St. John (1998) refer to the absolute and variable characteristics of ESP. The absolute characteristics of ESP courses are:

1 Designed to meet the needs of the learner.
2 Make use of the methodology and activities of the disciplines it serves.
3 Centred on the language, skills and genres appropriate to these disciplines.

The variable characteristics of ESP courses are:

1 May be related to specific disciplines.
2 May use different methodologies to English for general purposes (EGP).
3 Likely to be designed for adult learners.
4 Generally designed for intermediate or advanced leaners.

ESP is sometimes contrasted with to English for general purposes (EGP). This is somewhat controversial, with Dudley-Evans and St. John (1998) making a rather tongue-in-cheek reference to EGP as EFNOP – English for no obvious purpose. The basic tenet of ESP is that it is based on learner needs; of course, this can also be the case for EGP. However, to highlight the major characteristics of ESP, I have presented the commonly referred to differences between EGP and ESP in Table 1.1.

Generally, ESP courses tend to be for adult learners as they are more likely to have specific needs related to their study or occupation. However, there is a branch of ESP referred to as English for educational purposes, which is EAP for school age students (Cruickshank, 2009). ESP learners tend to have more focused goals than EGP learners. For example, an English for business purposes course focuses on the needs of business professionals in terms of a specific range of knowledge and skills, whereas an EGP course seeks to cover the whole range of grammar and lexis in the language with the goal of general language proficiency. ESP learners may have more externally oriented motivation. For example, an EAP learner may hope to enter an English-speaking university. EGP leaners, on the other hand, may have a range of motives for learning the language. In a school setting where

Table 1.1   Some typical characteristics of ESP and EGP courses

ESP	EGP
Adult learners	Any age learners
Learners have a common goal	Learners have a wide range of goals
Learners have high external motivation	Learners have a range of motivation
Are short term	Are long term
Based on needs analysis	May not bear in mind student needs
Have an academic, professional or workplace focus	Have no specific focus
Have specific content	Have general content
Are based on specific target communication	May include limited exposure to target communicative events
Learners usually have a basic command of English	Learners may be at all levels, including absolute beginners
Focus on specific lexis	A full range of lexis is included
May have a limited focus on grammar	Usually incorporates the full grammatical system. This may be the central organisational strand in the syllabus
A limited range of skills taught – for example, writing and speaking	All four skills are taught with equal focus
ESP courses may be taught with methodologies relevant to the content field	Methodology tends to be similar across courses adopting current thinking in English-language teaching in the region

English is mandatory, students may lack motivation. Given that ESP learners may have more focused learning goals and that the courses attempt to achieve these, it is likely for an ESP course to be for a specified period of time, whereas in EGP in schools, students may learn English for the entirety of their school and university education. Typically, an ESP course is based on a needs analysis arising from academic or workplace settings. As far as possible this setting will inform the informational content of the courses provided and will focus on the target communicative situations the learner is likely to encounter. EGP, on the other hand, may not reflect learner needs but be based on content which is selected based on potential interest. EGP courses do not always reflect the target communicative situations the learner will encounter. Because ESP courses are focused on a full range of lexis and grammar, these may not be included in the course, and the course is likely to be of limited duration. EGP, on the other hand, is often long-term, as is the case in school English. Finally, in terms of methodology, ESP courses often employ the dominant methodology from the content field rather than the prevalent view of English-language-teaching methodology. For example, problem-based learning (PBL) is popular in English for medical purposes because this is the dominant methodology in medical studies, while communicative-language-teaching methodology is the chosen approach in many EGP courses.

Of course, these are generalisations and we can find EGP courses with more of the characteristics of ESP, and ESP courses that have more features of EGP.

Reflection 1.1

Characteristics of English courses

What types of English course are you familiar with? Which of the characteristics listed in Table 1.1 do they reflect?

Task 1.1

Examples of English courses

Think about each of the characteristics of ESP and EGP courses listed in Table 1.1. Give an example how each of these may occur in courses you are familiar with. These characteristics are not absolute. Can you think of any situations where the above would not apply?

Classification of ESP

ESP is usually classified into two main branches: English for academic purposes (EAP) and English for occupational purposes (EOP). Within these two main divisions there are many subdivisions and overlaps based on the setting, level of experience and field of ESP.

Figure 1.1 presents a classification of EAP. EAP is primarily classified as English for general academic purposes (EGAP) and English for specific academic purposes (ESAP). In EGAP, the learners may come from a range of specialisations. So, for example, students who will study medicine, mathematics and history at university may be in the same English class. In this case, materials that are of general academic interest are used. The generally held belief of course designers and practitioners of EGAP is that academic English comprises a range of general academic language abilities that can be transferred to a range of different academic situations regardless of the setting or subject area. In ESAP, the learners are from similar backgrounds – for example, business. In this case, materials are directly relevant to the learners' intended area of study. This notion of specificity is a central theme in ESP and is discussed in detail in later chapters. ESP courses may also be classified by when they occur. For example, EAP courses may be pre-sessional, occurring before the students engage in academic study. These courses are often EGAP. Or they may be exam-oriented to train students in the skills and strategies necessary to achieve university-entry requirements, such as levels in IELTS or TOEFL. Foundation courses are a unique type of EAP course that includes EAP and subject tuition and are usually direct-entry programmes for entrance to a university. In this case, students often need a lower admission English score than for their chosen academic programme. They then complete a foundation course and are guaranteed entry to their academic programme provided they pass the foundation course. A further type of EAP course is the in-sessional course. Such courses are designed to help students while they are studying and are likely to be more specific. Each of these types of course is explored in more detail in Part 2, with examples of courses in Part 3.

Figure 1.2 illustrates a classification of EOP. As with EAP, specificity also plays an important role in EOP. EOP courses can be general. A general English for medical purposes course could be developed that includes

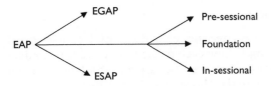

Figure 1.1   Classification of English for academic purposes (EAP)

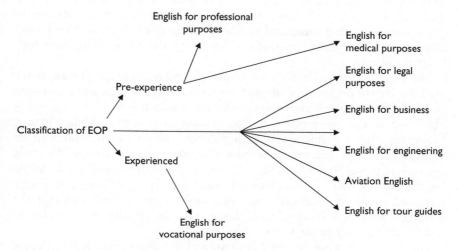

Figure 1.2 Classification of English for occupational purposes (EOP)

the essential features of medical discourse. There is a wealth of published textbooks available in this area – for example, Glendinning and Howard's (2007) *Professional English in use: Medicine.* This makes it possible to design a course without in-depth analysis of the participants' communicative needs. A course for a group with very specific needs – an example might be English for triage nurses in the accident and emergency unit at a hospital – would lie at the other end of the scale of specificity.

A further distinction in EOP is that of experience. Courses can occur before students have any work experience. In pre-experience EOP, the English course may be part of an undergraduate or graduate professional degree such as business, law or medicine. In this respect, there is an overlap between EOP and EAP. In EOP courses for learners with work experience, the learners will be able to make much more of a contribution to the identification of their communicative needs.

EOP is often classified by whether the area may be classed as professional or vocational. For example, English for legal purposes would be classified as professional, whereas English for tour guides would be classed as vocational.

History of ESP

ESP is a relatively recent branch of English-language teaching (ELT). It originated in the 1960s, driven by an accelerated world economy, itself driven by the increase in the demand for oil and an overall increase in international trade. There was a need to communicate on a global scale to facilitate and participate in this economic surge. English became the language of choice.

This led to an increase in international students at universities in English-speaking countries. ESP was a response to this need, and its aim was to equip learners with a command of English in an efficient manner by basing courses on what students actually needed rather than teaching the whole language system.

The earliest ESP was in the area of science and technology. The approach used for course design was labelled register analysis. It was sentence-based and focused on the grammar and vocabulary of scientific texts. The materials published in this early phase of ESP tended to follow a similar format, beginning with a technical and rather dense reading passage followed by manipulation-type grammar exercises and vocabulary exercises. An early example of this is Herbert's (1965) *The structure of technical English*. While Herbert's book was based on sound linguistic analysis, it focused on a very restricted range of vocabulary and grammar. Another issue was that the materials were very hard to teach because of the density of the passages and the complexity of the tasks.

The 1970s saw a move towards rhetorical functions. This approach saw a focus on functions such as comparison, definition and cause and effect. There was also a move away from the sentence as the unit of language. Again, the focus was mainly on science and technology, with an emphasis on how grammar and vocabulary relate to the rhetorical purpose of texts. It is from this background that ESP discourse analysis emerged in later years. Examples of early work in this area come from Swales (1971) and Bates and Dudley-Evans (1976–82). This work was sponsored by the British Council and focused on the oil and petroleum industry in the Middle East.

The 1970s also saw the advent of needs-based ESP courses with Munby's (1978) *Communicative syllabus design*. Munby classified needs based on interlocutors and situations in the learners' target communicative situations. This sounds quite logical, but Munby's model of a Communicative Needs Processor (CNP) based on his PhD is very complex, with a large number of subcategories. The model sought to capture a wide range of contextual influences – for example, by taking into account the status and background of the speakers and the intended purpose of communication. However, the CNP was not practical enough for application to the average ESP teaching course.

The 1980s saw a focus on study skills in EAP for the first time with the University of Malaya project *Skills for learning* (1980). The approach emphasised skills such as "getting to know the parts of a book". These were accompanied by the rationale for the skill. A similar approach was taken by the *Reading and thinking in English* series published by Oxford University Press, which shifted from a focus on functions, such as definition and describing a process, and notions, such as time. The authors attempted to focus on discourse, which examines the text beyond the sentence level.

The work of Hutchinson and Waters (1985) has had a significant impact on ESP. Their work in the 1980s was characterised by an emphasis on the target situation of the learners. This encompassed both immediate learning needs and future needs. They proposed a 'learning centred' approach to ESP, which they claim is based on "the principle that learning is totally determined by the learner". While giving voice to learner needs, this perspective has been expanded in recent years to consider the context of the learning and the needs of stakeholders involved in the ESP process. They also claimed that there was no such thing as ESP language, which, again, has been contradicted in recent years through corpus studies that have investigated patterns of language in large-scale corpora (Handford, 2010).

The 1990s saw a diversification of research in ESP, with a wide range of courses emerging. For example, there was more focus on vocational types of ESP (Johns, 2013). A key scholar during this era was John Swales. Building on previous work on rhetorical structure, Swales focused on identifying genres with an emphasis on generic stages or moves within a given type of text. Genre as the basis of course design remains very significant in current research and practice in ESP. The attraction of this approach to course design is that any text can be analysed for genre – that is, regular features and text moves. By establishing a corpus of texts and analysing these with the help of technology, regular features of texts can be identified and translated into an ESP syllabus

The use of corpora of lexis or texts and computer technology has led to corpus studies. Corpus studies use computer databases to identify lexical and grammatical patterns found in large numbers of texts to inform ESP course design. For instance, Lee and Swales (2006) developed a course for non-native-speaker doctoral students based on existing and student generated corpora.

The role of English

English plays a special role in the world today. It is often referred to as 'English as a lingua franca' (ELF), as it is frequently used as a means of communication between non-native speakers of English. English is the language of communication of business, of professions and of academia. In the early days of ESP, the model of English promoted was that of native-English-speaking countries. This model of English privileged speakers from native-speaker cultures over non-native speakers of English. However, in a seminal work, Kachru (1992) outlined a framework of world Englishes that acknowledged models of English that are used in countries other than native-English-speaking countries such as the UK, USA and Australia. For example, Indian English has its own characteristics, which are entirely appropriate in the setting in which it is used. Kachru's framework comprises three circles: the inner circle, the outer circle and the expanding circle. The inner circle represents native speakers. It is estimated that there are more than 400 million users of English in this category (Simons et al., 2015). The outer

Table 1.2 Timeline of ESP

Time	Approach	Example
1960s	Register analysis	Herbert, A. J. (1965) *The structure of technical English* Ewer, J. R. & Latorre, G. (1969) *Course in basic scientific English*
1970s	Rhetorical functions	Allen, J. P. B. & Widdowson, H. G. (1974) *English in physical science* (*English in focus* series). Bates, M. & Dudley-Evans, T. (1976–82) *Nucleus* series Swales, J. (1971) *Writing scientific English* Trimble, L. (1985) *English for science and technology: A discourse approach* Munby, J. (1978) *Communicative syllabus design*
1980s	Study skills	University of Malaya (1980) *Skills for learning* Moore, J. (1980) *Reading and thinking in English*
	Learning-centred	Hutchison, T. & Waters, A. (1985) *ESP at the crossroads*
1990s–present day	Genre	Swales, J. (1990) *Genre analysis: English in academic and research settings* Paltridge, B. (2001) *Genre and the language learning classroom* Swales, J. (2004) *Research genres, exploration and applications.*
	Corpus	Biber, D. & Conrad, S. (2009) *Register, genre and style* Coxhead, A. (2000) *A new academic word list*

circle represents ESL speakers where English is a widely spoken language – for example, India and Malaysia. It is estimated that there are more than 400 million users in this category (Simons *et al.*, 2015). The expanding circle represents EFL speakers where English is a foreign language – for example, China and Egypt. It is estimated that there are more than 400 million users in this category (Simons *et al.*, 2015). The emphasis on the number of users has had an enormous effect on ESP thinking and the teaching of English and has brought into question the ownership of English. Native speakers can no longer be thought of as the proprietors of the language as they constitute a minority of the total number of English users. Today, the boundaries between the circles is blurring, with the important distinction being the level of proficiency in English (Graddol, 2006). The focus on geographic regions is no longer as significant because of the rapid adoption of ELF, which is a reflection of the wide use of English by non-native speakers.

ELF has had a great influence on English for business, leading to the term 'business English as a lingua franca' (BELF) (Nickerson, 2013). English has become an essential aspect of the job for many business professionals (Kankaanranta & Louhiala-Salminen, 2010). This has great implications for ESP course design. In particular, the level of specificity of ESP and the use of appropriate models of English are determined by the contexts in which communication will occur.

As well as an increase in English-language learners and users there has been a similar development in the number and status of non-native-speaker teachers. There are many more non-native than native English teachers.

Task 1.2

ELF and ESP

How do you think ELF influences the following types of ESP?

1   English for business purposes
2   English for academic purposes
3   English for professional purposes

To what extent do you think a native-speaker norm is relevant to each?

Types of ESP

There are many different terms for types of ESP, although, in reality, many of these overlap. Thus an English for science and technology (EST) course could be a pre-experience course at university for engineering students so could be classed as an EAP course. If the EST course was designed for post-experience engineers then it could be classed as an EOP course. The following section presents a few of the types of course commonly referred to in the field of ESP. These types of courses are further explored in Part 2, and examples are provided in Part 3.

English for science and technology (EST)

This branch of ESP was the first area of ESP to evolve. Generally, the focus of EST is on the technical and semi-technical vocabulary of scientific texts, the commonly found grammatical structure in them and their genres – for example, a laboratory report. In EST, perhaps more than many other areas of ESP, there is often a mismatch between the ESP teacher's disciplinary knowledge and experience (Parkinson, 2013) and that of the target group, with many ESP teachers coming from a humanities or social-sciences background.

The current trend in EST, as with other areas of ESP, focuses on the target disciplinary community – for example, postgraduate research students investigating biochemistry. The role of the EST teacher is to help the learners integrate into their intended disciplinary community by using accepted ways of communicating. This community may be within an academic setting or a professional setting.

English for academic purposes (EAP)

English for academic purposes focuses on students' communicative needs at university. This is a very large area that has received a great deal of research interest. Students at English-language universities need to learn the appropriate forms, lexis and genres relevant to their discipline and academic level. So, for example, English for undergraduates will be different from English for research students; English for chemistry students will be very different from English for social-work students. Again, the notion of context is central to current thinking in EAP. As in EST, there are disciplinary differences, with each disciplinary community having its own communicative norms. Unlike EST, most EAP teachers have direct personal knowledge of academic requirements, as probably all EAP teachers have at least some experience of studying at university.

One of the biggest problems facing EAP is the notion of specificity: how specific should or can an EAP course be? The emphasis of a large amount of EAP in many countries is on preparatory courses. These courses prepare students for entry to university and may be delivered in the student's home country prior to departure or in the destination country prior to commencing academic study. Such preparatory courses prepare students to pass university language entry requirements – for example, IELTS and TOEFL. In addition, many universities stipulate that students need to study and pass courses at a language centre prior to entry. These courses are nearly always general in nature. There is much discussion as to the level of efficacy (transfer) of such courses (Green, 2015), suggesting that preparatory EGAP courses may be of limited value. For example, general academic texts may use very different language and concepts from discipline specific texts.

Business English

English for business purposes (EBP) is often referred to today as business English (BE). This is addressed in detail in Nickerson and Planken's (2016) book in this series, *Introducing business English*. EBP is distinct from other types of ESP in the extent to which English is used to facilitate intercultural communication between non-native English speakers. English is the global language of business communication and transaction and, as indicated above, the concept of BELF is very important in ESP research. The use of English in the business world is so prevalent today that it has become a necessary tool for international business professionals.

A similar distinction in terms of specificity is drawn with BE as with EAP. English for general business purposes (EGBP) refers to courses that usually aim to instruct in business as well as language and can be classed as pre-experience. Many universities feature such courses as part of their curriculum. Cambridge English Examinations offers a series of Business English Certificates targeting pre-experience students. English for specific business purposes (ESBP) is more likely to be aimed at experienced or in-service professionals who need English to do their job.

English for occupational purposes

English for occupational purposes (EOP) covers a broad range of types of ESP, some of which are explored below (other terms are 'English for vocational purposes' (EVP) and 'English for professional purposes' (EPP)). EOP is likely to be very specific and quite narrow in focus. Where an EGBP course for general business may mirror a general English course, presenting a full range of grammatical structure and vocabulary, EOP is likely to offer only those structures and vocabulary relevant to the communicative needs of the occupation. For example, Gordon (2002) presents an ESP course for entry-level manufacturing workers. The workers' course enabled them to talk about their work processes, complete orders, understand safety measures and communicate with other workers and supervisors.

English for work and the workplace (E4W and E4WP) sees the workplace as being the curriculum and classroom (Roberts, 2005). This area of ESP has an increasing research base (Marra, 2013). Typically, a workplace course would be based on a discourse analysis of the language that is used to complete the work tasks. However, recent research has paid attention to relational language, which enables the student to adapt to the culture of the workplace by emphasising the language of social interactions with workmates (Marra *et al.*, 2011).

English for medical purposes

While English for medical purposes (EMP) may be considered as a branch of EOP, it represents a large sector of ESP. There are two main considerations in EMP research. The first focuses on English as the international language of medical research. In this respect, it shares some features of EAP. For example, the teaching focus may be on the generic structure of a medical-journal article or on presenting research at a conference (Ferguson, 2013). The second consideration stems from the large numbers of migrant medical workers needing English to execute their work. This includes both clinical communication concerning medical procedures and treatments, and doctor–patient interactions, such as adopting an appropriate 'bedside manner'. In addition, EMP may provide pre-experience for medical students or for experienced doctors – for example, the case of a migrant doctor taking up employment in an English-speaking country. EMP course design tends to be localised. Typically, the discourse in a given clinical setting is analysed and courses developed on this basis (Shi *et al.*, 2001).

English for nurses

Within EMP, English for nursing is a somewhat recent phenenomen, which contrasts the use of English of doctors and other healthcare professionals with that of nurses. Recent years have seen a growing demand for nurses in Western countries, resulting in large numbers of international students enrolling in nursing degrees in native-English-speaking countries and an increase in the recruitment of nurses from non-English-speaking backgrounds, such as South America.

Cultural understanding is very important in nursing. Differing cultures have different norms concerning death, illness and sexuality. It is important nurses understand the norms of the target community, be these academic norms of supervisors or those of patients (Bosher, 2013).

English for legal purposes

English for legal purposes (ELP), or legal English (LE), is another expanding area of ESP and worthy of a separate category. As is the case with occupational types of ESP, it may be divided, into English for academic legal purposes (EALP), English for occupational legal purposes (EOLP) and English for general legal purposes (EGLP). EALP focuses on the communicative needs of students of law, while EOLP focuses on the needs of practitioners. EGLP focuses on very general legal language, and it may focus on legal texts that require specialist knowledge. The issues in ELP reflect the distinct features of legal language (Northcott, 2013). Legal language poses problems for ESP teachers and translators because of the specificity and complexity of the use of language (Northcott & Brown, 2006).

English for socio-cultural purposes

The final section in this chapter concerns English for socio-cultural purposes. It should be remembered that all ESP benefits from a socio-cultural focus. This means taking into consideration the social and cultural setting in which the communication occurs. This is the central tenet of an academic-literacies approach to EAP (Lea & Street, 1999). English for socio-cultural purposes (ESCP) is typically used to refer to the type of English course provided for immigrants and refugees. Research in Australia is prominent in this field, as the country has a high number of immigrants and refugees who are provided with English classes on arrival. De Silva Joyce and Hood (2009) refer to these types of course as "English for community membership". The aim of these courses is not only to improve English skills but to enable students to integrate into the local community. Morgan and Fleming (2009) use the term 'citizenship' to cover the aims of such courses. First-language literacy may be an issue with some refugees originating from troubled areas in the world. This means that transfer from L1 literacy to L2 literacy is not possible, so such ESP courses need to have basic literacy skills included.

Summary

This chapter serves as an introduction to the history and classification of ESP. It has presented a brief description of the different areas of ESP defined by student purpose, such as English for academic purposes, business English, English for occupational purposes and English for vocational purposes. Each of the types of ESP referred to in this chapter will be investigated in more depth in Part 2 and followed by examples of courses in Part 3.

Task 1.3

Types of ESP course

What type of ESP course do you think each of the following is? Think about whether the course is general or specific, pre- or post-experience.

1   A course for a group of ten Swiss mountain guides who need English to take groups of tourists into the mountains. They are being released for half a day per week to study English.
2   A course for a group of recently arrived refugees, from various countries, in Australia. Ultimately, they want to find jobs. The government provides English classes for 10 hours per week.
3   A group of students who will be studying for various Master's degrees at a UK university. They study English full-time at the language centre attached to the university. They need to pass the English course to continue with their studies.
4   A group of 10 international education undergraduates who are at risk of failing their teaching practice because of poor oral skills. They only have two available hours per week for an English class.
5   A group of newly recruited doctors at a UK hospital. The doctors are from non-English speaking backgrounds. They have a four-week intensive English course before they take up their positions.

Further reading

Lawrence Anthony's book in this series, *Introducing English for specific purposes* (forthcoming), is a solid up-to-date overview of the field. Dudley-Evans and St. John (1998) have a good chapter on the background to ESP until the 1990s; they also describe the classification of ESP. For the history of ESP, Swales' (1985) *Episodes in ESP* provides many examples of approaches and courses of ESP from the 1960s to the late 1980s.

References

Allen, J. P. B., & Widdowson, H. G. (1974). *English in physical science (In focus series)*. Oxford: Oxford University Press.

Anthony, L. (forthcoming) *Introducing English for specific purposes*. London: Routledge.

Bates, M., & Dudley-Evans, T. (1976). *Nucleus: General science*. Harlow: Longman.

Bates, M., & Dudley-Evans, T. (1976–82). *Nucleus* series. Harlow: Longman.

Biber, D., & Conrad, S. (2009). *Register, genre and style*. Oxford: Oxford University Press.

Bosher, S. (2013). English for nursing. In B. Paltridge & S. Starfield (Eds.), *The handbook of English for specific purposes* (pp. 263–82). Oxford: Wiley-Blackwell.

Coxhead, A. (2000). A new academic word list. *TESOL Quarterly, 34*(2), 213–38.

Cruickshank, K. (2009). EAP in secondary schools. In D. Belcher (Ed.), *English for specific purposes in theory and practice* (pp. 22–40). Ann Arbor, MI: University of Michigan Press.

De Silva Joyce, H., & Hood, S. (2009). English for community membership: Planning for actual and potential needs. In D. Belcher (Ed.), *English for specific purposes in theory and practice* (pp. 244–63). Ann Arbor, MI: Uiversity of Michigan Press.

Dudley-Evans, T., & St. John, M. (1998). *Developments in English for specific purposes: A multi-disciplinary approach*. Cambridge: Cambridge University Press.

Ewer, J. R., & Latorre, G. (1969). *Course in basic scientific English*. Harlow: Longman.

Ferguson, G. (2013). English for medical purposes. In B. Paltridge & S. Starfield (Eds.), *The handbook of English for specific purposes* (pp. 243–62). Oxford: Wiley-Blackwell.

Glendinning, E., & Howard, R. (2007). *Professional English in use: Medicine*. Cambridge: Cambridge University Press.

Gordon, J. (2002). An ESP program for entry-level manufacturing workers. In T. Orr (Ed.), *English for specific purposes* (pp. 147–60). Alexandria, VA: TESOL.

Graddol, D. (2006). *English next: Why global English may mean the end of 'English as a foreign language'*. London: British Council.

Green, A. (2015). Teaching for transfer: Hugging and bridging revisited. *English for Specific Purposes, 37*(1), 1–12.

Handford, M. (2010). What can a corpus tell us about specialist genres? In A. O'Keefe & M. McCarthy (Eds.), *The Routledge handbook of corpus linguistics* (pp. 255–69). London: Routledge.

Herbert, A. J. (1965). *The structure of technical English*. Harlow: Longman.

Hutchinson, T., & Waters, A. (1985). ESP at the crossroads. In J. Swales (Ed.), *Episodes in ESP* (pp. 174–87). Oxford: Pergamon.

Johns, A. M. (2013). The history of English for specific purposes research. In B. Paltridge & S. Starfield (Eds.), *The handbook of English for specific purposes* (pp. 5–30). Oxford: Wiley-Blackwell.

Kachru, B. B. (1992). *World Englishes*. Cambridge: Cambridge University Press.

Kankaanranta, A., & Louhiala-Salminen, L. (2010). "English? – Oh, it's just work!": A study of BELF users' perceptions. *English for Specific Purposes*, 29(3), 204–9. doi: 10.1016/j.esp.2009.06.004.

Lea, M., & Street, B. (1999). Writing as academic literacies: Understanding textual practices in higher education. In C. Candlin & K. Hyland (Eds.), *Writing: Texts, processes and practices* (pp. 62–81). London: Longman.

Lee, D., & Swales, J. (2006). A corpus based EAP course for NNS doctoral students: Moving from available specialised corpora to self-compiled corpora. *English for Specific Purposes*, 25(1), 56–71.

Marra, M. (2013). English in the workplace. In B. Paltridge & S. Starfield (Eds.), *Handbook of English for specific purposes* (pp. 175–92). Oxford: Wiley-Blackwell.

Marra, M., Holmes, J., & Riddiford, N. (2011). Language in the workplace project: Workplace communication for skilled migrants. In M. Krzanowski (Ed.), *English for work and the workplace: Approaches, curricula and materials* (pp. 93–106). Reading: Garnet.

Moore, J. (1980). *Reading and thinking in English*. Oxford: Oxford University Press.

Morgan, B., & Fleming, D. (2009). Critical citizenship practices in ESP and ESL programmes: Canadian and global perspectives. In D. Belcher (Ed.), *English for specific purposes in theory and practice* (pp. 264–88). Ann Arbor, MI: University of Michigan Press.

Munby, J. (1978). *Communicative syllabus design*. Cambridge: Cambridge University Press.

Nickerson, C. (2013). English for specific purposes and English as a lingua franca. In B. Paltridge & S. Starfield (Eds.), *The handbook for English for specific purposes* (pp. 445–60). Oxford: Wiley-Blackwell.

Nickerson, C., & Planken, B. (2016). *Introducing business English*. Abingdon and New York: Routledge.

Northcott, J. (2013). Legal English. In B. Paltridge & S. Starfield (Eds.), *The handbook of English for specific purposes* (pp. 213–26). Oxford: Wiley-Blackwell.

Northcott, J., & Brown, G. (2006). Legal translator training: Partnership between teachers of English for legal purposes and legal specialists. *English for Specific Purposes*, 25(3), 358–75.

Paltridge, B. (2001). *Genre and the language learning classroom*. Ann Arbor, MI: University of Michigan Press.

Parkinson, J. (2013). English for science and technology. In B. Paltridge & S. Starfield (Eds.), *The handbook of English for specific purposes* (pp. 155–74). Oxford: Wiley-Blackwell.

Roberts, C. (2005). English in the workplace. In E. Hinkel (Ed.), *The handbook of language teaching and research* (pp. 117–36). Mahwah, NJ: Lawrence Erlbaum.

Shi, L., Corcos, R., & Storey, A. (2001). Using student performance data to develop an English course for clinical training. *English for Specific Purposes, 20*(3), 267–91.

Simons, G. F., Lewis, P. M., & Fenning, C. D. (2015). *Ethnologue: Languages of the world*. Retrieved 3 March 2015 from www.ethnologue.com/.

Swales, J. (1971). *Writing scientific English*. London: Thomas Nelson.

Swales, J. (1985). *Episodes in ESP*. Oxford: Pergamon Press.

Swales, J. (1990). *Genre analysis: English in academic and research settings*. Cambridge: Cambridge University Press.

Swales, J. (2004). *Research genres: Exploration and applications*. Cambridge: Cambridge University Press.

Trimble, L. (1985). *English for science and technology: A discourse approach*. Cambridge: Cambridge University Press.

University of Malaya Press. (1980). *Skills for learning*. Kuala Lumpur: University of Malaya Press.

Chapter 2

Needs analysis and ESP course design

Needs analysis is the backbone of ESP course design. This chapter aims to provide an up-to-date overview of current thinking in needs analysis in relation to course design and guidance on how to conduct an appropriate needs analysis. The chapter addresses how to identify needs, whose needs should be considered and which methods can be used to collect needs data. The chapter traces the development of a course based on needs analysis. Examples of needs-based courses are presented in Part 3, and examples of needs analysis are included in Chapter 15. This chapter covers the following topics:

- What is needs analysis?
- Types of need
- Stakeholders' perspectives
- Methodologies of needs analysis (reflecting on how needs can be identified)

  o quantitative methods
  o qualitative methods

- From needs analysis to course design

Defining needs analysis

Needs analysis is the first step in the course-design cycle in ESP and refers to the systematic analysis of what learners need in order to operate in the target communicative situation. This is contrasted with the learner's current communicative ability. The ESP course is usually based on the gap between these two. A present-situation analysis may be conducted to discover the learners' immediate needs. These are likely to differ from target needs. Brown (2016, 4) defines needs analysis in ESP very succinctly as "the systematic collection and analysis of all information necessary for defining and validating a defensible curriculum".

Reflection 2.1

Experience with needs analysis

All language courses are informed by a needs analysis to a greater or lesser extent.

If you have teaching experience, give an example where you tried to accommodate learners' needs in your teaching.

If you do not have teaching experience, how do you think you might be able to reflect student needs in your teaching?

To what extent do you think the needs of the student can be reflected in an ESP course?

Whose needs are important?

How do you think needs can be assessed?

When do you think needs analysis should be carried out?

A focus on needs analysis emerged in the early 1970s with the work of the Council of Europe (Richterich & Chancerel, 1977), driven by the language needs of the European Union. In this early work, needs were conceived as a 'target situation' analysis. This refers to the language required to function in the discipline setting – for example, in EBP, an analysis of the language and vocabulary of a business report may be conducted. Based on this idea, John Munby investigated how needs could inform course design in a systematic way. His communicative needs processor (CNP) is a text-based model that identifies parameters of processing to produce a profile of needs. It analyses needs with a high level of precision by considering variables of interlocutor, setting, content, variety of English, attitude and purpose. Munby's work has been extremely influential in the area of ESP course design. Any course designer who plans to engage in a form of needs analysis will find food for thought in Munby's classification of needs by language and pragmatics. However, the micro-focus of the CNP is rather complex and not easily applied to practice.

Much of the early work in needs analysis tended to focus on an analysis of the language used in the target situation (Trimble, 1985). This continues today in a much more contextualised manner with work in genre (see Chapter 9), discourse analysis (see Chapter 10) and the use of corpora (see Chapter 11). Huchinson and Waters (1987) were the first to focus on the learner rather than exclusively on the discourse of the target situation, making ESP more relevant to the individual.

In addition to considering the end goal – the target communicative situation – it is necessary to consider where the learners are currently in terms of language competence. This is referred to as 'present situation'

wants	gaps	requests
desires	motivations	pre-requisites
necessities	deficiencies	essentials
lacks	requirements	x + 1 (x = what the students know already)

Figure 2.1   Synonyms for needs analysis

Source: adapted from Brown (2016).

analysis (Robinson, 1991). Further considerations include the analysis of 'lacks' (Hutchinson & Waters, 1987); this focuses on the difference in skills between the current situation and the target situation. West (1994) also considers learners' pedagogic needs: the learning strategies required to follow an ESP course. We can also consider what a learner 'wants' or thinks he or she needs; and it should be noted that this perception of needs may not be accurate, as the student may not be fully aware of what the target situation requires. The final part of this puzzle is consideration of 'constraints' (Hutchinson & Waters, 1987), also referred to as 'means analysis' (Holliday, 1994). This refers to possible resources, such as staff, materials and classrooms.

Brown (2016) lists some of the large number of synonyms for needs, as shown in Figure 2.1.

Stakeholders' perspectives

The early view of ESP tended to view needs analysis as objective and neutral. However, in any ESP course there are a number of stakeholders: the students, teachers, governing bodies, sponsors and employers. The perceptions of needs, wants, lacks and constraints may differ between the different stakeholders and with the actual requirements of the target communicative situations. Varying levels of power within the stakeholder network can impact on the ESP course that eventuates. For example, Jasso-Aguilar's (2005) seminal study into the needs of hotel maids in Hawaii found that the stakeholders had different perceptions of the target situation and thus of needs and wants. This was in opposition to the actual communicative needs of the maids themselves, which were identified by participant observations. This study highlighted the critical perspective in ESP, whereby the rights of students are also taken into consideration (Benesch, 2001). A further perspective is that stakeholders may not know what the students need. For example, a student who enrols on an EAP course prior to postgraduate study at an English university may have limited knowledge of

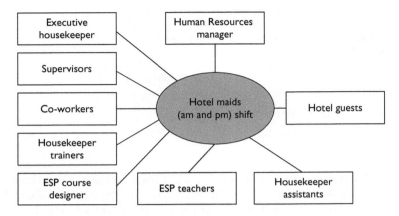

Figure 2.2 Network of stakeholders in ESP course: needs analysis

Source: based on Jasso-Aguilar (2005).

the writing skills required during the postgraduate course. Conversely, the subject specialist on the postgraduate course may have limited knowledge of the language needs and limitations of international students. Hutchinson and Waters (1987) make the distinction between student needs and wants. For example, in Jasso-Aguilar's (2005) study, the hotel maids did not really need much English, but the hotel wanted them to have English skills to enhance the hotel's image. The communicative situation can be conceptualised as a network with all members impacting on the needs. As an example I have used Jasso-Aguilar's (2005) study to generate a network of stakeholders who may impact on a needs analysis. Figure 2.2 shows the network of interlocutors in this situation.

As well as the immediate network of interlocutors in the target situation, a course designer may consult current practitioners, domain experts, past students and past teachers. Inherent in a broad view of needs analysis is research methodology. In addition, the published and unpublished literature on needs analysis of similar courses and the work of researchers in the field should be consulted. Considering needs and data from a large range of sources will make it more likely that the needs identified for analysis will be met.

Methodologies used in collected data about needs

Information about learner needs can be collected using quantitative methods, such as questionnaires, language audits and language tests, and/or qualitative methods, such as interviews, observations and discourse analysis.

Questionnaires and surveys
Text analysis
Language assessment
Previous research filed
Discussions with stakeholders
Interviews (unstructured, semi-structured and structured)
Target-situation observations (participant, non-participant)
Learning-situation observations
Learner diaries, logs and journals
Language audits
Expert and non-expert intuitions
Role-plays and simulations
Corpus analysis
Ethnography

Figure 2.3   Some methods that can be used to collect needs-analysis data

Traditionally, data is collected from stakeholders using questionnaires. Typically, a single questionnaire is given to the sponsor and the intended students. The data is then analysed according to frequency. However, rather than using a universal approach, Long (2005) recommends that data should be collected from a range of sources including research in the area, previous students and courses and domain experts. He argues for triangulation of data sources and methods.

Needs-analysis data may be collected in a range of ways (Figure 2.3) and may involve the students, teachers and domain specialists. This type of data collection would also include information about the present situation, reflecting what the students already know and their preferred learning styles. While these methods provide essential information to help with course design, there is a need for empirical data, too. Empirical data can be collected from target communicative events using methods such as discourse analysis, text analysis and authentic target task observation. Such data is very useful in accurately identifying the actual linguistic and pragmatic requirements of the target situation.

An example of how different methods may be used to collect data is that of Wozniak's (2010) study of the language needs of French mountain guides (see the needs-analysis example in Chapter 15). The analysis started with unstructured interviews with different stakeholders which led to the generation of a needs-analysis questionnaire. In addition, the students' proficiency and issues relating to certification were collected. Such triangulation can minimise the occurrence of error and enhance the credibility of the data (Cowling, 2007).

Task 2.1

Methods of needs analysis

Choose a potential or existing ESP course. Using the list of methods in Figure 2.3:

1 Discuss which of the methods would be most appropriate.
2 Who would you consult?
3 How would you collect the data?

How could you achieve triangulation? (sources and methods)

Settings of needs analysis

The setting of an ESP course influences needs analysis and subsequent course design.

In an academic setting the focus of ESP tends to be on skills. Reading and writing are often highlighted, as these are the major vehicles for the transmission of information and for academic assessment in the target situation. Needs analysis in this setting is often less likely to involve the learners, as institutional demands tend to be inflexible. What this means is that the students are obliged to adhere to norms laid down by the institution rather than be involved in the negotiation of needs as may be the case in other types of ESP course. Benesch questions the power balance inherent in this type of EAP and suggests a critical approach to EAP by proposing a rights analysis. She defines this as "a theoretical tool for EAP teachers and students to consider possible responses to unfavourable social, institutional and classroom conditions" (Benesch, 1996, 102). In critical EAP, the context is viewed as an instrument of social change (Macallister, 2016).

EOP may occur in different settings. It may happen in universities and training institutions or in the workplace. Needs in such settings will differ: in universities and training institutions the present-situation needs of the students will differ greatly from the target-situation needs as students are in the process of learning about the subject and need to fulfil course requirements. As the students are also likely to be pre-experienced, they will be less able to contribute to needs analysis as they have limited knowledge of the communicative situations they will experience in the workplace. In workplace ESP needs analysis can be very focused as the content field may be narrow. Typically, a workplace needs analysis involves the analysis of authentic tasks through on-site observations and ethnographic research.

The learner and needs analysis

It seems only common sense to place the learner at the centre of any needs analysis. Such analysis should take into consideration the learners' lacks and present-situation and target-situation communication needs. However, learners are not always aware of their needs. For example, EGAP students enrolled on a pre-sessional course may be unaware of their academic needs in relation to their chosen degree programme as the educational settings of their prior experience may be quite different. However, it is a good idea to include learners in the needs-analysis process because then they have a sense of ownership and responsibility which can be a motivating force. Holme and Chalauisaeng (2006) refer to needs analysis as an iterative process and formulate a series of qualitative techniques focusing on participatory appraisal to involve learners more in the process of identifying needs and solutions to learning problems. The methods focused on reading and involved class and group discussions and brainstorming.

Task 2.2

Application of methods in needs analysis

Chapter 15 shows three needs analyses:

Example 1	Mountain guides' needs analysis
Example 2	English for engineering
Example 3	Academic Legal English

1 What areas do the instruments target?
2 What do you think are the strengths and weaknesses of each instrument?
3 What would you do with the information gained from these needs analyses?
4 Could these instruments be used or adapted to suit your ESP teaching situation?

Figure 2.4 presents a framework comprising the major areas that can be used to inform needs analysis as a basis for ESP course design.

Why?		
Who?		**What?**
students		necessities
managers		needs
supervisors		lacks
sponsors		constraints
governing bodies		target communicative event
gate keepers		target communicative skills
teachers		target discourse
colleagues		present situation
domain experts		communication
past students		learning strategies
Where?		**When?**
workplace		pre-service
language school		in-service
university		
training institution		
	How?	
	intuitions	
	interviews	
	questionnaires	
	observations	
	literature review	
	ethnography	
	language audit	
	language test	
	task analysis	
	discourse analysis	
	corpus analysis	
	text analysis diaries,	
	journals and logs	

Figure 2.4   A framework for needs analysis

Task 2.3

Needs-analysis framework

Using Figure 2.4, discuss the framework in relation to a potential or existing ESP course

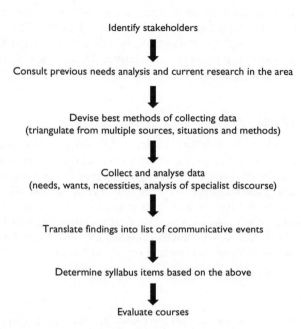

Identify stakeholders

Consult previous needs analysis and current research in the area

Devise best methods of collecting data
(triangulate from multiple sources, situations and methods)

Collect and analyse data
(needs, wants, necessities, analysis of specialist discourse)

Translate findings into list of communicative events

Determine syllabus items based on the above

Evaluate courses

Figure 2.5   Steps in needs analysis in ESP course design

Moving from needs analysis to course design

Needs are the basis of most courses in ESP. Needs-analysis data is translated into course objectives and teaching aims though a series of steps. A suggestion of how needs can be translated into syllabus items is outlined in Figure 2.5.

Figure 2.5 presents a linear process of course design; however, the needs of learners do not remain static but vary over the duration of the ESP course. This means that needs analysis is an ongoing process and that the relationship between needs analysis and course design is cyclical. Information obtained from the evaluation of courses by major stakeholders can then lead to further refinements in the course itself.

Summary

In this chapter the role of needs analysis in ESP has been discussed. The chapter has covered the emergence of needs analysis in ESP in the last century, which focused on purely linguistic needs and viewed ESP as essentially neutral, to current thinking, which considers a range of learner needs and a critical perspective on those needs. The chapter has discussed the sources from which needs information can be obtained, presented a range of methods for collecting needs-analysis data and suggested that triangulation is an essential aspect of current analysis of needs. The chapter has highlighted the relationship between needs and course design that will be explored in the following chapters. In Chapter 15 there are three examples of needs-analysis instruments.

Further reading

James Dean Brown has a book in the *Introducing ESP* series, *Introducing needs analysis and English for specific purposes*, which is essential reading for those interested in designing needs-based courses in ESP. For a very practical perspective on designing an ESP course from needs see Marjiatte Huhta *et al.* (2013). Richard's West's seminal article on needs analysis provides a state-of-the-art portrait of needs analysis relevant in the 90s. It gives a good historical overview. Michael Long's edited book on second-language needs analysis considers the topic from a wide range of perspectives and may be classed as essential reading in the area.

References

Benesch, S. (1996). Needs analysis and curriculum development in EAP: An example of a critical approach. *TESOL Quarterly, 30*(4), 723–38. doi:10.2307/3587931.

Benesch, S. (2001). *Critical English for academic purposes: Theory, politics, and practice*. Mahwah, NJ: Lawrence Erlbaum.

Brown, J. D. (2016). *Introducing needs analysis and English for specific purposes*. Oxford: Routledge.

Cowling, J. D. (2007). Needs analysis: Planning a syllabus for a series of intensive workplace courses at a leading Japanese company. *English for Specific Purposes, 26*(4), 426–42.

Holliday, A. (1994). *Appropriate methodology and social context*. Cambridge: Cambridge University Press.

Holme, R., & Chalauisaeng, B. (2006). The learner as a needs analyst: The use of participatory appraisal in the EAP classroom. *English for Specific Purposes, 25*(4), 403–19.

Huhta, M., Vogt, K., Johnson, E., & Tulggi, K. (2013). *Needs analysis for language course design*. Cambridge: Cambridge University Press.

Hutchinson, T., & Waters, A. (1987). *English for specific purposes: A learning centred approach*. Cambridge: Cambridge University Press.

Jasso-Aguilar, R. (2005). Sources, methods and triangulation in needs analysis in a case study of Waikiki hotel maids. In M. Long (Ed.), *Second language needs analysis* (pp. 127–68). Cambridge: Cambridge University Press.

Long, M. (Ed.) (2005). *Second language needs analysis*. Cambridge: Cambridge University Press.

Macallister, C. J. (2016). Critical perspectives. In K. Hyland & P. Shaw (Eds.), *The Routledge handbook of English for academic purposes* (pp. 283–94). Oxford: Routledge.

Munby, J. (1978). *Communicative syllabus design*. Cambridge: Cambridge University Press.

Richterich, R., & Chancerel, J.-L. (1977). *Identifying the needs of adults learning a foreign language*. Oxford: Pergamon.

Robinson, P. (1991). *ESP today: A practitioner's guide*. Oxford: Pergamon.

Trimble, L. (1985). *English for science and technology: A discourse approach*. Cambridge: Cambridge University Press.

West, R. (1994). Needs analysis in language teaching. *Language Teaching, 27*(1), 1–19.

Wozniak, S. (2010). Language needs analysis from a perspective of international professional mobility: The case of French mountain guides. *English for Specific Purposes, 29*(4), 243–52.

Chapter 3

Language and skills in English for specific purposes

This chapter addresses language and skills in designing an ESP course. More in-depth consideration of language issues in course design can be found in Chapter 4, about vocabulary, and in Part 2 about the use of genre (Chapter 9), discourse analysis (Chapter 10) and corpora (Chapter 11).

Many ESP courses focus on skills and content rather than on language forms. An explicit focus on grammar tends to play a lesser role in ESP than in general English, where it may be the central organisational strand in the course. This chapter introduces the role of the following language areas in ESP course design:

- Grammar
- Reading
- Writing
- Speaking
- Listening

Reflection 3.1

Language and ESP

As a teacher or learner of ESP:

1 How important is a focus on grammar in ESP?
2 What model of grammar should be used in ESP?
3 How important is a focus on skills?
4 Which skills are important in ESP?

It stands to reason that language plays an essential role in any ESP course, but how is language conceptualised? That is to say, what is language? The central issue is what the course designer believes language competence is, and this should be based on evidence. For example, does language competence mean a good knowledge of grammar? Or a wide range of vocabulary? Or an ability to deal with a range of communicative situations? Perhaps the most influential view of language competence is the notion of communicative competence put forward by Canale and Swain (1980). The term 'communicative competence' was coined by Dell Hymes (1966) in an attempt to extend Chomsky's 1965 distinction between competence and performance. Canale and Swain's conceptualisation of communicative competence comprises the following sub-competences:

1 Grammatical competence, which refers to knowledge of grammar, lexis, morphology, syntax, semantics and phonology.
2 Sociolinguistic knowledge: knowledge of the socio-cultural rules of language use.
3 Discoursal competence: knowledge of coherence and cohesion that connect spoken and written text.
4 Strategic competence: knowledge of verbal and nonverbal communication strategies.

Douglas (2000) neatly summarises ESP language knowledges as being made up of linguistic, textual, functional, communicative and sociolinguistic knowledge. Canale and Swain (1980) and Douglas (2000) provide a useful starting point for ESP course designers in terms of conceptualising language.

Task 3.1

Communicative competence and ESP

1 Canale and Swain (1980) identify four components of communicative competence:

> Grammatical competence
> Sociolinguistic knowledge
> Discoursal competence
> Strategic competence

What do you think each aspect refers to?

2 Find an example of ESP materials.* Look at the course syllabus and a sample unit. Think about how each type of competence is reflected in the materials. Think about how this might be reflected in an ESP course.

* Sample units and course overviews are freely available online from ESP book publishers. For example, Garnet: www.garneteducation.com/; and Cambridge: www.cambridge.org/gb/cambridgeenglish/catalog/business-professional-and-vocational/.

Specificity of content and language

The next important issue that needs to be addressed in relation to the treatment of language in ESP course design is one of specificity. In ESP specificity can refer to language and to content. In terms of language, the course designer needs to consider to what extent particular examples of language in the ESP discipline are unique to the field and to what extent particular forms are generic across all areas. Early course designers analysed target texts in terms of lexico-grammar and used these as syllabus items in the belief that the grammar and vocabulary used are unique to the setting. However, there is general agreement that there is a large body of generic language knowledge. This is referred to by Bloor and Bloor (1986) as the common core. This common core overlaps varieties of language common in all types of communication with those specific to particular communicative situations.

The notion of a basic command of language necessary to be able to communicate in a given language emerged through the conceptualisation of the threshold level in work leading to the Common European framework (van Ek, 1975, 1980). The taxonomy of communicative objectives prepared for the Council of Europe (van Ek, 1975) is based on a functional/notional conceptualisation of language described in the section below.

From an ESP perspective, the threshold level is conceived of as a level at which specific language instruction can optimally commence. For example, most university pre-sessional courses in university language centres start EAP at an intermediate or upper intermediate level. Typically, ESP courses, which are informed by needs analysis, are more expensive than general English courses, so there is a financial advantage to both the student and the provider to introduce ESP courses at a time when they can be comparatively short.

In terms of specificity of content in ESP, there are two perspectives connected with the notion of the common core of ESP language in relation to the specificity of language. ESP courses can be classified as English for general specific purposes and English for specific purposes (Dudley-Evans & St. John, 1998). Thus we have courses in English for general academic purposes (EGAP) or English general business purposes (EGBP) and courses in English for specific academic purposes (ESAP) or English for specific business purposes (ESBP). The level of generality is usually dictated by the homogeneity of the students and the resources available, such as materials, courses designers and specialised teachers. A general ESP course will be applicable to a much wider range of students and purposes, and it can use published materials and be taught by ESP practitioners without subject expertise. At the most specific end of the continuum of specificity are content-based courses taught in English. This has developed into an approach in its own right, labelled by some as 'content-based instruction' (CBI) and others as 'content and language integrated learning' (CLIL), depending on the setting. These are discussed in more detail in Chapter 13.

ESP and grammar

In EGP courses there is generally an emphasis on grammar, this typically being one of the major sequencing strands in the syllabus. Traditionally, grammar focuses on syntax, tense and aspect, and syllabuses usually begin with the simplest forms of these and continue through to the most complex – for example, from the verb 'to be' and the simple present tense to the use of gerunds. The assumption is that learners acquire these structures in this fashion. However, this belief has been challenged on a number of fronts. For example, as experienced English teachers know, the acquisition of verbs using the third person 's' form often takes learners a very long time. This lockstep approach reflects the fact that what is taught is not always what is learned (Nunan, 1998). In communicative-language teaching this often resulted in shifting the primary focus on to meaning rather than grammar. However, this does not mean grammar teaching has been rendered useless. A recent perspective on grammar teaching is a 'focus on form' (FonF). In contrast with 'focus on forms', which focuses on the deductive, explicit teaching of specific grammatical rules and forms (Doughty & Williams, 1998), FonF emphasises a communicative and inductive approach to grammar.

A course designer needs to decide to whether a focus on grammar will be included in the course and, if so, which aspects of grammar it will focus on and which description of language will inform the course. The decision about which grammatical items should be included in an ESP course can be informed by discourse analysis (see Chapter 10) that can indicate common linguistic forms in the target situation. In addition, diagnostic procedures such as a grammar test or language audit conducted at the needs-analysis stage can identify areas of language and grammar that learners need to be included in the course.

There is not just one grammar of English. Typically, a traditional grammar is used in English-language courses. However, a functional grammar based on systemic functional linguistics (SFL) may be used (Halliday, 1976). Systemic functional grammar (SFG) is more common in ESP than in EGP courses. SFG attempts to account for communicative settings, register, genre and interlocutors in the language description. The description focuses on field (what's going on), tenor (who's involved) and mode (channel of communication). This is very popular in some parts of the world, notably Australia, where SFG is the grammar taught in mainstream schools and is often referred to as the Sydney School. In practice, however, SFG may be complex to include in course design, both from the perspective of the course designer and, more importantly, that of the student.

Despite moves within mainstream EFL on FonF, ESP courses do not always include a grammar strand in the syllabus. There are a number of reasons for this. Perhaps the most significant is that learners are often heterogeneous. Classes may be grouped according to job or academic discipline, in contrast to EGP courses, where students are usually grouped according to language level. This means that learners with varying levels of language proficiency may be in the same class. Further, because ESP courses often commence once the threshold level is attained, some (students and instructors) may believe that a focus on grammar is no longer essential as the basic forms have already been acquired by the learners. In published ESP courses there may not be a focus on grammar or a grammar syllabus strand. This does not mean that grammar is not important in ESP, but it is often left to the ESP practitioner to supplement a given ESP course with frequent and common grammar forms taken from the target communicative situation and as the need arises.

ESP and functions and notions in language

In the latter part of the twentieth century, which saw an emphasis on communicative-language teaching, course designers focused less on grammar in favour of functions and notions. A function represents language that can achieve communicative aims, defined by White as "the intentional or purposive use of language" (White, 1988, 75) – for example, the request "could you open the window please?". A notion refers to concepts such as time, movement and cause. The functional–notional conceptualisation of language has been hugely influential on approaches to ESP course design and is the basis of the work on the levels of the Council of Europe framework (CEF). van Ek and Trim's taxonomy of functions (1998) is a very useful tool for course designers. This is an in-depth list of possible functions needed in everyday communication and is divided into the levels of the CEF.

Task 3.2

Grammar, functions and notions in published ESP materials

Using some ESP materials – for example, a coursebook or in-house materials – consider to what extent the materials focus on:

Functions

Notions

Grammar

Skills

A focus on skills is central to ESP course design and often takes precedence over a focus on linguistic form(s). One reason for this may be that skills and texts are central to many areas of ESP and are relatively easy to identify in ESP settings.

The first consideration is whether skills are receptive (reading and listening) or productive (speaking and writing). Figure 3.1 presents a taxonomy of receptive and productive texts commonly found in an EAP setting.

ESP skills are referred to and discussed extensively in many of the other chapters in this book – for example, Course 5 – in Part 3 – is a postgraduate course in academic writing.

The starting point for course designers in terms of skills is to ascertain what view of the construct or skill is adopted. For example, what do we mean by reading ability? Does it refer to a bottom-up type of processing whereby the reader moves from the smallest unit in the text to the overall meaning of the text? Or does the reader use top-down processing whereby the reader works from whole text meaning to smaller units of comprehension? Or some of both? Spoken and written texts form the mainstay of ESP course design. Based on needs analyses, texts are identified and collected from the target situations by key stakeholders. This is usually the ESP practitioner and/or course designer, but contributions can also be made by employers, subject specialists and the students themselves. Texts are collected and analysed using varying methodologies – for example, discourse analysis – and incorporated into course objectives and ultimately into classroom activities.

Writing

Very often writing plays a very important role within ESP. In EAP, for example, academic writing is extremely important because the majority of academic assessment is made though the vehicle of writing. The notion of academic literacy has received a lot of attention in recent years. Today literacy is considered as plural literacies (this is discussed in Chapter 13) and is something that members of an academic community do rather than acquire (Hyland, 2013). In EAP there is a rich tradition in writing approaches and theorising: a product approach to writing focuses on the technical aspects and the correctness of a final text, whereas a process approach incorporates drafting and re-drafting of writing; a genre approach to writing focuses on identifiable types of text and how these are typically structured (see Chapter 9); and an academic literacies approach to writing views writing being informed by context, setting, purpose and interlocutor (see Chapter 15). These approaches are not mutually exclusive and can be combined. For an excellent overview of approaches in EAP see Paltridge (2004). ESP writing using different approaches is addressed in Part 2 of this book.

Reading

The focus on reading in ESP has followed a similar trajectory to writing, with a move from a sentence-level focus to one on larger chunks of text, such as the moves within a business report. Selecting texts to use in an ESP course is very important. Central to this is the notion of authentic materials. This refers to texts which are used by the target interlocutors in communication. For example, an EAP course designer would probably include texts from academic journals in the students' discipline. Ideally the selection of texts is done in cooperation with major stakeholders in the field, such as subject lecturers. It is important to reflect the reciprocity between reading and writing in course design. Hirvela (2016) proposes a reading into writing perspective. This reflects the process of reading, extracting information, interpreting this information and using it in an academic written text. This is the usual process students follow when producing an academic assignment. Authentic materials are discussed throughout this book.

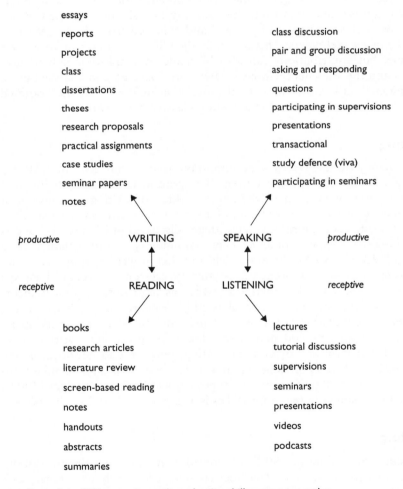

essays

reports

projects

class

dissertations

theses

research proposals

practical assignments

case studies

seminar papers

notes

class discussion

pair and group discussion

asking and responding

questions

participating in supervisions

presentations

transactional

study defence (viva)

participating in seminars

productive   WRITING   SPEAKING   *productive*

receptive   READING   LISTENING *receptive*

books

research articles

literature review

screen-based reading

notes

handouts

abstracts

summaries

lectures

tutorial discussions

supervisions

seminars

presentations

videos

podcasts

Figure 3.1   EAP receptive and productive skills: some examples

Speaking

Speaking is a central aspect of many ESP courses. English has become the language of business and international communication (Kankaanranta & Louhiala-Salminen, 2010) and speaking is a vital tool to execute commerce. It is important in international settings that norms are established and adhered to. These norms are not necessarily native-speaker norms. For example, in aviation English lives may depend upon the accuracy and fluency of communication (Wang, 2007). The development of corpora of spoken texts has done much to enhance our understanding of spoken English, particularly in academic settings (see, for example, the Michigan Corpus of Academic Spoken English (MICASE)).

Listening

As between reading and writing, there is a close relationship between speaking and listening. Interaction involves both speaking and listening. Listening can be one-way, based on a monologue, as is the case with talks, presentations and lectures, or interactive, or dialogic, as is the case with conversations, interviews and discussions. Vandergrift and Goh (2012) distinguish between the core comprehension skills which can be used individually or in combination:

1   Listen for details
2   Listen for main ideas
3   Listen for global understanding
4   Listen and infer
5   Listen and predict
6   Listen selectively

These listening skills apply to all language, whether EGP or ESP. However, in ESP there is a focus on the strategies experts use in decoding typical texts in the field. For example, in EAP a course may focus on methods of extracting the most important points in an academic lecture and translating these into comprehensible notes.

Task 3.3

Skills and ESP

1   Based on your experience as a teacher and/or learner, what are the receptive and productive skills needed in EAP?
2   Using the classification presented in Figure 3.1, draft a chart for an area of ESP you are familiar with.

> 3   Look at an ESP course or textbook and make a list of the skills and subskills featured.
> 4   Compare this list with another ESP coursebook or with a fellow teacher. Are they the same or different? In what ways?

Summary

This chapter has examined the role of language and skills in ESP. It has looked at the role of grammar and functions in ESP courses. The four language skills have been discussed in relation to ESP course design. Unlike EGP, ESP courses can vary in the importance given to language and skills. EAP, for example, needs a greater emphasis on writing skills as this is the major medium for assessment.

Further reading

van Ek and Trim (1998) provide a large taxonomy of functions which can be very useful for course designers. For an analysis of the characteristics and major issues in teaching spoken and written business English see Nickerson and Planken (2016) in this series. Paltridge and Starfield (2013) has a chapter on each of the skills: Feak, Chapter 2 (pp. 35–54), ESP and speaking; Goh, Chapter 3 (pp. 55–76), ESP and listening; Hirvela, Chapter 4 (pp. 77–94), ESP and reading; Hyland, Chapter 5 (pp. 95–114), ESP and writing.

References

Bloor, T., & Bloor, M. (1986). *Languages for specific purposes*. Dublin: Trinity College.
Canale, M., & Swain, M. (1980). Theoretical bases of communicative approaches to second language teaching and testing. *Applied Linguistics, 1*(1), 1–47.
Chomsky, N. (1965). *Aspects of the theory of syntax*. Cambridge, MA: MIT Press.
Doughty, C., & Williams, J. (1998). *Focus on form in second language acquisition*. Cambridge: Cambridge University Press.
Douglas, D. (2000). *Assessing languages for specific purposes*. Cambridge: Cambridge University Press.
Dudley-Evans, T., & St. John, M. (1998). *Developments in English for specific purposes: A multi-disciplinary approach*. Cambridge: Cambridge University Press.
Halliday, M. A. K. (1976). *System and function in language: Selected papers*. Oxford: Oxford University Press.
Hirvela, A. (2016). Academic reading into writing. In K. Hyland & P. Shaw (Eds.), *The Routledge handbook of English for academic purposes* (pp. 127–38). Abingdon and New York: Routledge.
Hyland, K. (2013). ESP and writing. In B. Paltridge & S. Starfield (Eds.), *The handbook of English for specific purposes* (pp. 95–114). Oxford: Wiley-Blackwell.

Hymes, D. H. (1966). Two types of linguistic relativity. In W. Bright (Ed.), *Sociolinguistics* (pp. 114–58). The Hague: Mouton.

Kankaanranta, A., & Louhiala-Salminen, L. (2010). "English? – Oh, it's just work!": A study of BELF users' perceptions. *English for Specific Purposes, 29*(3), 204–9.

Michigan Corpus of Academic Spoken English (MICASE). Accessed 12 April 2017 at http://quod.lib.umich.edu/cgi/c/corpus/corpus?page=home;c=micase;cc=micase.

Nickerson, C., & Planken, B. (2016). *Introducing business English*. Abingdon: Routledge.

Nunan, D. (1998). Teaching grammar in context. *ELT Journal, 52*(2), 101–9.

Paltridge, B. (2004). Academic writing: The state of the art. *Language Teaching, 37*(2), 87–105.

Paltridge, B., & Starfield, S. (2013). *The handbook of ESP*. Oxford: Wiley-Blackwell.

van Ek, J. A. (1975). *The threshold level*. Strasbourg: Council of Europe.

van Ek, J. A. (1980) *Threshold level of English: Council of Europe Modern Languages Project*. Strasbourg: Council of Europe.

van Ek, J. A., & Trim, E. M. (1998). *Threshold 1990*. Cambridge: Cambridge University Press. Retrieved 28 February 2017 from www.coe.int/t/dg4/linguistic/Threshold-Level_CUP.pdf.

Vandergrift, L., & Goh, C. C. M. (2012). *Teaching and learning second language listening: Metacognition in action*. London: Routledge.

Wang, A. (2007). Teaching aviation English in the Chinese context: Developing ESP theory in a non-English speaking country. *English for Specific Purposes, 26*(1), 121–8.

White, R. W. (1988). *The ELT curriculum*. Oxford: Basil Blackwell.

Chapter 4

Vocabulary and English for specific purposes

The area of vocabulary has received more attention within ESP in recent years due to the availability of large-scale corpora and user-friendly text-analysing software. This chapter addresses the nature of ESP vocabulary and the role it plays in course design. The chapter touches on the use of corpora, but this is explored in more detail in Chapter 11. The following areas are explored in this chapter:

- What is ESP vocabulary?
- Vocabulary levels
- Sources of ESP vocabulary
- Teachers and vocabulary knowledge
- Teaching vocabulary
- Learners and vocabulary

Vocabulary is essential in any area of language learning. As with the issue of language discussed in the previous chapter, ESP attempts to focus on the most essential elements of the target communicative events to deliver a course in the most efficient way. With vocabulary in ESP, the important task for the course designer is to identify the vocabulary ESP learners need in order to communicate effectively in the target situation. Once identified, this vocabulary needs to be included systematically in the course design along with the most effective method of teaching and promoting learning.

Vocabulary can be the major organisational strand in a syllabus. Willis and Willis (1988) introduced lexical syllabuses in EGP. This approach included a grammatical focus, but syllabuses were organised according to the frequency of lexis. The frequencies were based on one of the first English-language corpora, produced by the publisher Collins and reflected in their COBUILD dictionary (they published a series of coursebooks based on the COBUILD dictionary). The approach had limited success when it was introduced in the 1980s; however, the approach and the corpus are very popular today. Collins have a free online dictionary which is a very useful resource for both teachers and students (Collins, online).

Reflection 4.1

Vocabulary and ESP

What experiences have you had teaching and/or learning foreign language vocabulary?

What do you think is the best way to learn vocabulary?

How do you think vocabulary can be selected for inclusion in an ESP course?

What is ESP vocabulary?

There is a range of terms used to talk about the types of ESP vocabulary, reflecting the degree of specialisation. ESP vocabulary may be classified in three main types. The first type is technical vocabulary, also called specialist, or specialised, vocabulary; this refers to vocabulary specific to the discipline and not widely used or understood outside this area. The second type is semi-technical vocabulary, also called sub-technical vocabulary; this refers to terms commonly used in the discipline which may have a specific usage or meaning. These terms may be used or understood outside the field but may be used in a different way (Dudley-Evans & St. John, 1998). The third type is general vocabulary: common everyday vocabulary necessary for any communication in the language. Table 4.1 provides some examples of these types of vocabulary. All three types are necessary for the learner to successfully integrate into the target community, be that an academic, legal or business setting. Communities use lexis in ways unique to them, and usage identifies participants in that community. For example, the use of the term 'prac' in a pre-service teachers' course in Australia refers to the practicum. This is the term used for the practice teaching students undertake in government schools as part of their assessment.

Task 4.1

Technical, semi-technical and general vocabulary

Using Table 4.1, think of some examples of technical, semi-technical and general vocabulary and definitions in a field of ESP or a subject discipline you are familiar with.

As well as individual vocabulary items it is important to include lexical patterning in an ESP course. Lexical patterning refers to words which

Table 4.1   Some examples of technical, semi-technical and general vocabulary and definitions in ESP

Field	Technical	Semi-technical	General
Law	alienability – possibility to be transferred in legal usage	duty – obligation by law	clerk – person who takes records, files
Tele-communications	photoresist, etching – technical in telecommunications	loop – closed circuit	resistant
Linguistics	speech act – utterance as a function of communication	syntax – arrangement of words and phrases in a sentence	discourse
General academic	conferment – gaining an academic degree	seminar – presentation of student paper	lecture

commonly occur together. Again, there is a range of terms used to describe vocabulary clusters – for example, 'multi-word units' refer to words linked together in an idiomatic way, while 'collocations' refer to two or more words commonly used together (for example, fast food, fast track), and 'lexical bundle' is the term used to refer to chunks of language such as 'Can I have?' and 'I don't know'. Using corpus analysis, Hyland (2008) investigated lexical bundles in EAP and produced a frequency list. While he found many similarities across different subjects, the frequency of three-word, four-word and five-word lexical bundles varied in occurrence and use across disciplines. This is an important aspect to remember when considering which vocabulary to include in a course.

Task 4.2

Multi-word units and collocations

Using Table 4.2, think of some examples of multi-word units and collocations in a field of ESP or a subject discipline you are familiar with.

As mentioned, beyond collocations there is formulaic language. Formulaic language refers to chunks of language commonly used in the field that have a single meaning or function (Martinez & Schmitt, 2012). Learning such phrases can be an efficient way to learn vocabulary and usage within an ESP field. With the aid of technology it is now quite easy for researchers, teachers and even students to be able to make, use and exploit specialist corpora. Martinez

Table 4.2 Some examples of multi-word units and collocations in ESP

Field	Multi-word unit	Collocation
Law	By the book	Acquired company
Business	Cash cow	Work–life balance
General academic	Keep tabs on	Trial and error

and Schmitt (2012) established a bank of phrasal language, the PHRASal Expressions List, relevant to general English. In contrast, corpora can reflect usage within a narrow field. Such focused corpora can identify connections between vocabulary patterns and context of use. For example, Grabowski (2015) established a corpus of key words and lexical bundles within certain pharmaceutical texts (patient information leaflets, summaries of product characteristics, clinical-trial protocols and chapters in academic textbooks). Chapter 15 includes a list of corpora useful to ESP course designers.

Vocabulary levels

One important consideration in vocabulary is the notion of vocabulary levels. Vocabulary is often classified into levels according to frequency of occurrence. Nation (2001) proposed four levels of frequency, with the top level accounting for the most frequent 2000 words. This level covers around 80 per cent of words in academic texts and newspapers and 90 per cent of novels and conversation (Chung & Nation, 2003).

The Academic Word List (AWL) developed by Coxhead (2000) is organised by levels of frequency. The list emerged from the categories in West's 1953 General Service List (GSL) and is based on a written academic corpus of 3.5 million words. Since its development, the AWL has made a significant contribution to EAP course design. The list has been exploited to produce further, more specialised lists (Hyland & Tse, 2007; Ward, 2009; Wang *et al.*, 2008). It has also been exploited pedagogically (Coxhead, 2006), with a large number of materials available for teachers and students. See, for example, the materials made available by the University of Nottingham (online), and Cobb's *Compleat lexical tutor* (online).

The AWL is based on the concept of a common core of vocabulary required to process discipline-specific spoken and written texts. Specific technical vocabulary tends to occur in the lowest level of common core lists of academic vocabulary, if at all, yet it is essential for learners to acquire these terms to be able to function in their target discourse community.

Teacher vocabulary knowledge

Technical vocabulary can present a great challenge for the ESP practitioner. Hutchinson and Waters (1987) claim that it is not the role of the

ESP practitioner to teach technical vocabulary but the role of the subject specialist. However, it is the ESP practitioner's job to ensure that students can operate in the target communicative situation; therefore he/she needs to ensure the essential vocabulary is mastered. Students often have far fewer problems with technical vocabulary than with other types of vocabulary as it is within their field of knowledge and may be similar to terms they have already learned. ESP practitioners should attempt to understand the technical vocabulary so they can facilitate mastery of it.

Sources of ESP vocabulary

The ESP course designer needs therefore to access both technical and semi-technical vocabulary. This may present a challenge for the course designer, who is probably not an expert in the disciplinary field. Sources of vocabulary that may be used are subject specialists, subject dictionaries, vocabulary lists and corpora. These sources are valuable to the course designer and each has its advantages and disadvantages. Subject specialists have a deep knowledge of the subject and the genres required therein. However, they are not usually language specialists and may not be able to identify the most important vocabulary that students need to learn. Subject dictionaries can be very helpful for course designers; however, these do not indicate the significance of the frequency of the vocabulary. Vocabulary lists are very useful for course designers, especially those that are very focused on the subject area (examples of available vocabulary lists are presented in Chapter 15). For example, Ward (2009) produced a basic engineering English word list for foundation engineering undergraduates.

Perhaps the most appropriate source of vocabulary is a corpus. With computer technology, corpus-analysis techniques are now accessible without the need for sophisticated analytical skills. This means that course designers, teachers and students can collect a corpus and analyse this corpus for lexis within very specific areas. Corpora are discussed in Chapter 11. Figure 4.1 summarises the sources of vocabulary available to ESP course designers, using an example of graduate EAP in the field of education.

Teaching vocabulary

In the syllabus-design process it is necessary to think beyond which vocabulary items and vocabulary clusters need to be included. Any ESP course has an implicit view of how vocabulary is learned, which influences the teaching and learning activities.

A distinction is usually made between receptive and productive vocabulary. That is, vocabulary an individual understands and the vocabulary an individual can produce. Obviously, the former is much larger.

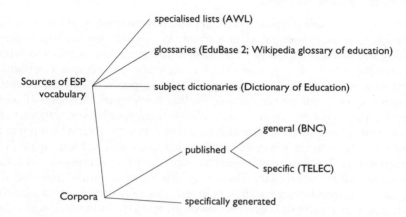

Figure 4.1 Sources for vocabulary with graduate education students as an example

Key: AWL: Academic Word List (Coxhead, 2000); BNC: British National Corpus; TSLC TELEC: secondary learner corpus (Allan, 2002); Dictionary of Education (Wallace, 2015); https://en. wikipedia.org/wiki/Glossary_of_education_terms (accessed 1 March 2017).

Nation (2001, 2007) proposes four strands to provide balanced vocabulary instruction:

- Meaning-focused input (reading and listening)
- Meaning-focused output (speaking and writing)
- Language focused learning (linguistic study of item)
- Fluency development

Task 4.3

Using Nation's strands for course design

How can Nation's four strands be reflected in an ESP course? Pick a specific course – for example, business English (BE) or English for academic purposes (EAP).

What types of ESP vocabulary-language-learning tasks exemplify these strands?

1 Meaning-focused input (reading and listening)
2 Meaning-focused output (speaking and writing)
3 Language-focused learning (linguistic study of item)
4 Fluency development

Vocabulary and learners

In addition to the selection of vocabulary and how to teach it, attention needs to be given to how vocabulary is learned. Vocabulary learning may occur incidentally through exposure – for example, by watching movies and listening to music – or explicitly, where the learner sets out to acquire a particular word or vocabulary set. While comprehensible input is one of the essential components of language acquisition, explicit learning of vocabulary is considerably more efficient. In order to explicitly learn vocabulary, learners need to use strategies. These are typically considered as cognitive, which refers to conscious efforts to learn words, or metacognitive – that is, focusing on *how* to learn words. Teachers may present a range of learning strategies which can help students learn vocabulary. These range from memory and retrieval strategies, such as remembering vocabulary in semantic networks, to metacognitive strategies, which refer to consideration of preferred learning techniques and planning learning (see the work of Schmitt (2000), and Nation (online) for more information). Harding (2007) recommends the use of personal learning dictionaries for learners of specialist vocabulary, whereby learners develop their own dictionaries of the most useful words in their field and include information valuable to them – for example, definitions, pronunciation, synonyms and authentic example of use.

Task 4.4

Using vocabulary lists

Look at one of the sources of ESP vocabulary listed in Chapter 15. How do you think this could be used in course design and teaching?

Summary

This chapter has presented the major issues in ESP vocabulary. It has provided possible sources of ESP vocabulary and offered advice as to how these could be incorporated into course design. It has also considered issues in the teaching and learning of ESP vocabulary. Many of the issues covered in this chapter are further explored in Chapter 11, about ESP corpora, and Chapter 15 provides resources for vocabulary.

Further reading

For a good overview of issues in ESP vocabulary and discussion about the AWL see Averil Coxhead's chapter in Paltridge and Starfield (2013).

Paul Nation's webpage (Nation, online) is a valuable resource for EGP which contains many of his publications available for download.

The Academic Word List (Coxhead, online) is available for download. It contains 570 word families, excluding the most frequent 2000 words. Discussion about the development of the list can be found in Coxhead (2000, 2011).

Tom Cobb's *Compleat lexical tutor* (Cobb, online) is a very useful source for vocabulary. It includes concordances, lists tests and exercises.

References

Allan, Q. G. (2002). The TELEC secondary learner corpus: A resource for teacher development. In S. Granger, J. Hung, & S. Petch-Tyson (Eds.), *Computer learner corpora, second language acquisition and foreign language teaching* (pp. 195–211). Amsterdam: John Benjamin.

Chung, T. M., & Nation, P. (2003). Technical vocabulary in specialised texts. *Reading in a Foreign Language, 15*(2), 103–16.

Cobb, T. (online). *Compleat lexical tutor.* Retrieved 1 March 2017 from www.lextutor.ca/.

Collins, online. Accessed 12 April 2017 at www.collinsdictionary.com/dictionary/english.

Coxhead, A. (2000). A new Academic Word List. *TESOL Quarterly, 34*(2), 213–38.

Coxhead, A. (2006). *Essentials of teaching academic vocabulary.* Boston: Houghton Mifflin.

Coxhead, A. (2011). The Academic Word List 10 years on: Research and teaching implications. *TESOL Quarterly, 45*(2), 355–62. doi:10.5054/tq.2011.254528.

Coxhead, A. (2013). Vocabulary and ESP. In B. Paltridge, & S. Starfield (Eds.), *The handbook of English for specific purposes* (pp. 115–32). Oxford: Wiley Blackwell.

Coxhead, A. (online). *The Academic Word List.* Accessed 1 March 2017 from www.victoria.ac.nz/lals/resources/academicwordlist/.

Dudley-Evans, T., & St. John, M. (1998). *Developments in English for specific purposes: A multi-disciplinary approach.* Cambridge: Cambridge University Press.

Edubase 2. Retrieved 1 March 2017 from www.education.gov.uk/edubase/glossary.xhtml.

Graboswski, L. (2015). Keywords and lexical bundles within English pharmaceutical discourse: A corpus-driven description. *English for Specific Purposes, 38*(1), 23–33.

Harding, K. (2007). *English for specific purposes.* Oxford: Oxford University Press.

Hutchinson, T., & Waters, A. (1987). *English for specific purposes: A learning centred approach.* Cambridge: Cambridge University Press.

Hyland, K. (2008). As can be seen: Lexical bundles and disciplinary variation. *English for Specific Purposes, 27*(1), 4–21.

Hyland, K., & Tse, P. (2007). Is there an 'academic vocabulary'? *TESOL Quarterly, 41*(2), 235–53.

Martinez, R., & Schmitt, N. (2012). A phrasal expressions list. *Applied Linguistics, 33*(3), 299–320. Accessed 12 April 2017 at www.norbertschmitt.co.uk/resources.html. doi10.1093/applin/ams010.

Nation, P. (2001). *Learning vocabulary in another language*. Cambridge: Cambridge University Press.

Nation, P. (2007). The four strands. *Innovation in Language Learning and Teaching, 1*, 2–13.

Nation, P. (online). Webpage. Accessed 1 March 2017 at www.victoria.ac.nz/lals/about/staff/paul-nation.

Schmitt, N. (2000). *Vocabulary in language teaching*. Cambridge: Cambridge University Press.

Schmitt, N. (2010). *Researching vocabulary: A vocabulary research manual*. London: Palgrave.

University of Manchester. (online). *Academic phrasebank*. Retrieved 1 March 2017 from www.click2go.umip.com/i/academic_phrasebank/appe.html.

University of Nottingham. (online). Accessed 12 April 2007 at www.nottingham.ac.uk/alzsh3/acvocab/index.htm.

Wallace, S. (2015) *Dictionary of education* (2nd ed.). Oxford: Oxford University Press.

Wang, J., Liang, S. I., & Ge, G. (2008). Establishment of a medical academic word list. *English for Specific Purposes, 27*, 442–58.

Ward, J. (2009). A basic engineering English word list for less proficient foundation engineering undergraduates. *English for Specific Purposes, 28*(3), 170–82.

West, M. (1953). *General Service List*. Retrieved 1 March 2017 from www.academia.edu/4791005/Gsl-the-general-service-list-by-michael-west-1953.

Willis, D., & Willis, J. (1988). *Collins CoBUILD English course*. London: Collins.

Chapter 5

Teaching English for specific purposes

This chapter deals with pedagogical issues of teaching ESP. It addresses the expected qualities of ESP teachers, often referred to as ESP practitioners, and discusses the issue of specialist subject knowledge in teaching ESP. This chapter is directed towards both new and practising English-language teachers who are making the transition to ESP. It covers the following aspects, including major distinctions between EGP and ESP and appropriate and inappropriate general classroom practices:

- Differences between teaching ESP and English for general purposes (EGP)
- ESP teachers vs EGP teachers
- Roles of ESP practitioners
- Qualities of ESP practitioners
- Need for subject knowledge

Differences between teaching ESP and English for general purposes (EGP)

In Chapter 1 Table 1.1 presented the typical characteristics of ESP and EGP courses. These characteristics influence the way that ESP courses are taught – those approaches and activities that are appropriate and those that are not. The characteristics are summarised and discussed below in terms of what this means for ESP teaching. From a teaching perspective, the main differences between EGP and ESP are the learners themselves, teaching methodology and classroom activities. These differences are not always clear-cut, and Campion (2016) presents an interesting account of EGP teachers moving into EAP. She emphasises the need for further research concerning these differences.

ESP learners are goal-driven

To motivate learners EGP teachers often have to work hard, including fun activities such as games, songs and puzzles. These activities can take up a lot of time for minimal gain other than the fun factor. ESP learners, in contrast, usually have common goals and are arguably more highly motivated, particularly in terms of extrinsic motivation. Cook (2002) divides communication goals as being internal or external to the classroom. ESP focuses very firmly on out-of-class communication as a goal, while in EGP classes, particularly in an EFL setting where English is not a means of communication outside the classroom, the only communication in the target language may be in the classroom.

ESP learners may have varying levels of linguistic proficiency

Usually, EGP classes are organised into language levels, starting with beginners and moving through the levels to advanced. In ESP this is often not the case. Class groupings may be made based on the students' specialisation, resulting in groups of mixed ability. ESP practitioners need to bear this in mind when selecting material and making assumptions about students' knowledge. A further distinction is that ESP classes usually begin once a certain threshold of linguistic proficiency is reached.

Focus on skills rather than grammar

Typically, EGP courses have a strong focus on grammar. This can be seen in the majority of EGP coursebooks, where grammar is often the main organisational strand in the syllabus. This can be explicit, where grammatical terms are referred to, such as the present perfect tense. Or it can be implicit, where grammar terms are not explicitly referred to. In ESP, however, needs analysis usually identifies skills which emerge from the target communicative situations. While grammar is still important, it is not considered useful to systematically work through the English grammatical system as is often the case with EGP courses.

Classroom management

EGP lessons are typically organised in stages, starting with a warm-up. Staging a lesson is considered one of the basic skills of an EGP teacher and is assessed in training and development courses. In ESP this is less usual. Generally in ESP teaching, continuity throughout the whole course is emphasised, so teachers can pick up where they left off in the previous session (Martin, 2015).

Relationship with students

The relationship between students and the teacher in ESP is likely to be different from that in the EGP classroom. Where the focus is entirely on language, as is the case with EGP, the teacher has a very high status, as he or she is the expert, whereas in the ESP classroom language per se is only part of the picture. This means the ESP practitioner is an expert in one of the areas covered in the teaching. The ESP practitioner is rarely an expert in the disciplinary field. This may influence the relationship with the students, with ESP practitioners feeling insecure because of their lack of subject knowledge. Wu and Badger (2009) reported that teachers felt a lack of knowledge reflected badly on their competence. Campion (2016) reported a lack of knowledge as the major challenge facing new EAP teachers. This is discussed further below.

Appropriate teaching methodology

As mentioned in Chapter 1, disciplines in ESP have their dominant methodologies and these may be applied to the ESP classroom. For example, medical students may be familiar with problem-based learning and business students may be familiar with a case-study approach. These methodologies can be usefully employed in the ESP classroom and are discussed in Chapter 12. In EGP the current, widely adopted methodologies are communicative-language teaching (CLT) and task-based learning (TBL). CLT emerged in the 1970s and focuses on communication – meaning and interaction – as the major aim of language teaching. TBL develops the communicative notion to reflect classrooms that focus on the use of the target language to complete meaningful tasks, which then facilitates acquisition of the language (Van den Branden, 2012).

Roles of ESP practitioners

The term 'ESP practitioner' has been used throughout in this book rather than 'ESP teacher'. This terminology attempts to capture the range of demands within the profession (Dudley-Evans & St. John, 1998). Figure 5.1 illustrates some of the many roles an ESP practitioner may need to adopt.

Reflection 5.1

Role of ESP practitioners

What roles do you think an ESP practitioner should have? Discuss those in Figure 5.1.

Have you encountered further responsibilities as an ESP practitioner?

Are there any drawbacks in assuming these responsibilities?

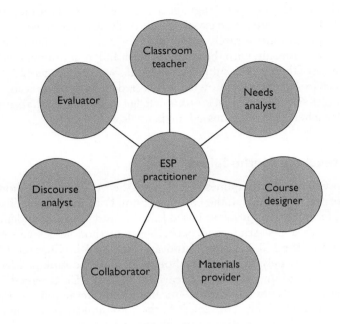

Figure 5.1 Roles of the ESP practitioner

The teacher as a course designer

An ESP practitioner does not usually follow an established ESP course with a set of materials. More often than not the ESP practitioner is expected to play a central role in all aspects of course design, from needs analysis and materials preparation to evaluation.

Starting with needs analysis: at the very least, the ESP practitioner will supplement a needs analysis with a short survey of his or her own focusing on the areas he or she feels need to be included in the course outline. Some ESP practitioners play a central role in course design by collecting and analysing needs data and collaborating with stakeholders; course aims and objectives are then generated.

Published materials very rarely meet the specific needs of students, so ESP practitioners are likely to be involved in course design and materials selection and/or adaptation of existing materials (Menkabu & Harwood, 2014; Grammatosi & Harwood, 2014). The ESP practitioner may choose to use an established coursebook as a starting point and supplement this. Often a coursebook provides a syllabus in the form of a grid of areas of focus. Table 5.1 shows a section of such a grid from a published EAP coursebook.

Task 5.1

Supplementing coursebooks

Using the grid for Unit 1 presented in Table 5.1, how do you think you would supplement this for an EAP class of your choice?

What authentic text do you think you could choose for a group of EAP students? What activities could be based on this text?

What output activities do you think you could choose?

Supplementary materials would normally be based on authentic source materials and tasks that mirror the target situation or the skill focus of the textbook syllabus. Authentic materials in ESP are spoken and written texts that have been produced for a specialist audience. For example, with English for an engineering class an engineering textbook or manual may be used. There are three criteria that should be used when selecting authentic texts: suitability, exploitability and readability (Gilmore, 2007). Suitability refers to the relevance of the text to the students' special field. Exploitability refers to the extent to which the text can be manipulated to generate

Table 5.1 Excerpt from course grid in a published EAP coursebook

Unit 1 Choices and implications	Reading	Listening and speaking	Writing skills	Grammar and vocabulary practice
	Researching texts for essays	Introducing your presentation	Understanding how essay types are organised	Avoiding repetition: that (of) and those (of)
	Skimming and scanning	Clarifying key terms	Drafting the introduction to an essay	Word families: linking parts of texts
	Identifying the sequence of ideas Understanding implicit meanings Inferring the meaning of words Vocabulary building		Language for writing: common knowledge	Verb–noun collocations

Source: Hewings (2012, p. 7).

pedagogic activities. Readability refers to the lexical and grammatical complexity of the text. The selection of suitable texts is an area students can be actively involved in as they will probably have more subject knowledge than the ESP teacher. Authentic texts need to be accompanied by authentic tasks; that is, reflecting real-life communicative situations. A good example of how authentic texts can be exploited can be found in Palmero (2003).

Specificity – that is, how subject-specific the ESP course is – is an area which influences the selection of authentic texts and generation of learning activities. For example, with a general academic class, such as found in pre-sessional English courses, selecting appropriate authentic texts for use with a class is quite challenging because the students are from different fields. The usual solution to this is to use general academic texts taken from low-level textbooks or magazines. Such sources may not be relevant, as they are written for a non-academic audience. One solution to this dilemma is to involve the students in finding authentic texts and generating tasks relevant to their intended field of study.

What makes an ESP practitioner?

Most ESP practitioners move from EGP to ESP without any training in ESP. There are relatively few training courses focusing on ESP, although these are gaining in availability, with some universities offering MA courses in ESP or with an ESP module included in the provision. This lack of training can pose problems for both the ESP practitioner and the resulting ESP course. Ding and Campion (2016) discuss this in EAP in detail. Generally, the methodologies and techniques highlighted on EGP teacher-preparation courses do not reflect those required by various forms of ESP. For example, a communication game where students have to verbally work out the contents of a stick-it note attached to their own heads would not be appropriate for a group of high-level Chinese university administrators. So new ESP teachers need to consider the appropriateness of the methodology and methods they choose to deliver the ESP course.

As mentioned earlier, one of the concerns of new ESP practitioners is a lack of subject knowledge. Teachers may feel insecure when faced with a lack of knowledge in classroom situations (Wu & Badger, 2009). The degree of specialist knowledge needed by the practitioner depends very much on the students. Ferguson (1997) discusses the variables that may influence the amount of specialist knowledge an ESP practitioner may need. Among these are whether the students are experts or apprentices in the field; students' needs; class sizes (the larger the class the more diverse it may be); and the nature of the materials.

Problems may arise when new ESP practitioners have little knowledge of the students' target communicative setting yet are put in a position of power within the classroom. This can be ameliorated by the ESP practitioner acknowledging that their expertise lies in English, not in knowledge of the subject, and adopting a willingness to learn about the subject. Subject knowledge undoubtedly enhances the teaching of ESP. One way of achieving this is by working in collaboration with subject specialists. In addition, genre and discourse analysis can promote a deeper understanding of the terminology, structure and applications of ESP language. These issues are discussed in more detail in Part 2.

Aside from subject knowledge, there are skills and other areas of expertise that ESP teachers should have. The British Association of Lecturers in English for Academic purposes (BALEAP) devised an EAP teacher-competency framework based on survey research and practitioner debate. The purpose of this framework was to inform good practice and provide input for EAP teacher development (2008), and it could be adapted to inform other types of ESP. The overall competency framework is reproduced in Table 5.2.

The framework may seem daunting to new ESP teachers and has been criticised as such by Ding and Campion (2016) and Campion (2016). However, the whole framework, which is available as an ebook, is useful for ESP course designers because it systematises the major elements of ESP. That is, understanding and identifying ESP contexts, identifying student needs, developing a syllabus and materials and, finally, teaching practices and methodologies and assessment (BALEAP, 2008).

Task 5.2

Qualities of ESP practitioners

What do you think are the most important qualities of ESP practitioners?

How do you think the BALEAP framework can be realised in your ESP teaching?

Would you add anything to this framework?

The teacher as an evaluator

In ESP, evaluation and assessment play an important role, as stakeholders typically want to know how effective the programme is. The ESP practitioner plays a pivotal role in this as he/she may be solely responsible for student assessment. Assessment can be informal and formative, involving classroom tasks and tests that aim to consolidate and inform learning. Assessment can also be summative, measuring student performance at a more formal level. The continuum of formative to summative testing in ESP is shown in Figure 5.2. At the other end of the spectrum from formative

Table 5.2 Summary of EAP teacher-competency statements

Academic practice	An EAP teacher will –
Academic contexts	Have a reasonable knowledge of the organizational, educational and communicative policies, practices, values and conventions of universities
Disciplinary differences	Be able to recognise and explore disciplinary differences and how they influence the way knowledge is expanded and communicated
Academic discourse	Have a high level of systematic language knowledge including knowledge of discourse analysis
Personal learning, development and autonomy	Recognize the importance of applying to his or her own practice the standards expected of students and other academic staff
EAP students	*An EAP teacher will understand –*
Student needs	The requirements of the target context that students wish to enter as well as the needs of students in relation to their prior learning experiences and how these might influence their current educational expectations
Student critical thinking	The role of critical thinking in academic contexts and will employ tasks, processes and interactions that require students to demonstrate critical skills
Student autonomy	The importance of student autonomy in academic contexts and will employ tasks, processes and interactions that require students to work effectively in groups or independently as appropriate
Curriculum development	*An EAP teacher will understand –*
Syllabus and programme development	The main types of language syllabus and will be able to transform a syllabus into a programme that addresses student needs in the academic context within which the EAP course is located
Text processing and text production	Approaches to text classification and discourse analysis and will be able to organize courses, units and tasks around whole texts or text segments in ways that develop students' processing and production of spoken and written texts
Programme implementation	*An EAP teacher will be –*
Teaching practices	Familiar with methods, practices and techniques of communicative-language teaching and be able to locate these within the academic context and relate them to teaching the language and skills required by academic tasks and processes
Assessment practices	Able to assess academic language, skills and tasks using formative and summative assessment

Source: BALEAP (2008, p. 3).

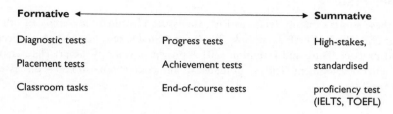

Figure 5.2 ESP assessment practices

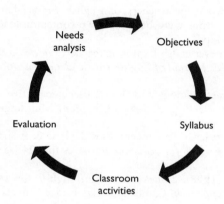

Figure 5.3 ESP course-design cycle

assessment are high-stakes, independent tests, such as the Test of Business English or the academic IELTS test (Hughes, 2003). The assessment of ESP is dealt with in more detail in Chapter 8.

Course evaluation is an essential part of the course-design cycle, as illustrated in Figure 5.3. The cycle starts with needs analysis and this leads to the drawing up of course objectives and aims. This then leads to a syllabus. Lessons and classroom activities are designed based on the ESP syllabus. Student and teacher evaluation of courses leads to course revision and a closer match between student and stakeholder needs, which will inform future course design. The whole course-design process is thus cyclical, with needs influencing course content and teaching practices.

Summary

This chapter has addressed some of the issues in teaching ESP. It has identified the major differences between EGP teachers and ESP practitioners and discussed some of the roles of an ESP practitioner. These roles are linked to issues in course design, and the course-design cycle has been presented.

Further reading

While these sources mainly relate to EAP, the issues identified may apply to other types of ESP. The BALEAP handbook (2008) is a valuable resource covering aspects of good practice. Ding and Campion (2016) present a state of the art chapter on EAP teacher development. The use of materials and coursebooks in ESP is discussed in Chapter 14.

References

BALEAP (2008). Competency framework for teachers of English for academic purposes. Retrieved 13 April 2017 from www.baleap.org/wp-content/uploads/2016/04/teap-competency-framework.pdf.

Campion, G. C. (2016). 'The learning never ends': Exploring teachers' views on the transition from general English to EAP. *Journal of English for Academic Purposes, 23*, 59–70.

Cook, V. (2002). Language teaching methodology and the L2 user perspective. In V. Cook (Ed.), *Portraits of the L2 user* (pp. 325–43). Clevedon: Multilingual Matters.

Ding, A., & Campion, G. (2016). EAP teacher devlopment. In K. Hyland & P. Shaw (Eds.), *The Routledge handbook of English for academic purposes* (pp. 247–59). Abingdon: Routledge.

Dudley-Evans, T., & St. John, M. (1998). *Developments in English for specific purposes: A multi-disciplinary approach*. Cambridge: Cambridge University Press.

Ferguson, G. (1997). Teacher education and LSP: The role of specialised knowledge. In R. Howard & G. Brown (Eds.), *Teacher education for languages for specific purposes* (pp. 80–9). Clevedon: Multilingual Matters.

Gilmore, A. (2007). Authentic materials and authenticity in foreign language learning. *Language Teaching, 40*(2), 97–118.

Grammatosi, F., & Harwood, N. (2014). An experienced teacher's use of the textbook on an academic English course: A case study. In N. Harwood (Ed.), *English language teaching textbooks: Content, consumption and production* (pp. 178–204). Basingstoke: Palgrave Macmillan.

Hewings, M. (2012). *Cambridge academic English: An integrated skills course for EAP. Students' book*. Cambridge: Cambridge University Press.

Hughes, A. (2003). *Testing for language teachers*. Cambridge: Cambridge University Press.

Martin, P. (2015). Teachers in transition: The road to EAP. In P. Breen (Ed.), *Cases in teacher identity, diversity and cognition in higher education* (pp. 287–316). Hershey: IGI Global.

Menkabu, A., & Harwood, N. (2014). Teachers' conceptualization and use of the textbook on a medical English course. In N. Harwood (Ed.), *English language teaching textbooks: Content, consumption and production* (pp. 145–77). Basingstoke: Palgrave Macmillan.

Palmero, N. C. (2003). The ESP teacher as a materials designer: A practical example. *Estudios de linguistica inglesa aplicada, 4*, 189–200.

Van den Branden, K. (2012) Task-based education. In A. Burns & J. C. Richards (Eds.), *The Cambridge guide to pedagogy and practice in second language teaching* (pp. 132–9). Cambridge: Cambridge University Press.

Wu, H., & Badger, R. G. (2009). In a strange and uncharted land: ESP teachers' strategies for dealing with unpredicted problems in subject knowledge during class. *English for Specific Purposes, 28*(1), 19–32.

Chapter 6

Learning English for specific purposes

This chapter considers ESP from a learning perspective; its focus is therefore on ESP learners and their characteristics. The chapter also presents some further discussion on common types of ESP course from a learning perspective. The following areas are covered:

- General features of ESP learning
- Different types of EAP
- Different types of EBP
- Legal English
- Medical English
- The role of learners

In ESP the learner is at the centre of course design. Typically, courses emerge from needs analyses conducted with major stakeholders (see Chapter 2). This chapter seeks to address issues concerning the learning of ESP that may need to be taken into consideration when designing an ESP course. It discusses different types of ESP, as learning, attitude and approach may vary between these.

General features of ESP learning

Table 1.1 presented some of the typical characteristics of EGP and ESP courses, with a focus on learners. ESP learners are usually adult learners who have mastery of their first language. Course designers can assume these students already have preferred learning styles and strategies. ESP learners in many teaching and learning contexts are also likely to be motivated with clearly articulated goals. They may already have specialist knowledge which can be exploited in the course-design process. ESP learners may also have clearly defined expectations of a given language course.

In terms of learning ESP, there are three main considerations: level of experience, the ESP context and variations in communication across fields.

The level of subject or job experience and prior knowledge of the students will greatly influence the content of the ESP course (Dudley-Evans & St. John, 1998). For example, in an English for legal purposes course will the learners have to learn about law, perhaps to qualify as a lawyer, or is the focus on typical language and communicative patterns used in legal settings?

A further consideration that features in many ESP courses is that of academic context. A large proportion of ESP occurs in universities. In this setting consideration needs to be paid to the subject area – for example, accounting, which may vary from arts subjects in terms of language needs and expectations. These issues reflect multiple academic literacies. This is addressed in more detail in Chapter 13.

The use of language in ESP is central to the notion of identity. Flowerdew distinguishes between professional and individual identities, which, he argues, are constructed through writing and speaking in the ESP domain (Flowerdew, 2011). Professional identity reflects the stylistic features of a particular profession. For example, professional identity is reflected in the discourse of managers and junior members of staff in a given cultural environment. Individual identity refers to the presentation of self based on the intended perception of others.

ESP learners are often highly motivated. Their purpose for learning English is very specific and goal-driven. Learners have to achieve a specific goal – for example, give a presentation in English within a given timeframe. This means that it is often not necessary for the teacher to devote a lot of consideration to motivation as is the case in EFL. In EFL the use of songs, games and fun communicative activities can engage otherwise unmotivated learners. In ESP such motivating techniques may be viewed by the ESP student as irrelevant to the goals of learning and, rather than being embraced enthusiastically, may be resisted. However, there are some advocates of games within ESP. For example, Alex Case blogs about games and communicative activities in EAP and has a selection of activities and worksheets freely available for teachers to use (Case, 2015).

Subject knowledge is the main area which distinguishes ESP learners from EFL learners. It is often the case that an ESP learner has a much wider knowledge of the subject than the ESP practitioner. There are a number of approaches to this dilemma. One approach is to work closely with subject specialists; this is discussed in Chapter 13, about content-based methodologies. Another is to use the learners as experts, as is the case in problem-based learning and case study discussed in Chapter 12, and students as researchers, as discussed in Chapter 13.

Learning strategies

In any course design attention should be paid to the preferred learning practices of the learners. Referred to as language-learning strategies, this area has received great deal of attention over the years in EGP (Oxford, 2011a). Strategies are typically classified into three broad categories: cognitive strategies relating to actions taken to help with learning, such as memorising; metacognitive strategies relating to the planning of learning; and social strategies that utilise others in the learning process. Oxford's *Strategy inventory for language learning* (SILL) is a widely used instrument for measuring learning strategies (Oxford, 1990). It lists 50 possible strategies which could be used when learning a language. This is a general strategy inventory which classifies strategies into six categories: memory, cognitive, compensatory, metacognitive, affective and social; and as well as general language-learning strategies it investigates skills-specific strategies. Language-learning-strategy research has also focused on more specific areas, such as reading (Grabe & Stoller, 2002), writing (Anderson, 2005), listening (Graham *et al.*, 2007), speaking, vocabulary and grammar (Oxford, 2011b). In ESP learning-strategy research has focused on very specific areas, such as strategies in ELF communication between domestic helpers and employers (Kwan & Dunworth, 2016), EAP test-taking strategies (Yang, 2012) and oral presentation strategies (Chou, 2011).

Task 6.1

Learning strategies

Find a list of language-learning strategies you believe are relevant to a specific ESP course.

For example, Oxford (1990) or Chou (2011).

How do you think a course designer could include these in a course design?

The following section presents some varieties of ESP and the implications for teaching and learning.

Types of EAP

EAP occurs in a range of settings often based on the stage of education of the learners. EAP may be provided before university studies, such as school-based EAP, university-entry-examination training, pre-sessional and foundation courses. Once a learner is enrolled on a university course, in-sessional EAP may be provided. Examples of the types of EAP course are explained in more detail below.

Reflection 6.1

Types of EAP

What types of EAP course are you familiar with?

What are the major considerations in developing a course for these types of EAP?

Foundation EAP courses

Foundation courses are aimed at upper high-school students and comprise subject and language instruction. Typically, students attend full-time courses. Foundation courses often replace traditional entry requirements for undergraduate courses. Such courses are often referred to as direct-entry courses. They may be delivered in the student's home country or in the intended country of study or a combination of the two. Some Western universities have set up training centres in the home country to do this.

Pre-sessional EAP courses

Pre-sessional courses tend to be EGAP, as the classes are inevitably heterogeneous, with students from different disciplines in one class. Full-fee-paying international students are often required to enrol in full-time language courses prior to academic study. For example, most large universities in the UK offer pre-sessional English courses that last one or more months prior to the beginning of academic courses. These may be voluntary but more commonly they are mandated, often based on English-exam results. The motivation for this provision is not necessarily driven by the need to enhance the student university experience, as such courses generate much needed funding for the university. Aside from this, there are other problems inherent in the pre-sessional model. In the UK, for example, there is a large demand for short-contract EAP teachers in the two months prior to university admission in October – so universities need to recruit quite large numbers of teachers for just one or two months. This obviously dilutes the quality of the EAP teachers employed, as many may have no EAP or even EFL experience. While this a good opportunity for aspiring EAP teachers to acquire good experience, it obviously can have an effect on the quality of the EAP provision.

The rationale behind EGAP is transfer. It is assumed that by learning general EAP skills and language, knowledge can be applied (transferred) to a range of more specific communicative situations. James (2014) reviewed studies in this area and found evidence to support transfer to a certain degree from EAP courses to subject courses. He examined a wide range of studies on different areas of transfer – for example, on the quality of student work. However, his review suggested, and it is generally believed, that the more specific an EAP course is the more effective it is likely to be (Gillett, 2014).

In-sessional courses

In-sessional EAP is often provided to support students while they are engaged in their academic study. These courses take various forms. Courses may be provided based on diagnostic language tests, such as the Diagnostic English Language Needs Assessment (DELNA) at the University of Auckland (University of Auckland, 2015; Elder, 2003) and the Measuring the Academic Skills of University Students procedure (MASUS) at the University of Sydney (Bonanno & Jones, 2007). These tests assess student deficiencies in academic communication, with an emphasis on reading and writing. Based on the results of these tests, students can enrol on targeted EAP courses. These courses may be voluntary, as is the case with MASUS, or compulsory, as is the case with DELNA. These courses tend not to be for credit.

In the MASUS procedure students are typically set an academic writing task – for example, to write a short essay about a given topic based on set texts. These are then assessed using assessment grids comprising analytical descriptors. These grids come in forms that can be used by subject tutors or literacy experts, depending on the type of provision. An example of a typical grid used by literacy experts is presented in Table 6.1.

Task 6.2

Using the MASUS

Decide how you can best use MASUS diagnostic assessment sheet (Table 6.1) with a group of in-sessional EAP students.

Decide on the target group of learners and target communicative situations within their disciplines.

Decide what action could be taken informed by the results provided on this form. How could you make the diagnostic form and task more relevant to a specific group of EAP learners you are familiar with?

Another type of EAP course in university settings is an EAP course for credit. This may be compulsory for all students, including native English speakers – for example, core English-composition classes mandated by many US universities (Tardy & Jwa, 2016) – or may be elective, as is the case with English in academic settings in Course 5 in Part 3.

Table 6.1 MASUS diagnostic assessment sheet

DIAGNOSTIC ASSESSMENT SHEET (EXPERT LITERACY RATERS)

Cohort: Name: SID:

KEY TO RATING

4 = excellent / no problems / accurate / very appropriate

3 = good / minor problems / mainly accurate / largely appropriate

2 = only fair / some problems / often inaccurate / often inappropriate

1 = poor / major problems / inaccurate / inappropriate

A = appropriate

NA = not appropriate

CRITERIA				
A. *Use of source material – information retrieval and processing*	4	3	2	1
<ul><li>Relevant information selected</li><li>Information integrated into the answer</li><li>Free from plagiarism</li></ul>		A	NA	
B. *Structure and development of answer*	4	3	2	1
<ul><li>Generic structure appropriate to the task</li><li>Focused position statement</li><li>Critical evaluation of evidence</li><li>Appropriate statement of conclusion</li></ul>				
C. *Control of academic writing*	4	3	2	1
<ul><li>Language appropriately abstract and technical</li><li>Generalisations qualified where appropriate</li><li>Logical flow of ideas</li></ul>				
D. *Grammatical correctness*	4	3	2	1
<ul><li>Accurate sentence structure</li><li>Correct subject/verb agreement</li><li>Consistent and appropriate tense choice, correctly formed</li><li>Correct use of articles</li></ul>				
E. *Qualities of presentation*	4	3	2	1
<ul><li>Spelling generally correct</li><li>Handwriting legible</li><li>Paragraphing reflects essay structure</li></ul>				

Source: Bonanno & Jones (2007).

Types of business English

When looking at business English, a distinction can be made between EBP and EOP. While, strictly speaking, they may fall under the umbrella term 'EOP', the term 'EBP' is widespread and often functions as a discipline in its own right. Like EAP, EBP has various forms, and three main types will be addressed here: independent examination courses, academic EBP and job-experienced EBP.

Task 6.3

Types of business-English course

What do you think are the major differences and similarities between the following types of course?

- Business English Certificate (BEC) courses
- English for an MBA
- English for sales executives in a company
- One-to-one EBP for a senior manager in a company

Comment on typical settings, typical students, the role of needs analysis and implications for course design.

Business-English examination courses

Business-English examination courses are based on the usefulness of a knowledge of English for business, regardless of whether the user intends to have a career in business. Cambridge examinations offer three Business English Certificates (BEC) targeting different levels: BEC preliminary, which corresponds to the Common European Framework of Reference (CEFR) B1; BEC Vantage, which corresponds to CEFR B2; and BEC Higher, which corresponds to CEFR C1 (Cambridge English Business Certificates, online). These courses are often offered in senior high schools, private language schools or at an undergraduate level. The qualifications are very popular in Chinese universities.

University-level business English

The second type of business English occurs in universities and may be at an undergraduate or graduate level – for example, English for MBA students. With this type of course, students need to learn about academic English to fulfil their course requirements, which may include typical academic essays. They also need to know about communication in real-world business communication.

Business English for professional purposes

The last type of business-English course is for job-experienced learners. Such courses may be conducted in the workplace and are based on contextually relevant needs. They are typically tailored to specific groups. The group may share knowledge of the workplace and professional practice – for example, in a manufacturing company – but may be very different in terms of job level and English proficiency. This has implications for course design. A special brand of EBP is the one-to-one course, usually provided for senior company staff.

English for occupational purposes

We can distinguish between academic EOP and EOP for job-experienced learners. In academic EOP the learner needs to acquire expert knowledge from the discipline but also needs to be able to communicate in an academic setting. In workplace settings provisions for job-experienced EOP students are the same as those discussed for business English for professional purposes. Within EOP there are many specialised divisions, such as English for legal purposes, English for medicine, English for science and technology and English for engineering. Some of these are discussed below.

English for legal purposes

In learning legal English there are many distinctions and constraints. Legal English is something everyone who studies the law needs to master, regardless of whether English is their first or additional language. Northcott (2013) claims that legal English is a particularly specialised branch of ESP that poses many problems for non-legal experts. It might be argued that teachers of ELP should be experts in law as well as language experts. However, in reality, few ESP practitioners are expert in both areas (Northcott & Brown, 2006). In Part 3, Course 3, Northcott's *English for lawyers* is an example of a legal English course for job-experienced students.

English for medical purposes

Medical English has a similar distinction concerning whether it is practice-focused or academically focused. The skills required for medical communication are varied. Students need to be able to access and communicate medical knowledge, which tends to be very formal and technical. They also need to communicate with patients using an appropriate bedside manner, which necessitates mastery of informal colloquial language. Further, medical English may be subdivided into specialisms such as anatomy, dentistry, pharmacy and nursing (Ferguson, 2013). In Part 3, Course 2, Bosher's *English for cross-cultural nursing* focuses on English for nurses.

Learner issues in ESP

There are many differences between learners in EFL and ESP. To start with, EFL learners in a school setting must attend class, while ESP learners often attend voluntarily. Compulsory attendance has its own problems where learners may see a lack of relevance or may not be interested in learning English. In ESP there may be a tension between subject and language that may influence the quality of engagement. For example, in EAP learners may attend a class because of perceived weaknesses in their English. However, this deficiency will undoubtedly reflect a difficulty with academic work in general. What this means is that the most at-risk students have the least time to devote to language studies and may attend classes sporadically and not do prescribed tasks. From an EOP perspective, on-site ESP is notoriously difficult to implement. As learners are in their workplace it is very easy to be distracted by work duties and again the ESP course takes a lower priority. These issues and how to minimise them must considered in course design.

The role of the learner in ESP

In ESP learners are more likely to play an active role in course design than in regular EGP classes. ESP learners may have a clear idea of their current and future needs. They often have greater knowledge of the subject area and may have a much wider subject-specific vocabulary. It is also likely that they will be able to access specialist texts – for example, lectures and seminars in EAP. For this reason, it is sensible to utilise learners' expertise as much as possible in designing the ESP course.

Reflection 6.2

The role of learners in ESP course design

What is your experience in designing ESP/EFL courses?

As a language learner do you have any experience with ESP/EFL course input?

What role do you think the ESP learners should play in the course-design procedure?

How much influence do you think learners should have on the course content?

Reflect on your experience as a teacher and as a language learner.

In its strongest form a learner-centred approach to course design is informed by a process syllabus which sees courses negotiated between learners and teachers in contrast to the usual approach to course design, which sees the syllabus framework in place before the course commences. In a negotiated syllabus the responsibility for course content is shared, thus empowering students (Breen & Littlejohn, 2000). Such syllabuses are more appropriate in certain settings, such as with heterogeneous groups, where no materials are available and where there is little shared knowledge between learners and the teacher. These types of syllabus are challenging to implement from a practical point of view because of the absence of planning and structure. It is particularly difficult for teachers who generally prefer a course outline prior to the beginning of the course. For these reasons, they are rarely implemented.

In a lot of approaches to ESP course design the learner plays a central role. For example, in Woodrow's course *English in academic settings* (Part 3, Course 5) the notion of students as researchers (Johns, 1997) is applied to an in-sessional, graduate EAP course. This approach sees the learner as a researcher investigating the communicative needs and norms of his or her own discourse community. In Maggie Charles' course *Writing in your field with corpora* (Part 3, Course 7) students are trained to generate and analyse personal subject-specific corpora.

Summary

This chapter has focused on the learner and learning in ESP. It has discussed the role of learning strategies and provided links to ESP strategy research. It has also presented some types of ESP from a learning perspective. These were linked to sample courses in Part 3.

Further reading

For comprehensive coverage of EAP, Hyland and Shaw (2016) is an excellent resource. The volume presents a range of types of EAP and each chapter has excellent links to further research.

Paltridge and Starfield's 2013 edited volume includes chapters on a range of research into types of ESP and EOP.

A good resource for learning strategies is Oxford (2011b). While this refers to EGP, many of the issues are relevant to ESP. The book is an updated view on researching and teaching learning strategies.

References

Anderson, N. J. (2005). L2 learning strategies. In E. Hinkel (Ed.), *Handbook of research in second language teaching and learning* (pp. 757–71). Mahwah, NJ: Lawrence Erlbaum.

Bonanno, H., & Jones, J. (2007). *The MASUS procedure: Measuring the academic skills of university students. A diagnostic assessment.* Learning Centre, University of Sydney. Retrieved 2 March 2017 from http://sydney.edu.au/stuserv/documents/learning_centre/MASUS.pdf.

Breen, M., & Littlejohn, A. (2000). *Classroom decision-making: Negotiation and process syllabuses in practice.* Cambridge: Cambridge University Press.

Cambridge English Business Certificates. (online). Retrieved 2 March 2017 from www.cambridgeenglish.org/exams/business-certificates/.

Case, A. (2015). EAP games and worksheets. Retrieved 2 March 2017 from https://tefltastic.wordpress.com/worksheets/eap/.

Chou, M.-h. (2011). The influence of learner strategies on oral presentations: A comparison between group and individual performance. *English for Specific Purposes, 30*(4), 272–85.

Dudley-Evans, T., & St. John, M. (1998). *Developments in English for specific purposes: A multi-disciplinary approach.* Cambridge: Cambridge University Press.

Elder, C. (2003). The DELNA initiative at the University of Auckland. *TESOLANZ Newsletter, 12,* 15–16.

Ferguson, G. (2013). English for medical purposes. In B. Paltridge & S. Starfield (Eds.), *Handbook of English for specific purposes* (pp. 243–62). Oxford: Wiley-Blackwell.

Flowerdew, J. (2011). Action, content and identity in applied genre analysis for ESP. *Language Teaching, 44,* 516–28.

Gillett, A. (2014). Does EAP work? A guide for students in higher education. Retrieved 2 March 2017 from www.uefap.net/blog/?p=440.

Grabe, W., & Stoller, F. (2002). *Teaching and researching reading.* Harlow: Pearson.

Graham, S., Macaro, E. & Vanderplank, R. (2007). A review of listening strategies: Focus on sources of knowledge and on success. In A. D. Cohen & E. Macaro (Eds.), *Language learner strategies: 30 years of research and practice* (pp. 165–85). Oxford: Oxford University Press.

Hyland, K., & Shaw, P. (2016). *The Routledge handbook of English for academic purposes.* London: Routledge.

James, M. (2014). Learning transfer in English-for-academic-purposes contexts: A systematic review of research. *Journal of English for Academic Purposes, 14,* 1–13.

Johns, A. M. (1997). *Text role and context.* Cambridge: Cambridge University Press.

Kwan, N., & Dunworth, K. (2016). English as a lingua franca communication between domestic helpers and employers in Hong Kong: A study of pragmatic strategies. *English for Specific Purposes 43,* 13–24.

Northcott, J. (2013). Legal English. In B. Paltridge & S. Starfield (Eds.), *Handbook of English for specific purposes* (pp. 213–26). Oxford: Wiley-Blackwell.

Northcott, J., & Brown, G. (2006). Legal translator training: Partnership between teachers of English for legal purposes and legal specialists. *English for Specific Purposes, 25*(3), 358–75.

Oxford, R. L. (1990). *What every teacher should know.* New York: Newbury House.

Oxford, R. L. (2011a). Strategies for learning a second or foreign language: A timeline. *Language Teaching, 44*(2), 167–80.

Oxford, R. L. (2011b). *Teaching and researching language learning strategies*. Harlow: Longman-Pearson.

Paltridge, B., & Starfield, S. (Eds.) (2013). *Handbook of English for specific purposes*. Oxford: Wiley-Blackwell.

Tardy, C. M., & Jwa, S. (2016). Composition studies and EAP. In K. Hyland & P. Shaw (Eds.), *The Routledge handbook of English for academic purposes* (pp. 56–68). Abingdon: Routledge.

University of Auckland. (2015). Diagnostic English Language Needs Assessment (DELNA). Retrieved 2 March 2017 from www.delna.auckland.ac.nz/en.html.

Yang, H.-C. (2012). Modeling the relationships between test-taking strategies and test performance on a graph-writing task: Implications for EAP. *English for Specific Purposes, 31*(3), 174–87.

Chapter 7

Technology and English for specific purposes

One area in ESP that has witnessed a great change over recent years is the use of technology. The internet, social media and digital technologies have had a massive influence on business, workplaces and education. These technologies need to be utilised and reflected in ESP course design, resources and management. However, it should be acknowledged that technology develops so rapidly that any discussion of the area will probably be redundant within five years. This chapter addresses the following areas in the role of technology in ESP:

- Technology and changing modes of communication
- Technology and pedagogy
- Technology and course management
- Technology and assessment
- Constraints of technology

Technology has had a tremendous influence on how we communicate, how we teach and how we learn. In recent years the way literacy is conceived has changed. Literacy is no longer considered as a singular attribute but as a pluralistic set of literacies. Included in this is digital literacy, which refers to the ability to communicate using different media and modes (Bloch, 2013). Multimodal literacies are essential in today's world and individuals who do not possess these literacies will be greatly disadvantaged in terms of communication, work and study. This chapter will discuss the uses of technology that have resulted in new forms of communication and the use of technology to facilitate teaching and learning, with a focus on EAP and ESP outside of university settings. Table 7.1 lists some examples of the types and uses of technology in ESP course design. Chapter 15 lists links and resources for these.

Reflection 7.1

Digital literacy

Would you class yourself as digitally literate?

What types of technology do you use on a daily basis?

How does technology help you learn?

How do you use technology in your teaching?

New ways of communicating

In today's digital age people communicate in very different and varied ways compared to a few years ago. A digital divide separates those who possess the literacies in current technology from those who do not (Arnó-Macià, 2012), with those who do not being at a great disadvantage. Digital modes of communication can occur in real time, referred to as synchronous communication, such as Twitter and chat, or with a time delay, referred to as asynchronous, such as email. With advances in technology, communication can take place in any setting through the use of mobile devices such as phones and tablets. In the workplace this means people are expected to be contactable at all times. In academia the geographical constraints of the university classroom and library no longer apply. This has affected where and how students study and how courses are offered. Courses no longer need to be designed and offered as classroom-based and exclusively face-to-face. Many academic courses are available in distance mode, whereby the student and the teacher are not in the same location. Hybrid, or blended, academic courses are increasingly popular, whereby instruction and learning take place both virtually and face-to-face. This also applies to language-learning courses, with most university-based EAP courses including an online component. The following section addresses some of the major forms of communication that have emerged in recent years to play an important role in ESP.

Email

Email is an essential medium of communication in EAP and in EBP. It is arguably the most common medium of daily communication. In academia it has replaced some face-to-face communication, particularly between academic staff, administrative staff and students. In EBP email has replaced business letters and memos.

Table 7.1   Some examples of types and uses of technology in ESP

Types and uses	Example
Finding authentic texts EAP EOP	TED Talks faculty homepage company's webpage
ESP-specific computer software Interactive exercises	Cambridge online IELTS practice

Ebook
Electronic readers
	A lot of publications come in three formats:
	    hardback book, softback book and ebook.
	The ebook is cheaper and publishers often
	    provide samples free of charge,

Electronic-document readers,
    which allow readers to highlight
    and take notes.
	Kindle and Garnet

Internet browsing Google Scholar	Using descriptors to find materials and subject specific information

E fora
Webinars
E villages
	Online discussions that focus on one topic
	    IATEFL run these regularly for teachers
	    TESOL's Electronic Villages Online (EVO)

Wikis
Tags within electronic texts
	These are electronic tags that occur in texts that
	    can link to other courses, expanding the
	    learning experience for students

University library sites	University library sites include a lot more than
	    electronic catalogues. For example, the use of
	    electronic databases has transformed literature
	    reviewing

Learning Management System (LMS)	LMS is an essential tool in academic study,
	    controlling all aspects of course delivery and
	    consumption

Corpora Concordance programmes	British National Corpus AntConc

Apps	Programs available for smart phones that are
	    useful for executing tasks away from the desk.
	    There are many thousands of apps available
	    for EAP and ESP learners

The role of email is central when participating in an academic community. Most students and staff will be assigned an exclusive email account as part of their university enrolment. They will receive all university communications through this mode. Email is now available across all devices, such as computers, tablets, mobiles and iPads. This means that students, staff and administrative staff may be in contact outside regular hours, such as at weekends and evenings. This has led to a need for etiquette within the university setting. For example, students and teachers need to establish whether it is reasonable to expect email interaction during the weekend. Register is another area that can problematic. Email language tends to be more informal than written forms of communication but more formal than texting or speaking. This can lead to problems for second-language students with inappropriate levels of formality, which may result in offence. It may be appropriate to focus on email etiquette and register in an ESP course.

In EBP business communication is frequently through email (Warren, 2013). One interesting and unique aspect of email communication is the nested chain (Kankaanranta, 2006) and the use of the cc facility to include others in the communication chain (Gimenez, 2000). These two phenomena present novel considerations for the interlocutors. Nested email chains enable continuity, with the communication chain being visible in one source. The cc facility often acts as a management tool. For example, a sales clerk in a disciplinary situation may be emailed by her supervisor with a cc to the head of department, thus lending authority and formality to the communication. A further departure in terms of types of communication is engaging with communication from more than one source at a time. Gimenez (2014) refers to the concept of multiple conversations and gives the example of a person writing an email or text while speaking to a client on the phone. An ESP course should prepare students to participate in such multimodal communication.

Blogging and microblogging

Another important influence in ESP and ELT in general has been blogging. Blogging refers to an interactive, web-based communication. Initially, in the 1990s, blogging tended to be restricted to monologues posted by individuals on a topic of their choice. Increasingly blogs have become dialogic and multi-authored, comprising chronological posts about a given topic (Darics, 2015) and can thus help form ESP communities in a way that other media cannot. In business, corporate blogs may promote products or the company. Amazon and Trip Advisor, for instance, use customer reviews, a form of blog, to promote products.

Individuals maintain blogs for a number of reasons. Professional blogs are common in academia, with academics keeping blogs about research in their fields. This makes blogs a useful resource for researchers and course designers. Microblogging refers to social media modes, such as Twitter and Facebook. A microblog provides brief interaction instantly and as such has greatly influenced the nature of communication. For example, business communication used to be characterised by precise, regulated business letters and reports in a prescriptive formal style. Today this formality has been replaced with instant communication across national borders (Gimenez, 2000), thus saving a vast amount of time and effort, although spontaneous communication can lack precision and may require more iterations and revisions to reach the communicative aim.

Reflection 7.2

Blogging and microblogging

Do you subscribe to any blogs?

Do you write blogs?

Do you use Twitter or Facebook?

For what purposes do you use these?

Where and when do you use these media?

Task 7.1

Blogs, blogging and ESP course design

How do you think the use of blogs could be included in an ESP course design?

How do you think student blogging could be included in an ESP course design?

Technology as a pedagogic tool

Computer-assisted language learning (CALL)

Computer-assisted language learning has been around since the early 1980s. Computers and technology can play a central role in ESP course delivery and also facilitate a link between the language-learning context and the authentic communicative context. In particular, technology enables teachers and learners to access and engage with authentic communication. Some ESP courses have a CALL component as a central strand – for example, *Career Express* (Butzphal & Maier-Fairclough, 2013) is a business-English course that has an online self-study component. Some publishers of ESP materials make companion websites available. For example, *Academic writing: A handbook for international students* (Bailey, 2015) has a companion website that offers further materials, topics and answers. The internet has had the largest influence on course design and has made it easier for course designers, teachers and students to source the authentic materials that are the mainstay of ESP courses.

Authentic resources

For the course designer, technology is extremely useful and has simplified the course-design task enormously. There is a vast array of authentic materials and spoken and written texts available free of charge on the internet. In EAP students can often access their academic courses, reading lists and academic tasks online prior to enrolment. This can help a course designer address individual students' needs by setting tasks based on the material. Some universities – for example, Yale (online) and MIT (online) – offer lectures, classroom materials and, in some cases, complete courses online free of charge. 'Massive open online courses' (MOOCs) is the term used to refer these provisions. An internet search of MOOCs will provide a long list of specialised courses, some affiliated with universities and free of charge. An example of a commercial provision of MOOCs is Open Classrooms (online), whereby the learner pays a monthly premium. Video-hosting sites such as YouTube have a vast array of potential resources for receptive and productive skills. Sites such as Skype allow video calling and conferencing, providing great potential for interaction and conversation. Podcasts are becoming common in academic and business settings, replacing radio broadcasts as a source for ESP material; and podcasts are usually freely available. For example, the BBC (online) has a series of podcasts on EAP.

The internet and course delivery

Computers and the internet play an important role in course delivery. Many institutions use learning management systems (LMS), such as Blackboard or Moodle, to manage teaching and learning. Blackboard is normally bought by the institution. Moodle (modular object-oriented dynamic learning environment) on the other hand is free and can be used by individuals. Using an LMS, students access materials, submit assessments and get feedback from tutors and peers. LMS are becoming increasingly sophisticated. For example, in many EAP settings the LMS can include text-matching software, such as Turnitin. Text-matching software identifies similarities between the text the student submits and others, both published texts and those submitted by other users of the system. It is a tool used primarily to combat plagiarism within academic settings, but it also includes tools such as Grademark that can be used by instructors to assess and provide online feedback on students' work.

In the fairly recent past students needed to access a desktop computer to engage with their academic course. Today many students rely on mobile devices such as smartphones and tablets to engage with materials, peers and teachers. As a result, engagement with ESP no longer has physical or temporal boundaries.

Computers and the internet are essential for course administration. Student records and performance can all be recorded and monitored using specific database-type programs.

The influence of technology on assessment

With the globalisation of English, there is a vast need to learn ESP. With this comes the need to be able to reliably measure English performance. This has led to a range of high-stakes ESP tests. EAP tests in particular are high-stakes, as they serve a gatekeeping function for university entry. Some of these tests are delivered electronically, either internet-based, such as the TOEFL iBT, or asynchronously, as in the computer-based version of IELTS. Cambridge offers a suite of business-English tests at different levels. For example, the Business Language Testing Service (BULATS) is a test administered online. The advantages of online testing are that it is quick, cheap and objective; however, such objectivity can present a problem when assessing communicative practices such as speaking and listening, which are subjective non-observable skills. Issues in ESP assessment are addressed in greater detail in Chapter 8.

Technology and the ESP practitioner

A challenge for teachers and students is how to select appropriate sources and media. Unlike published materials, online sources are not vetted nor have they undergone peer review. Anybody can post texts on any subject online, regardless of their expertise. Because of this, information collected online cannot necessarily be trusted, so ESP course designers need to have a system to evaluate online authentic texts they may wish to use on courses. Evaluation should be based on the reliability of the sources and whether the writer is an authority; consideration should also be given to the intended audience of the text and currency; how up-to-date the entry is matters too. Table 7.2 outlines these three criteria that can be used to assess the relevance of online texts. Chan (2009, 126) refers to three main criteria that need to be considered when evaluating ESP materials: "authenticity, suitability and credibility". She devised a checklist that could be applied to the teaching of English for business meetings. This is the basis for the template presented in Chapter 15.

Table 7.2 Criteria for evaluating internet texts for ESP

Audience	Who is the audience of the text?
	Does this reflect the target audience? For example,
	   a magazine article about engineering targets a lay audience,
	   while a research article targets an academic audience.

Authority	Is the writer of the text a recognised expert in the field? Texts with no named author are not appropriate for use in courses.
Currency	Is the text up-to-date? Sources remain on the internet forever. It is important sources are dated.

Task 7.2

Evaluating online authentic texts for ESP

Find some examples of authentic sources online. Using Table 7.2, evaluate how appropriate your source would be to an ESP course.

Another recent development that is greatly enhancing ESP course design is the use of language corpora. These are large collections of texts which can be analysed using concordancing software. This software is used to analyse the occurrence and frequency of words and expressions in corpora. Corpora and the analytical software are within the reach of most ESP practitioners. An example of an accessible concordance programme is *Wordsmith* (Lexical Analysis Software, online). By using corpora and concordancing software teachers and students can be very specific in the selection of texts and the exploration of common forms and expressions. Further discussion of the use of corpora can be found in Chapter 11. For a list of corpora and concordancing software see Chapter 15.

Issues with technology and ESP

The use of technology is dependent upon the social and economic setting of the ESP learners. In some countries technology is not widely available and internet connections may be unreliable. For example, in many areas, even in developed countries, mobile coverage is not available. This implies also that ESP learners who come from less developed regions may lack the computer and technological skills necessary to engage in an ESP course in more developed countries. In the case of EAP, for example, students may need to be instructed on how to access library catalogues or learning management systems. A further consideration is the expertise of the ESP practitioners. Teachers may be resistant to utilising new technologies because of a lack confidence or a lack of time.

A further consideration is the unique contribution technology brings to the teaching and learning of ESP. Course designers need to consider whether the use of a particular technology or program improves upon traditional printed material and in what way. In other words, course designers need to guard against using technology purely for its novelty effect. There is perhaps also an expectation from students to use technology.

Task 7.3

Using technology in ESP course design

How familiar are you with:

> Skype
> YouTube
> podcasts

Think about the different ways these could be exploited in an ESP setting.

Search for some potential authentic texts, spoken or written, that could be used in a specific ESP course.

> How did you choose these?
> How could you exploit the texts?

What are the major considerations when selecting authentic texts for student use?

How can ESP practitioners ensure students achieve the required digital literacies?

How can ESP practitioners develop their own digital literacies?

Summary

This chapter has considered some implications of technologies on ESP and ESP course design. It has identified its major uses within the field and provided some starting points for discussion of the impact of the digital age on ESP and on teaching and learning in a broader sense.

Further reading

For a good overview of the role of technology in ESP see Arnó-Macià (2012); Darics (2015) has an interesting edited book about the changing nature of business communication; Bloch (2013) has a chapter on the use of technology; and an example of a blog on EAP is Gillet (online).

References

Arnó-Macià, E. (2012). The role of technology in teaching languages for specific purposes courses. *Modern Language Journal, 96*(1), 89–104.

Bailey, S. B. (2015). *Academic writing: A handbook for international students.* London: Routledge. Accessed 2 March 2017 at www.routledgetextbooks.com/textbooks/9781138778504/.

BBC. (online). Accessed 2 March 2017 at www.bbc.co.uk/worldservice/learningenglish/general/talkaboutenglish/2009/04/090427_tae_al.shtml.

Bloch, J. (2013). Technology and ESP. In B. Paltridge & S. Starfield (Eds.), *The handbook of English for specific purposes* (pp. 385–402). Oxford: Wiley-Blackwell.

Butzphal, G., & Maier-Fairclough, J. (2013). *Career express.* Reading: Garnet. Accessed 2 March 2017 at www.garneteducation.com/selfstudy/career-express.html.

Chan, C. S. C. (2009). Forging a link between research and pedagogy: A holistic framework for evaluating business English materials. *English for Specific Purposes, 28*(2), 125–36.

Darics, E. (Ed.) (2015). *Digital business discourse.* London: Palgrave Macmillan.

Gillet, A. (online). Accessed 15 March 2017 at www.uefap.net/.

Gimenez, J. C. (2000). Business e-mail communication: Some emerging tendencies in register. *English for Specific Purposes, 19*(3), 237–51.

Gimenez, J. C. (2014). Multi-communication and the business English class: Research meets pedagogy. *English for Specific Purposes, 35*(1), 1–16.

Kankaanranta, A. (2006) Hej Seppe, could you pls comment on this! A study of BELF users' perceptions of English. *English for Specific Purposes, 29*(1), 204–29.

Kankaanranta, A., & Louhiala-Salminen, L. (2010). "English? – Oh, it's just work!": A study of BELF users' perceptions. *English for Specific Purposes, 29*(3), 204–9.

Lexical Analysis Software. (online). Accessed 2 March at www.lexically.net/wordsmith/.

MIT. (online). Accessed 2 March 2017 at http://ocw.mit.edu/index.htm.

Open Classrooms. (online). Accessed 18 April 2017 at https://openclassrooms.com/.

Warren, M. (2013). "Just spoke to...": The types and directionality of intertextuality in professional discourse. *English for Specific Purposes, 32*(1), 12–24.

Yale University. (online). Accessed 2 March 2017 at http://oyc.yale.edu/.

Chapter 8

Assessment of English for specific purposes

This chapter addresses the essential element of assessment and evaluation in course design. This includes formal assessment, such as high-stakes EAP tests like TOEFL and IELTS, and business-English tests like the Cambridge Business English Certificates. The chapter also addresses less formal classroom assessment and includes guidelines for conducting some more formative types of ESP assessment. Course evaluation, which is an essential part of the course-design cycle, is also discussed. The chapter addresses the following areas:

- Need for assessment
- Purpose of assessment
- Types of ESP assessment

  - Formal assessment
  - High-stakes testing
  - Informal assessment

- Course evaluation

Assessment in ESP is a very broad term and includes many aspects. Language assessment can be used to identify needs, to place students into groups, to ensure course objectives are met, as a learning tool, to monitor progress, as an exit measure and as an external entry measure. In this chapter, course evaluation is included under the umbrella term 'ESP assessment'.

In principle ESP assessment is no different from EGP assessment and might include entry tests, exit tests and progress tests. However, in some forms of ESP – for example, EOP – there may be no formal assessment.

Within ESP, EAP tends to include more formal, high-stakes assessment than EOP because of the external need for standardisation. Universities need to ensure that qualifications gained from one institution are in line with those from another, so an undergraduate degree is standardised at least on a national level. EOP on the other hand has no such constraints, and assessment is likely to be much less formal and more likely to rely on teacher or classroom assessment.

Reflection 8.1

Experience with language assessment

What is your experience with language testing/assessment?

As a test taker?
As a test giver?

What was the purpose of the test?

Did you think the purpose was achieved?

The major consideration in assessment in ESP or otherwise is purpose: why is the assessment being conducted? Examples of ESP assessment purposes include evaluating performance on an ESP course, diagnosing linguistic weaknesses, meeting university-entry criteria and fulfilling an immigration requirement. Whatever the purpose, assessment needs to be thoroughly analysed and thought through for relevance. In many cases, particularly in EAP, the purpose of the assessment is specific – for example, entry to university – yet the test itself cannot be classed as an ESP test, since it reflects general language proficiency. An example of this is IELTS.

Assessment relevant to ESP courses

A primary concern for a course designer in ESP assessment is alignment. Alignment refers to the extent to which the assessment task accurately reflects the content and learning objectives of the course and the target communicative situation. In language assessment a distinction is made between direct and indirect testing. Direct testing reflects target-language use. For example, in EBP report writing is a common skill that would be on the syllabus; in direct testing the assessment task would be to write a report. Indirect testing is where it is assumed that performance on the assessment task can be generalised to target-language use. Indirect testing is common in large-scale proficiency tests such as TOEFL and is widespread because a high level of reliability and objectivity can be achieved. Reliability refers to the stability of a test, so that test items always measure the same thing, the testing conditions are the same and the rating is the same.

In relation to ESP language tests, designers need to consider test purpose, test-taker characteristics and the target-language-use situation (Douglas, 2013). However, linguistic competence in the target communicative situation is often difficult to define, as it is impossible to untangle the relationship between language and subject expertise in ESP.

Common types of assessment in ESP

There are a number of assessment types that are common in both ESP and EGP (Brown & Abeywickrama, 2010). These depend on the purpose of the assessment and may vary in specificity. One of the central notions in language assessment is construct representation or construct validity (Fulcher & Davidson, 2007). This refers to what is being measured – for example, EAP reading – and how this is done. So, for example, a reading test that involves writing long answers cannot be said to have construct validity in terms of reading. In ESP this is complicated further because we have to be clear about what is being measured in terms of language compared to content knowledge. The construct here reflects ESP competence – so designers need to articulate what this is and how it can be measured.

Diagnostic tests

Diagnostic tests are used to identify the strengths and weaknesses of the students. They may be used as part of needs analysis, used for placement (see next section) or as a tool to measure progress. Pilbeam introduced the term 'linguistic audit' (1979), which refers to gathering information and analysing stakeholder language needs. Inherent in diagnostic tests is the notion that action will be taken on the results. For example, if a diagnostic test shows that that a large number of EAP students cannot critique an academic text, this shortcoming would then be addressed in the ESP course.

Published diagnostic tests are available, although these are general in nature and do not reflect ESP. Perhaps the most well known is DIALANG, which is linked to the Common European Framework and is available in a number of languages. Oxford University Press (online) publishes diagnostic grammar tests which link to their grammar books.

Some EAP institutions offer diagnostic tests which feed into their own EAP courses. An excellent example of an EAP diagnostic procedure is the Diagnostic English Language Needs Assessment (DELNA) used at the University of Auckland, New Zealand. This is a mandatory post-entry diagnostic test for all undergraduate and doctoral students, regardless of language background (Read, 2015). Based on the results students may receive targeted help with EAP. It is interesting to note that it implies an academic literacies approach to EAP. This approach assumes that all students need to learn appropriate academic skills, not just those who are from non-English-speaking backgrounds. An academic-literacies approach to EAP is discussed in more detail in Chapter 13.

Placement tests

Placement tests usually reflect a diagnostic procedure. With ESP projects where more than one group will be studying ESP, some form of placement tool is required. A typical example of this is in a university pre-sessional course, where large numbers of international students enrol prior to starting their academic courses. A placement test is often used to measure students' proficiency according to levels such as advanced, intermediate and elementary. Classes are then formed on this basis. In a placement test it is important that the aspects measured are matched by syllabus items for the respective levels – so if basic textual cohesion is included in the intermediate course, a student would need to demonstrate this ability in order to be considered eligible for the next level.

Entry tests

This type of assessment shares some similarities with placement tests. They are used to measure whether a student has the basic proficiency to be able to successfully study the ESP course. The main difference is that an entry test may be used to exclude entry on to a course, while a placement test is conducted after entry. Entry tests assume that there is a common core of language. A typical example of this is a language assessment determined to decide whether a student has reached the threshold level that will allow him/her to enrol on an ESP course rather than a EGP course. Some language tests are used as entry measures but are not specific to the setting. For example, TOEFL and IELTS are high-stakes tests used to gate-keep entry to academic programmes and even for immigration purposes. High-stakes tests are discussed further below.

Exit tests

In a similar vein, exit tests assess whether the student has achieved the aims of the ESP course or whether they need further study. These tend to be very specific to the setting in which they occur. Again, these are widely used in university language centres to assess whether the student is ready for entry to their academic courses.

Achievement and progress tests

These are assessments directly related to the ESP course that are used to, as the name suggests, measure progress. These tests measure how much the learner has learned during the ESP course.

Task 8.1

Types of ESP assessment

Think of some possible assessment tasks for the following common types of assessment in ESP. Think of the students, the purpose of the assessment task, the nature of the assessment task and how the results can be reported.

Diagnostic test
Entry test
Exit test
Progress test
Achievement test

High-stakes tests

The demand for education in English-speaking countries has greatly increased in recent years. Pre-sessional training and coaching for English exams is now big business in many countries and high-stakes proficiency tests such as IELTS and TOEFL are much in demand. Success or failure in these tests can influence an individual's future. For example, if a student gets the required entry band on IELTS, they will be allowed to follow their chosen academic pathway, and, if not, they will be obliged to rethink their future. While high-stakes tests offer more rigour, reliability and validity than other methods of assessment, there are some undesirable aspects. The first is the issue of washback (Cheng *et al.*, 2004). Because these tests are so important, teachers and students may perceive that only classroom activities and materials relevant to the test are of use and therefore make these the primary focus of teaching and learning. In this case learners will experience problems when embarking on their academic course, because IELTS and TOEFL are not ESP tests and do not reflect the target communicative situation of the students. Research into the predictive validity of IELTS shows that low language proficiency (Band 6 or lower) impedes academic performance; however, high language proficiency (Band 6.5 and higher) does not predict achievement (Woodrow, 2006). There are many other factors contributing to academic success, such as motivation and cognitive ability (Phakiti *et al.*, 2013).

An example of an EOP test is the Occupational English Test (OET), developed at the University of Melbourne, Australia (McNamara, 1996; Elder *et al.*, 2013). This is a test for health professionals in 12 health disciplines, including nursing and dentistry. The test was developed

Table 8.1   Occupational English Test

Test development	Commonalities	Skills	Texts	Test tasks
Analysis of target communicative situation	Assessment of patient including history-taking	Listening	Simulated health professional/ patient consultation Lecture about health-related topic	Note-taking Answering questions
Consultation with clinical educators, professionals and EFL teachers	Physical examination	Reading	Two scientific texts relating to a health issue	Multiple-choice questions
	Explanation to patient of diagnosis and treatment	Writing	Health-related scenario	Write letter of referral
	Treatment	Speaking	Patient/carer health-professional interview	Role-play: candidate plays role of health professional
	Patient/client education and counselling.			

Source: The OET Centre (online).

through analysis of target situations based on consultation with major stakeholders (clinical educators, practitioners, ESP teachers). The findings revealed that there are commonalities across health-professional language needs. Table 8.1 shows a breakdown of the test's components. The handbook published for the test is a useful resource for course designers in the health-sciences field. It provides examples of tasks and sample answers. It also has a useful section on preparing students for the test.

Common European Framework of Reference for Languages (CEFR)

A useful tool for course designers is the CEFR. This is a series of descriptions of language ability across six levels, from the lowest to the highest

Table 8.2   Equivalences of widely used tests with ESP

CEFR level	Description	IELTS	TOEFL iBT	Cambridge	Pearson	BEC	TOEIC	BULATS
C2	Upper advanced	8.5–9	NA	CPE	NA	NA	NA	90–100
C1	Advanced	6.5–7	110–20	CAE	76–84	BEC Higher	945–90	75–9
B2	Upper intermediate	5–6.5	87–106	FCE	59–75	BEC Vantage	785–940	60–74
B1	Intermediate	4.00–4.5	57–86	PET	43–58	BEC Preliminary	550–780	50–9
A2	Elementary	3.5–4	NA	KET	30–42	NA	225–545	20–39
A1	Beginner	NA	NA	NA	10–29	NA	120–220	0–19

Key: IELTS (International English language Testing Service); TOEFL iBT (Test of English as a Foreign Language: internet-based test); Cambridge CPE (Cambridge Proficiency English); Cambridge CAE (Cambridge Advanced English); Cambridge FCE (Cambridge First Certificate); Cambridge PET (Preliminary English Test); Cambridge KET (Key English Test); Pearson Test of English; Cambridge BEC Higher (Business English Certificate Higher); Cambridge BEC Vantage (Business English Certificate Vantage); Cambridge BEC Preliminary (Business English Certificate Preliminary); TOEIC (Test of English for International Communication); BULATS (Business English Language Testing Service).

(A1, A2, B1, B2, C1, C2). The descriptors reflect linguistic ability in a range of settings and across all four skill areas: setting, interlocutors, grammar and vocabulary. The system can be applied to a range of contexts but is particularly useful for intercultural communication – for example, in business. There has been a great deal of research into the framework and it has been used to inform the course design and assessment of a vast number of language courses (Council of Europe, 2001). The Council of Europe web page has a great deal of information about the CEFR (Council of Europe, online). It is extremely useful to have internationally comparable levels of language proficiency. The CEFR features in most comparisons of language tests. In assessment, comparing tests is referred to as equivalences and can be useful to the course designer; however, as the tests often measure different skills and types of language, they should be regarded with caution. Table 8.2 is an equivalence table for some of the major English language tests in use.

Assessment methods

There is a range of methods available to course designers when designing assessment tasks. These may be formal pen and paper tests, such as multiple-choice and short-answer tests, which are widely used to test receptive skills, such as reading and listening (Brown & Abeywickrama, 2010). However, when assessing productive skills pen and paper tests are not adequate. With speaking and writing tests, samples of language need to be elicited from the student which then need to be assessed. This can be done by using a rating scale that describes the performance using descriptors. There are two types of rating scale: those that use holistic descriptors and those that use analytical descriptors. In a holistic scale the overall performance is described, while analytical scales break down the performance into components (Hughes, 2002).

Reflection 8.2

Assessment purpose and techniques

What types of assessment are you familiar with?

What was the purpose of the assessment task?

Make a list of assessment techniques you have experience with (for example, end-of-term tests).

How was performance assessed? By grade? Through feedback?

What did you think about these assessments?

Eliciting language to assess

ESP ability can be assessed formally or informally. It can be assessed by designing assessment tasks that replicate the target communicative situation. An example of this in EAP could be getting students to take notes from a lecture, or in EBP asking students to give an oral presentation. There are many ways of assessing general language proficiency. Usually, some form of test or assessment task is given to the students and their performance is measured, based on a framework. This normally consists of a list of descriptors, which students either have achieved or not. The best known such framework is the Common European Framework, as discussed above. This framework is a useful starting point for course designers because the levels are universally understood (Council of Europe, 2001).

However, scales and descriptors of general proficiency cannot measure ESP performance because they do not take into account the needs of the target situation or the disciplinary field. Such descriptors need to be designed by the course designer.

Task 8.2

Using analytical assessment scales

Look at the CEFR scales for assessment available at: https://rm.coe.int/
CoERMPublicCommonSearchServices/DisplayDCTMContent?
documentId=090000168045b15e

Using one or several of these, devise a rating scale for a particular ESP
assessment task.

The ESP practitioner as assessor

In large-scale language institutions reliable, validated tests are more likely to
be used. Such tests could be commercial tests, such as the Cambridge Business English Certificate (BEC) or IELTS, or specific tests developed in-house.
The test-development procedure is an iterative process, very much like the
process of course design itself. Weigle and Malone (2016, 616) recommend
the following steps in EAP test development:

1   Determining test purpose
2   Defining objectives
3   Creating test plan or test specification
4   Writing items
5   Reviewing and revising items
6   Assembling a complete test
7   Pilot testing
8   Statistical analysis
9   Creating a plan for administration, scoring and score reporting
10 Ongoing monitoring of the test.

However, in specific EOP courses, assessment is likely to be more specialised,
so it may rest with the ESP practitioner to assess the students. In a small-scale EOP course students may be at different linguistic levels, which will
impact on the types of assessment that are possible and meaningful. In such
cases negotiation with the stakeholders is necessary to find out exactly what
constitutes successful target-situation communication.

Formative and summative assessment

Course designers need to consider the role of assessment in the course. Summative assessment refers to the type of assessment task used to assess whether a student has achieved the aims of the course or not. It provides a snapshot of learner achievement. Such tests would include exit tests and progress and achievement tests. An example of a summative assessment is a language test used to provide information to stakeholders; however, such a test does not help the learner improve. Formative assessment on the other hand is designed to facilitate learning. Diagnostic procedures could be classed as formative. Most classroom assessment that reflects objectives can be classed as formative. Formative assessment has learning as its aim. It comprises assessment tasks that inform the learner of areas for improvement, and the assessment act itself should promote learning. For example, setting an EAP class a literature review will help with critical reading and the acquisition of content knowledge.

Feedback

Within the field of assessment, feedback is a very important aspect of teaching and learning. Feedback can come from the teacher or from classmates. The type of feedback in the assessment process needs to be considered carefully and be in line with stakeholders' expectations. Feedback on productive skills of speaking and writing is particularly important as success in these skills is not as readily measurable as in reading and listening. In writing, feedback is able to facilitate writing as a process because it promotes drafts of writing. Peer review is particularly important to this end as it takes pressure off the teacher to provide feedback on multiple drafts of work (Paltridge *et al.*, 2009). Peer feedback may be appropriate for a range of ESP-type courses as it may reflect real practice. For example, in a business-oriented EOP course, group decisions and negotiations which may be classed as forms of feedback are probably normal, everyday working activities. Part 3, Course 6 of Paltridge's *Writing for publication* provides an excellent example of how peer review can be included in an ESP course.

Evaluation

Course evaluation is an essential part of the course-design cycle. Course evaluation provides reflection on the effectiveness and relevance of the ESP course and indicates what needs to be improved. Evaluation data should be obtained from all the stakeholders, students, ESP practitioners and employers to ensure everyone's needs are being met. This data can be collected, as with needs, using a variety of methods. Student questionnaires regarding their satisfaction concerning the ESP course are widely used. When designing evaluation procedures, it is important that measures are focused and, importantly, that the results can be acted upon. So, for example, the question "Did you find teacher feedback sufficient for this course?" presupposes that it is feasible to offer more teacher feedback. Figure 8.1 illustrates the cycle of course design incorporating assessment and course evaluation.

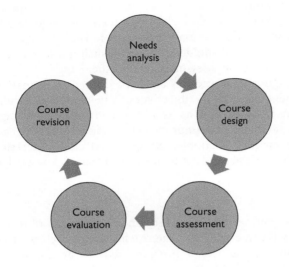

Figure 8.1 Course design and assessment cycle

Task 8.3

Course evaluation

Consider how course evaluation can be conducted

What methods can be used?

Think of an ESP course you are familiar with. How was the course evaluated?

What action was taken informed by evaluation?

Summary

This chapter has discussed the role of assessment in ESP. Assessment occurs at a number of levels of ESP course design from the classroom level, ensuring lesson aims are achieved, to the course level, assessing whether the student has attained the required level. Inherent in this is the importance of assessment purpose. Assessment and evaluation overlap with needs analysis in that they may use similar methodological techniques and all contribute to the course-design cycle. Figure 8.1 illustrated the course-design cycle, incorporating assessment and evaluation.

Further reading

Douglas (2013) provides a short and up-to-date overview of assessment in ESP, while Douglas (2000) provides an in-depth survey of the issues in ESP assessment and how to do it.

This latter publication is part of a comprehensive series of books on language assessment published by Cambridge University Press. Other books in the series include: Alderson (2000), *Assessing reading*; Buck (2001), *Assessing listening*; Cushing-Weigle (2002), *Assessing writing*; and Luoma (2004), *Assessing speaking*. In 2012 *The Modern Language Journal* published a focus issue on ESP. Sullivan's article in this issue is a good source for developments in ESP assessment. For an accessible introduction to the principles and practice of language assessment see Brown and Abeywickrama (2010). For a list of links to widely used tests in ESP see Chapter 15.

References

Alderson, C. J. (2000). *Assessing reading*. Cambridge: Cambridge University Press.

Brown, H. D., & Abeywickrama, P. (2010). *Language assessment: Principles and classroom practice*. Harlow: Pearson Longman.

Buck, G. (2001). *Assessing listening*. Cambridge: Cambridge University Press.

Cheng, L., Watanabe, Y., & Curtis, A. (2004). *Washback in language testing: Research contexts and methods*. Mahwah, NJ: Lawrence Erlbaum.

Council of Europe. (2001). Common European Framework of Reference for Languages: Learning, teaching, assessment. Retrieved 3 March 2017 from https://rm.coe.int/CoERMPublicCommonSearchServices/DisplayDCTMContent?documentId=090000168045b15e.

Council of Europe. (online). Accessed 3 March 2017 at www.coe.int/t/dg4/linguistic/cadre1_en.asp.

Cushing-Weigle, S. (2002). *Assessing writing*. Cambridge: Cambridge University Press.

Douglas, D. (2000). *Assessing languages for specific purposes*. Cambridge: Cambridge University Press.

Douglas, D. (2013). ESP assessment. In B. Paltridge & S. Starfield (Eds.), *The handbook of English for specific purposes* (pp. 367–83). Oxford: Wiley-Blackwell.

Elder, C., McNamara, T., Woodward, R., Woodward-Kron, R., Manias, E., McColl, G., Webb, G., Pill, J., & O'Hagan, S. (2013). Developing and validating language proficiency standards for non-native English speaking health professionals. *Papers in Language Testing and Assessment, 2*, 114–18.

Fulcher, G., & Davidson, F. (2007). *Language testing and assessment: An advanced resource book*. London: Routledge.

Hughes, A. (2002). *Testing for language teachers*. Cambridge: Cambridge University Press.

Luoma, S. (2004). *Assessing speaking*. Cambridge: Cambridge University Press.

McNamara, T. (1996). *Measuring second language performance.* Harlow: Longman.

The OET Centre. (online). Retrieved 3 March 2017 from www.occupationalenglish
test.org/resources/uploads/2015/08/OET-Preparation-Support-Pack-180515.pdf.

Oxford University Press. (online). Accessed 15 February 2017 at www.
oxfordenglishtesting.com/.

Paltridge, B., Harbon, L., Hirsh, D., Shen, H., Stevenson, M., Phakiti, A., &
Woodrow, L. (2009). *Teaching academic writing: An introduction for teachers
of second language writers.* Ann Arbor, MI: University of Michigan Press.

Phakiti, A., Hirsh, D., & Woodrow, L. (2013). It's not only English: Effects of
other individual factors on English language learning and academic learning of
ESL international students in Australia. *Journal of Research in International
Education, 12*(3), 239–58.

Pilbeam, A. (1979). The language audit. *Language Training, 1*(3), 6–9.

Read, J. (2015). Issues in post-entry language assessment in English-medium universities. *Language Teaching, 48*(2), 217–34.

Sullivan, B. (2012). Assessment issues in languages for specific purposes. *Modern
Language Journal, 96* (focus issue), 71–88.

Weigle, S. C., & Malone, M. E. (2016). Assessment of English for academic purposes.
In K. Hyland & P. Shaw (Eds.), *The Routledge handbook of English for academic
purposes* (pp. 608–20). Abingdon: Routledge.

Woodrow, L. (2006). Academic success of international postgraduate education students and the role of English proficiency. *University of Sydney Papers in TESOL,
1,* 51–70.

Part 2

Approaches to ESP course design

Chapter 9

Genre

In Part 2 the current major theoretical influences on course design are discussed. Chapter 9 focuses on genre, Chapter 10 on discourse analysis and Chapter 11 on corpora. These three perspectives are often used together and rely upon each other. This chapter discusses how theoretical and research perspectives on genre have influenced ESP course design and how genre analysis can be used as a course-design tool. Genre is a very important conceptualisation in ESP thinking and course design. The chapter discusses the following prominent aspects of genre:

- Background to genre
- Discourse communities
- Genre and needs analysis
- Genre networks
- Generic structure
- Application of genre to course design

Background to genre

Genre is arguably one of the most significant influences on ESP in recent years.

Genres can be understood at the most basic level as types of text – for example, an academic journal article. These genres are constructed by the community in which they occur and are subject to change. Norms of published research have evolved over the years and so journal articles may look very different from similar texts of 30 years ago. One change is that there are many more writers who use English as an additional language rather than a dominance of native English writers.

Conceptualisations of genre are rooted in three main traditions: the systemic functional linguistics (SFL) perspective, the rhetorical genre studies (RGS) perspective and the English for specific purposes (ESP) perspective. SFL originated from the work by Michael Halliday in the 1960s. For an accessible introduction to SFL see Eggins (2004). SFL attempts to capture the social and contextual element of language. In the acronym SFL 'systemic' refers to the systems of choices available to language users, while 'functional' refers to the uses and roles of language in a given context. The SFL approach to genre analysis is often labelled as the Sydney School, as much of the work originated at the University of Sydney, Australia. Key researchers in the area are Jim Martin and colleagues, who have made a significant contribution to SFL and genre studies. Martin defines genre as "a staged goal oriented purposeful activity in which speakers engage as members of our culture" (1984, 25). The SFL approach to language has also been extremely influential in educational settings in Australia, with this description of language having replaced traditional grammar for the teaching of writing in some Australian schools (Rose, 2006).

For the ESP course designer, an SFL framework can be used to generate a text-based syllabus, as this is the nature of the SFL framework of genres and genre families. An example of how SFL is used in a syllabus can be found in Feez (1998).

The RGS perspective on genre, originating in the US, focuses on the social actions that genres fulfil, rather than the actual discourse. The emphasis is on first-year writing and often from a native-speaker perspective. This has greatly influenced the area of composition studies in US undergraduate programmes (Tardy & Jwa, 2016). A seminal work in this area is Miller's (1984) notion of genre as social action. The recent focus in RGS has been on the use of ethnographic research methods to investigate dimensions of genres such as membership of systems and multimodality (Molle & Prior, 2008).

For the ESP course designer the implications of an RGS perspective are more nebulous than those of the other perspectives. This is because the focus of these researchers is on real settings with real participants, which are impossible to recreate in a classroom. However, the emphasis that is useful to the course designer is that of community (Flowerdew, 2011).

Within ESP, genre is defined by Swales as:

> a class of communicative events, the members of which share some set of communicative purposes. These purposes are recognized by the expert members of the parent discourse community and thereby constitute the rationale for the genre. This rationale shapes the schematic structure of the discourse and influences and constrains choice of content and style.
>
> (Swales, 1990, p. 58)

For the ESP course designer an ESP perspective on genre is valuable and informs many current teaching materials. An example of the application of the 'creating a research space structure' (CARS) framework

Table 9.1 Discourse communities

A discourse community	Examples from Graduate TESOL setting in a UK university
Has a broadly agreed set of common public goals	To facilitate students' knowledge about theory and practice of TESOL and underlying theory; to facilitate research into TESOL related areas; to enhance professional practice; to gain a Master's degree
Has mechanisms of intercommunication among its members	Through LMS, emails, face-to-face, blogs, Facebook
Uses its participatory mechanisms primarily to provide information and feedback	Attend lectures, tutorials, supervisions, additional seminars, online webinars
Utilises and hence possesses one or more genres in the communicative furtherance of its aims	Essays, seminar presentations, conversation analysis, dissertation, research plans, ESL course outlines
In addition to owning genres, a discourse community has acquired some specific lexis	Conversation analysis, second-language acquisition (SLA), flowchart (research), seminar, dissertation, module
Has a threshold level of members with a suitable degree of relevant content and discoursal expertise (Swales, 1990, 24–7)	Students need English proficiency (6.5 IELTS for international students), a recognised degree in a related subject. Staff have PhDs, experiences in TESOL and TESOL-related academic publications

(discussed in the 'Investigating genres' section on p. 103) can be found in Feak and Swales (2011). An ESP approach highlights the need to consider audience, purpose and setting in terms of genre.

Discourse communities

Central to the conceptualisation of genre in Swales' view is therefore a consideration of the social community within which the genre occurs, which he refers to as a "discourse community". This discourse community is a group of people who are engaged in similar activities and engage in disciplinary communication – so an academic discourse community shares communicative goals and interests.

According to Swales, a discourse community has six defining characteristics, which are influenced by the setting in which they are located. Table 9.1 presents these six characteristics with examples from a graduate TESOL setting.

Task 9.1

Discourse communities

Think about a discourse community you are a member of. This could be a professional community based on your job, an academic community based on your studies or a general community based on a free-time activity – for example, a language class or gym membership. Using the table below fill in examples for each of Swales' characteristics.

A discourse community	Examples
Has a broadly agreed set of common public goals	
Has mechanisms of intercommunication among its members	
Uses its participatory mechanisms primarily to provide information and feedback	
Utilises and hence possesses one or more genres in the communicative furtherance of its aims	
In addition to owning genres, a discourse community has acquired some specific lexis	
Has a threshold level of members with a suitable degree of relevant content and discoursal expertise (Swales, 1990, 24–7)	

In any discourse community members have varying levels of expertise and power in using and determining genres. For example, in a university department a professor would be viewed as an expert in the genre and has a great deal of power in determining what constitutes this genre, whereas a newly enrolled international student is viewed as a novice in the genre and has very little say in its constitution. This raises the issue of an imbalance of power within EAP. Critical ESP attempts to redress the imbalance of power relations within the communicative domain, particularly in universities, to help empower students in their academic experience (Benesch, 2001).

Genre and needs analysis

A course designer can consider genre at the needs level by identifying and collecting samples of the types of genre or text the learners will encounter in the target communicative situation. As recommended in Chapter 2, needs analysis should be triangulated in terms of stakeholders and methods. So, examples of genres can be collected from major stakeholders, such as employers, experts and students. In addition, the decision as to which genres to choose should be informed by previous research and experience. The classification of genres in academic settings was investigated by Nesi and Gardner (2012). With colleagues they established the British Academic Written English Corpus (BAWE) (online), which is made up of student assignments at various levels, from first-year undergraduate to postgraduate, and in a range of majors: arts and humanities, social sciences, life sciences and physical sciences. Based on their analysis of this corpus they identified 13 genre families (Table 9.2). This is a very useful corpus, as student assignments are rarely shown to others and are thus classed as occluded genres (Swales, 1996). Nesi and Gardner's book on genres across the disciplines (2012), their article (Gardner & Nesi, 2013) and the BAWE corpus may help the course designer identify the genre needs of EAP students in UK academic settings.

Task 9.2

Genres and discourse communities

Using the grid you completed in Task 9.1, make a list of genres associated with your discourse community.

Genre networks

As well as discrete genres, it is important to consider how genres are related to other genres. Genres do not occur in isolation but in networks. Swales (2004) uses the terms 'genre sets', which refers to the range of genres in a field, and 'genre chains', which capture the chronological aspect of genres. Figure 9.1 presents a possible genre chain for a job application.

Investigating genres

Swales (1981) introduced the notion of moves within a genre. This reflects commonly occurring stages within a given genre. His best known work was on research-article introductions. Using a corpus of research-article texts, he identified the 'creating a research space' (CARS) model, which describes the structure of the typical research-article introduction as a set of moves and steps, starting with outlining the research area, then establishing a research gap and finally stating the purpose of the research. This is presented in Figure 9.2. The model has been applied to other texts, such as thesis and dissertation introductions (Paltridge & Starfield, 2007).

Table 9.2 Classification of genre families

Genre family	Examples	Characteristics
Case study	Business report, medical/patient report	An exemplar, often professional and includes recommendations
Critique	Academic-paper review, project evaluation, financial report evaluations	Show understanding of area and an ability to evaluate and assess significance
Design specification	Application design, website design	Show ability to design product or procedure
Empathy writing	Advice to industry, information leaflet, news report	Show understanding and ability to communicate academic ideas to non-specialist audience
Essay	Discussion, exposition, commentary	Show ability to construct argument; reflects critical skills
Exercise	Data analysis, short answers	Practice in key skills, demonstrate understanding of key concepts
Explanation	Methodology explanation/system/process; disease account	Show understanding of and ability to describe object of study
Literature survey	Literature review, annotated bibliography	Develop understanding of literature relevant to field Summarise, synthesise and evaluate sources
Methodology account	Show familiarity with procedures and methods for research conducted by writer	Data-analysis report, forensic report
Narrative recount	Show awareness of motives, recount historical description	Accident report, character outline, biography
Problem question	Practise applying methods to professional problems	Business scenario, law problems
Proposal	Show ability to make a case for future action	Research proposal, business plan, catering plan
Research report	Show ability to undertake research and associated skills	Research article, topic-based dissertation

Source: Gardner & Nesi (2013, pp. 37–40).

Since the development of Swales' CARS framework, move analysis has featured in many ESP studies. Bhatia (1993; 2008) extended Swales' work to the field of business English and legal English. He identified three levels of analysis: lexico-grammatical features of the text – that is, the words and grammar of the text; chunks that are typically used in the text; and the

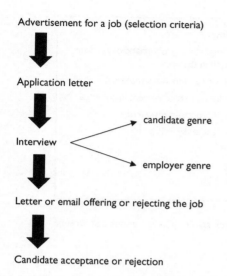

Advertisement for a job (selection criteria)

Application letter

Interview → candidate genre

→ employer genre

Letter or email offering or rejecting the job

Candidate acceptance or rejection

Figure 9.1   Genre chain for a job application

structural organisation of the text. This is similar to Swales' CARS. In his analysis he compared sales letters and job-application letters and found the moves to be similar because both texts have the same communicative purpose: one is product promotion and the other self-promotion. Bhatia (1993, 48–9) suggested the following moves for these genres:

1   Establishing credentials
2   Introducing the offer/candidate

    a   offering product/service/candidature
    b   essential detailing of offer/candidature
    c   indicating value of offer/candidature

3   Offering incentives

    a   Enclosing documents
    b   Soliciting response
    c   Using pressure tactics
    d   Ending politely

Further examples of the application of move analysis in professional settings can be found in Pinto dos Santos (2002), who examined business negotiation letters. Morton (2016) examined the genre of desk-crit in architecture education. The desk-crit is a spoken genre involving the presentation and review of students' in-progress design work in a design studio.

Move 1 Establishing a research territory
      a   Show research area is important, problematic or relevant
      b   Review previous research in the area

Move 2 Establishing a niche (gap in literature/previous research)
      a   Indicate gap in knowledge or extend current knowledge

Move 3 Occupy the niche (purpose of proposed research)
      a   Outline purpose of current study
      b   List research questions
      c   Outline main findings
      d   Present value of study
      e   Describe structure of paper

Figure 9.2 Swales' 'creating a research space' (CARS) generic structure

Source: Swales (1990).

Task 9.3

Move analysis

Take a research-article introduction, a sales-promotion letter or a job-application letter and apply either Swales' CARS or Bhatia's move analysis to the text.

Genre and course design

Genre can play an important part in course design. By including common genres from the students' target communicative situation, the texts are more meaningful and relevant to their needs. Students can play an important role in a genre approach to ESP. They can collect samples of genres, identify genre networks and analyse generic structure and moves.

Genre in academic writing is sometimes compared to a product approach because in some interpretations the focus is entirely on producing a text. Genre analysis thus may run the risk of being restrictive and prescriptive. It is important that when a genre approach is used in the ESP classroom teachers are aware that the analysis should be located within a context that reflects texts, purposes and interlocutors rather than a prescriptive presentation of the rules and moves which occur in a given text. This issue is explored in Badger and White (2000), who suggest combining a genre and process approach to academic writing to avoid an inflexible and unrealistic attention to product.

Needs analysis:	identify genres in target situation through consultation with stakeholders, expert informants and literature
Collect:	samples of target genres (include student input)
Identify:	genre chains
Analyse:	regular features of genres (include student input)
Organise:	texts in order in ESP course from least challenging to most challenging
Devise:	secondary syllabus strands focusing on the skills, organisation and lexico-grammatical features

Figure 9.3 Steps in genre-informed course design

Task 9.4

Genre analysis

Find a few examples of a common genre, spoken or written, in an area of ESP. What are the common features of these texts? Can you identify the steps within the text?

Look at the genres in terms of:

    purpose
    audience
    skills
    structure
    grammar and vocabulary

Figure 9.3 illustrates the possible steps that course designers and ESP practitioners can follow to utilise genre in course design.

Summary

This chapter has introduced the important role of genre in ESP course design. It has considered the major issues in genre. Although the majority of research into genre focuses on EAP and academic writing, it is a useful concept for ESP in all settings (Paltridge, 2013; 2014). The chapter has provided some guidelines on how to include genre and genre analysis in an ESP course.

Further reading

Brian Paltridge (2014) has developed a research timeline which provides an excellent overview of genre studies. His book on implementing genre in the classroom is very useful for ESP practitioners (Paltridge, 2001). Nesi and Gardner (2012) and Gardner and Nesi (2013) provide useful taxonomies of academic genres. Badger and White's (2000) seminal article is useful reading for EAP practitioners who are teaching and designing courses in academic writing.

References

Badger, R., & White, G. (2000). A process genre approach to teaching writing. *ELT Journal, 54*(2), 153–60.

Benesch, S. (2001). *Critical English for academic purpose: Theory, politics, and practice.* Mahwah, NJ: Lawrence Erlbaum.

Bhatia, V. K. (1993). *Analysing genre – Language use in professional settings.* London: Longman.

Bhatia, V. K. (2008). Genre analysis, ESP and professional practice. *English for Specific Purposes, 27*(2), 161–74.

British Academic Written English Corpus (BAWE). (online). Accessed 10 September 2016 at www.coventry.ac.uk/bawe.

Eggins, S. (2004). *Introduction to functional systemic linguistics* (2nd ed.). London: Continuum Press.

Feak, C. B., & Swales, J. M. (2011). *Creating contexts: Writing introductions across genres.* Ann Arbor, MI: University of Michigan Press.

Feez, S. (1998). *Text-based syllabus design.* Sydney: Macquarie University.

Flowerdew, J. (2011). Action, content and identity in applied genre analysis for ESP. *Language Teaching, 44*(4), 516–28.

Gardner, S., & Nesi, H. (2013). A classsification of genre families in university student writing. *Applied Linguistics, 34*(1), 25–52.

Martin, J. (1984). Language, register and genre. In F. Christie (Ed.), *Language studies: Children's writing: A reader* (pp. 21–9). Geelong: Deakin University Press.

Miller, C. R. (1984). Genre as social action. *Quarterly Journal of Speech, 70,* 151–67.

Molle, D., & Prior, P. (2008). Multimodal genre systems in EAP writing pedagogy: Reflecting on a needs analysis. *TESOL Quarterly, 42*(4), 541–66.

Morton, J. (2016). Adjacent worlds: An analysis of a genre at the intersection of academic and professional communities. *Journal of English for Academic Purposes, 22*(1), 54–63.

Nesi, H., & Gardner, S. (2012). *Genres across disciplines: Student writing in higher education.* Cambridge: Cambridge University Press.

Paltridge, B. (2001). *Genre and the language learning classroom.* Ann Arbor, MI: University of Michigan Press.

Paltridge, B. (2013). Genre and English for specific purposes. In B. Paltridge & S. Starfield (Eds.), *Handbook of English for specific purposes* (pp. 347–66). Malden, MA: Wiley-Blackwell.

Paltridge, B. (2014). Genre and second language academic writing. *Language Teaching, 47*(3), 303–18.

Paltridge, B., & Starfield, S. (2007). *Thesis and dissertation writing in a second language.* London: Routledge.

Pinto dos Santos, V. B. M. P. (2002). Genre analysis of business letters of negotiation. *English for Specific Purposes, 21*(2), 167–99.

Rose, D. (2006). Reading genre: A new wave of analysis. *Linguistics and the Human Sciences, 2*(2), 185–206.

Swales, J. M. (1981). Aspects of article introductions. *Aston ESP Research Reports,* No 1. Language Studies Unit, University of Aston at Birmingham. Republished University of Michigan Press (2011).

Swales, J. (1990). *Genre analysis: English in academic and research settings.* Cambridge: Cambridge University Press.

Swales, J. (1996). Occluded genres in the academy: The case of the submission letter. In E. Ventola & A. Mauranen (Eds.), *Academic writing: Intercultural and textual issues* (pp. 45–58). Amsterdam: John Benjamins.

Swales, J. (2004). *Research genres: Exploration and applications.* Cambridge: Cambridge University Press.

Tardy, C. M., & Jwa, S. (2016). Composition studies and EAP. In K. Hyland & P. Shaw (Eds.), *The Routledge handbook of English for academic purposes* (pp. 56–68). Abingdon: Routledge.

Chapter 10

Discourse analysis

Discourse analysis, like genre, has had a significant influence on ESP knowledge and course design. In terms of knowledge, discourse analysis provides deep insights into the demands of target communicative situations in ESP. By analysing authentic texts and interactions in the target communicative situation and translating these into ESP course components, ESP courses can be made very specific. Discourse analysis has progressed rapidly, with developments in technology that allow for the collection and analysis of large amounts of data. This chapter looks at how discourse analysis has influenced ESP. Discourse analysis is considered from the point of view of the course designer, the ESP practitioner and the students. This chapter covers the following areas of discourse analysis in ESP:

- Definition of discourse analysis
- Approaches to discourse analysis
- Discourse analysis and needs analysis
- Students and discourse analysis

Definition of discourse

Discourse may be classed as the central element of ESP courses. ESP learners need to know how to construct and understand situation-specific discourse in order to function effectively in the target communicative situation. Discourse analysis informs a variety of analytical frameworks that can be applied to written and spoken language. Hyland (2007) refers to discourse analysis as the most important tool in the ESP toolbox. For the purposes of course design it is important to distinguish between pedagogic types of discourse analysis and research types of discourse analysis. Perhaps the most important aspect of discourse analysis is that it considers discourse and its context. Paltridge (2012) defines discourse analysis as:

> Discourse analysis examines patterns of language across texts and considers the relationship between language and the social and cultural

contexts in which it is used. Discourse analysis also considers the ways the use of language presents in different views of the world and different understandings. It examines how the use of language is influenced by relationships between participants as well as the effects the use of language has upon social entities and relations. It also considers how views of the world and identities are constructed through the use of discourse.

(Paltridge, 2012, 2)

Approaches to discourse analysis

The investigation and description of authentic specialist discourse to inform ESP courses is now considered an important aspect of ESP course design compared to the past, when the identification of discourse was often based on intuition. At best this was based on the intuitions of discipline experts and at worst on the intuition of teachers outside the discipline. As the goal of ESP courses is to focus on communication and language use in the target situation, it is necessary to use a description of specialist discourse (Basturkmen, 2010). Such investigations may be formal research projects or more informal investigations conducted by teachers. Formal in-depth analysis can be time-consuming and require expertise in analysis. Informal discourse analysis is less rigorous. Task 10.1 reflects an informal, practitioner-based discourse analysis. While such an investigation may not be informed by the approaches to discourse analysis listed below, there is undoubtedly value in such an analysis. At the very least, such an investigation can raise awareness in ESP practitioners and students.

Task 10.1

Informal discourse analysis

How do you think you can use discourse analysis to help with ESP teaching?

Find some examples of discourse from a field of ESP you are familiar with.

What texts would you collect?

What data analysis would you do?

What could you do with the findings?

There are several different approaches to formal discourse analysis. Some of these lend themselves to ESP course design and pedagogy, while some are so complex that the EAP practitioner would not find much of practical use in terms of course design.

Genre analysis

This is one of the most common approaches to discourse analysis. Genre analysis focuses on identifying types of text within a field and identifying their common textual features – for example, identifying and analysing a range of texts required in the communication of a group of middle managers at a company. The procedure would involve collecting samples of the target texts and making a comparison between them based on given criteria. The analysis could focus on classifying texts in terms of purpose – for example, a company report; it could focus on moves within a certain genre; or it could focus on the lexico-grammatical analysis of genres. More detailed discussion of genre can be found in Chapter 9.

Conversation analysis

The analytical technique of conversation analysis takes several forms. Typically, stretches of authentic spoken conversation are recorded, transcribed and analysed from a given perspective. Conversational analysis uses a transcription scheme that can account for pauses, laughter and intonation patterns, all of which have meaning in spoken interactions. Figure 10.1 shows an example of a transcription scheme adapted from Jefferson (2004). Because of the level of detail in conversation analysis, selected texts tend to be quite short.

For steps in doing conversation analysis see www.kcl.ac.uk/sspp/departments/education/research/Research-Centres/ldc/knowledge-transfer/DATA/part3.pdf (accessed 20 April 2017).

Typically, conversation is analysed for turn-taking and how conversation is structured – for example, openings and closings. This may be useful for ESP courses that have a focus on oral skills, but conversation analysis is very time-consuming and may not be a practical course of action.

However, collecting samples of authentic oral data can be useful for course designers. The course designer collects samples of typical interactions from the target situation and then transcribes these. Such samples can reveal patterns of discourse which otherwise are not apparent. Sullivan and Girginer (2002) focused on aviation English in their study into interactions between pilots and air-traffic controllers. Their study produced hard data as to what these transactions involve and produced a valuable resource for aviation ESP. This is an area in ESP where accuracy is essential, as lives depend upon the communication between the pilots and air-traffic controllers.

Transcription symbol	Example
:: prolongation of the immediately prior sound	how are yo:::u.
(.) a brief interval (about a tenth of a second) within or between utterances	H. step right up (1.3)
(0.5) the time elapsed (by tenths of seconds) between the end of the utterance or sound and the start of the next utterance or sound	H. I said step right up. (0.8) J. are you talking to me (Atkinson & Heritage, 1984, x–xi)
= latched utterances – no break or gap between stretches of talk	Charlotte. Trey and I got engaged after only a month= Samantha= how long before you separated
now stress	Charlotte. we're together <u>NOW</u> and that's what matters. (.) when it's right you just know (Paltridge, 2012, p 92)
? rising intonation . falling intonation	R. Okay can we just clarify one or two points? Okay? A. yes.
, continuing/unfinished intonational contour	D. all the family's gonna go to the game today because, … sports are very important (Chafe, 1993, 213)

Figure 10.1 Sample transcription symbols

Source: Jefferson (2004).

Discourse and pragmatics

Pragmatics focuses on the meaning of utterances in relation to the context in which they occur. It examines the relationship between form and function. One influential perspective in pragmatics is speech act theory (Austin, 1962). In this perspective, pragmatic analysis looks at how action is achieved with words. Speech acts can be direct ("open the window") or indirect ("it's cold in here"). A functional approach to language and course design which is widespread in both EGP and ESP is based on speech act theory. A functional syllabus is organised according to functions such as requests, agreeing and disagreeing. This is discussed further in Chapter 3.

Discourse and grammar

Discourse analyses focusing on grammar abound in research studies into ESP. Typically, texts from the target situation are collected and analysed for grammatical and lexical features. These in turn may (or may not) be translated into course aims and activities. For example, Staples (2015) collected samples of 102 patient and nurse interactions. To these she applied a move analysis in the first instance and then a grammatical analysis. The moves are based on the phases of the interaction, from the interaction opening through describing the complaint to treatment and the closing sequence. This study presents an excellent example of the development of an ESP course from a linguistic analysis. Tables 10.1 and 10.2 present the results of her analysis. This analysis can then be translated into course aims, objectives and activities.

Task 10.2

Discourse analysis to course design

Using Staples' analysis of nurse–patient interaction in Tables 10.1 and 10.2, how could this be translated into an ESP course?

Comment on: objectives, syllabus, sample activities.

Recent ESP course design has tended to use a discourse perspective focusing on the grammar and structure of the whole text rather than a traditional sentence-based approach. When considering grammar from a discourse perspective, the notion of cohesion is central (Paltridge, 2012), as it addresses chunks of communication. Emphasis on this level of grammar needs to be reflected in an ESP course. Cohesion refers to how a text is structured based on phrases, clauses and words (Hasan, 1989). A discourse grammar analysis of a text would reflect both grammatical and lexical cohesion. Grammatical cohesion involves reference. This is classified as anaphoric (referring backwards), cataphoric (referring forwards), exophoric (referring outside the text) and homophoric (reflecting contextual knowledge). Examples of these types of reference are presented in Figure 10.2.

Lexical cohesion focuses on the relationship between lexical items and typically refers to repetition (repeating the same word), synonymy (using another word with the same meaning), antonymy (using the opposite word), hyponymy (classes of words), meronymy (referring to parts and the whole) and collocation (a word or phrase commonly used with another word or phrase). Examples of these are presented in Figure 10.3.

Table 10.1 Generic structure of patient–nurse interactions

Phase	Elements contained in the phase
Opening	Greetings Small talk Orientation of patient to environment and interaction Acknowledgements of patient's current condition
Complaint	Nurse's elicitation of primary complaint Patient's primary complaint
Exam	History Past health and medical history, family history, procedures and treatment Physical exam Indications of nurse's upcoming actions Online reports on patient's condition or reports from chart
Counsel	Diagnosis/possible diagnosis Health-related information Recommendations for treatment Counselling Reference to plan of care (e.g. doctor's follow-up) Discussion of goals
Closing	Summary of arrangements Asking for further questions or concerns Reminder of how to contact nurse Expressions of future contact (e.g. "if you need anything…") Terminal exchange (farewells, thank yous)

Source: Staples (2015, p. 126).

Intercultural rhetoric

This perspective on discourse analysis focuses on the cultural variations between L1 and L2 texts. This can be very important in ESP, which frequently involves interactions between different cultures. Originally referred to as contrastive rhetoric, this perspective emerged from work by Kaplan (1966) and was further developed by Connor (1996; 2004). In this analysis L1 and L2 texts are compared. For example, Vergaro (2004) compared the rhetorical differences between Italian and English sales letters. Her study revealed that these texts showed differences in terms of moves and how these are realised in terms of politeness. The issue of intercultural variation has received a lot of attention in medical English – for example, Bosher and Smalkoski (2002) found cultural differences in the interactions between international medical graduates and their patients which led to miscommunication, particularly in the interactions between patients and international medical graduates (and see Part 3, Course 2: Bosher's *English for cross-cultural nursing*).

Table 10.2   Lexico-grammatical features of patient–nurse interactions

Lexico-grammatical feature

1   Features of involvement

    a   Conditionals (e.g. "If you are in pain, see Dr. Carl")
    b   1st- and 2nd-person pronouns
    c   Mental verbs (e.g. think, feel)
    d   General emphatics (e.g. most)
    e   General hedges (e.g. kind of)
    f   Amplifiers (e.g. very)
    g   Downtoners (e.g. only)
    h   Present tense
    i   Causative subordination (e.g. "You have to practise relaxation techniques cause the stress is hard in your heart")

2   Narrative features

    a   Past tense
    b   Perfect aspect
    c   3rd-person pronouns
    d   Communication verbs (e.g. say, tell)

3   Stance features

    a   Modals of prediction (e.g. will)
    b   Modals of necessity (e.g. should)
    c   Modals of possibility (e.g. can)
    d   adverbs (e.g. truthfully)
    e   Attitudinal adverbs (e.g. surprisingly)
    f   Certainty adverbs (e.g. obviously)
    g   Likelihood adverbs (e.g. evidently)
    h   That complement clauses (verb, noun, adjective):

        i   controlled by verbs: "I just hope that I have plugged it in properly"
        ii   controlled by adjectives: "I'm not sure that they did very much at all"
        iii   controlled by nouns: "the fact that he will get away with attacking my daughter is obscene"

    i   clauses (verb, adjective, noun):

        i   controlled by verb: "I just want to make sure"
        ii   controlled by adjectives: "oh, I'm sorry to hear that"
        iii   controlled by nouns: "she has a strong tendency to argue"

Source: Staples (2015, p. 127).

Critical discourse analysis

A critical approach to discourse analysis has received attention in ESP, particularly in EAP. This approach attempts to account for underlying assumptions and power imbalances within the ESP context. Thus ESP

Reference

Anaphoric – the word or phrase refers back

> We had a presentation by <u>Ms Barbara Green</u> about the launch of the

> new product. <u>She</u> explained <u>the process</u> extremely well.

Cataphoric – the word or phrase refers forward

> When <u>she</u> started talking <u>Ms Green</u> seemed nervous

Exophoric – the word or phrase refers to something outside of the text

> That woman said that the bus is running late.

Homophoric – the word or phrase refers to shared cultural knowledge

> It's the Queen's ninetieth birthday in April. (Understood to be the Queen
> of the United Kingdom.)

Figure 10.2   Examples of grammatical cohesion

Repetition
>   <u>Mr Smith</u> manages the Nissan Plant in Washington. <u>Mr Smith</u> recently
>   moved to the area.

Synonymy (same meaning)
>   Mr Smith plans to expand <u>the plant</u> at Washington. <u>The factory</u> will provide
>   employment for the region.

Antonymy (contrastive meaning)
>   Mr Smith plans to <u>expand</u> production and <u>reduce</u> wastage.

Hyponymy (classes of lexical items)
>   Cars: saloon, hatchback, estate, all terrain.

Meronymy (classes of word that indicate a-whole-to-a-part relations)
>   Car engine: carburettor, cylinder, valves, spark plugs.

Figure 10.3   Examples of lexical cohesion

is viewed as being political rather than neutral (Benesch, 2001). Critical discourse analysis aims to "reveal some of these hidden and often out of sight values, positions and perspectives" (Paltridge, 2012, p. 187) and thus empower traditionally less powerful participants – for example, university students. Benesch argues that course designers need to be aware not only of needs but also who sets the course goals and why and whose interests are served by these goals. She emphasises that EAP practitioners should not be afraid of challenging these goals. In her book she gives examples of how this approach can be put into practice. One such example was introducing a gender balance in a psychology EAP course. The psychology course was dominated by contributions of male psychologists. She achieved more of a balance by her choice of EAP topics, including anorexia, a condition mainly suffered by females.

Using discourse analysis in course design

Needs analysis and discourse analysis

Discourse analysis frequently occurs in needs analysis. The course designer typically collects information about the target communicative situation and analyses this with a view to translating this into teachable sections. For example, an EAP practitioner may collect a range of typical student assignments from the target situation. She may then analyse these using some of the perspectives described above, as is illustrated in Staples' (2015) example.

Figure 10.4 presents a suggested list of steps an ESP course designer could follow to use a discourse analysis approach.

Identify most important texts in target communicative situation:
    Spoken/written
Use informants such as students, disciplinary experts, past students and other stakeholders
Collect a representative sample of these
Organise into a format suitable for analysis:
    Spoken texts need to be transcribed
    Written texts should be in electronic format
Look for distinguishing aspects of texts
Compare texts for similarities
Decide on one or more approach(es) to discourse analysis:
    Genre
    Conversation analysis
    Pragmatic analysis
    Lexico-grammatical analysis
    Intercultural rhetoric analysis
    Critical discourse analysis
Conduct analysis
Record most important results
Use focus of analysis as organising strand in syllabus –
    for example, grammar, vocabulary, conversation strategies

---

Figure 10.4 Steps in discourse-informed ESP course design

Task 10.3

Course design using discourse analysis

Focusing on an area in ESP and a target group of students, pick one of the approaches to discourse analysis:

Genre
Conversation analysis
Pragmatic analysis
Lexico-grammatical analysis
Intercultural rhetoric analysis
Critical discourse analysis

How would you collect texts?
What aspects would you focus on in the analysis?
How could these be reflected in an ESP course?

Students and discourse analysis

One interesting variation on the role of discourse analysis in course design is to get students to become discourse analysts. Students may be trained in techniques of discourse analysis. They then collect a sample of discourse from the target communicative situation and apply an analysis. This can provide deep insights into the target communicative situation. Riggenbach (1999) suggests the following stages when training students to use discourse analysis: predict, plan, collect data, analyse data, generate analysis and review.

Summary

This chapter has discussed the importance of discourse analysis in ESP course design. It has presented the major approaches to discourse analysis and discussed these in relation to course design. It has discussed Staples' (2015) article as an example of discourse analysis as it is typically used in ESP.

Further reading

Paltridge's (2012) *Discourse analysis* is an excellent introduction to the field. It presents the major types of discourse analysis and examples of analytical frameworks that can be applied to the investigation of specialist discourse.

Staples' (2015) article provides a good example of the levels of discourse analysis and how these can be translated into an ESP course.

Maria del Pilar Garcia Mayo's (2000) *English for specific purposes: Discourse analysis and course design* describes a discourse-analysis approach to course design in English for science and technology.

References

Atkinson, M., & Heritage, J. (Eds.) (1984). *Structures of social action*. Cambridge: Cambridge University Press.

Austin, J. L. (1962). *How to do things with words*. Oxford: Clarendon Press.

Basturkmen, H. (2010). *Developing courses in English for specific purposes*. Basingstoke: Palgrave-Macmillan.

Benesch, S. (2001). *Critical English for academic purposes: Theory, politics, and practice*. Mahwah, NJ: Lawrence Erlbaum.

Bosher, S., & Smalkoski, K. (2002). From needs analysis to curriculum development: Developing a course for health-care communication for immigrant workers in the USA. *English for Specific Purposes, 21*(1), 59–79.

Chafe, W. (1993) Prosodic and functional units of language. In J. Edwards & M. Lampert (Eds), *Transcription and coding in discourse research* (pp. 33–43). Hillsdale, NJ: Erlbaum.

Connor, U. (1996). *Contrastive rhetoric: Cross cultural aspects of second language writing*. Cambridge: Cambridge University Press.

Connor, U. (2004). Intercultural rhetoric research: Beyond texts. *Journal of English for Academic Purposes, 3*, 291–304.

García Mayo, M. d P. (2000). *English for specific purposes: Discourse analysis and course design*. Leioa: Universidad Del País Vasco.

Hasan, R. (1989). The structure of text. In M. A. K. Halliday & R. Hasan (Eds.), *Language, context and text: Aspects of language in a social-semiotic perspective* (pp. 52–96). Oxford: Oxford University Press.

Hyland, K. (2007). English for specific purposes: Some influences and impacts. In J. Cummins & C. Davison (Eds.), *International handbook of English language teaching* (pp. 391–402). New York: Springer.

Jefferson, G. (2004), Glossary of transcript symbols with an introduction. In G. H. Lerner (Ed.), *Conversation analysis: Studies form the first generation* (pp. 13–31). Amsterdam: John Benjamin.

Kaplan, R. B. (1966). Cultural thought patterns in intercultural education. *Language Learning, 16*(1), 1–16.

Paltridge, B. (2012). *Discourse analysis* (2nd ed.). London: Bloomsbury.

Riggenbach, H. (1999). *Discourse analysis in the language classroom. Volume 1. The spoken language*. Ann Arbor, MI: University of Michigan Press.

Staples, S. (2015). Examining the linguistic needs of internationally educated nurses: A corpus-based study of lexico-grammatical features in nurse–patient interactions. *English for Specific Purposes, 37*, 122–36.

Sullivan, P., & Girginer, H. (2002). The use of discourse analysis to enhance ESP teacher knowledge: An example using aviation English. *English for Specific Purposes, 21*(4), 397–404.

Vergaro, C. (2004). Discourse strategies of Italian and English sales promotion letters. *English for Specific Purposes, 23*(2), 181–201.

Chapter 11

Corpora

The use of corpora in ESP course design and research has gained in popularity in recent years. This has been facilitated by the development of user-friendly concordancing software that enables ESP practitioners, course designers and students to conduct analysis. This chapter explores what corpora are and their role in ESP course design, as follows:

- What is a corpus?
- Types of corpus
- Word lists
- Corpus analysis
- Developing an ESP corpus
- Corpora and course design

What is a corpus?

A search for 'corpus' in the journal *English for Specific Purposes* in 2017 revealed that 469 articles published since 1995 focused on the use of corpora in some way. A corpus is defined as "a collection of pieces of language text in electronic form, selected according to external criteria to represent, as far as possible, a language or language variety as a source of data for linguistic research" (Sinclair, 2004, p. 19). While a corpus does not necessarily have to be electronic, most uses in ESP depend upon computer storage and analysis of data. Nesi (2013) distinguishes between corpus-based and corpus-driven investigations. Corpus-based investigations focus on confirmatory analysis: that is, providing evidence for a view about language through analysis. Corpus-driven investigations on the other hand are exploratory in nature and seek to make discoveries about language. Both approaches to the analysis of corpora can be useful in ESP.

A corpus is the usual starting point for discourse-analysis course design (see Chapter 10) in ESP. An ESP corpus is based on authentic texts taken from the target communicative situation. These are then analysed from a linguistic perspective using discourse-analysis techniques – for example, the analysis of vocabulary frequency and grammatical structures using specialist software.

The advantages of using corpora are that real, authentic usage of language can be uncovered, as opposed to what is intuitively believed to be common usage.

Types of corpus

As technology becomes more sophisticated and user friendly, there is an increasing number of corpora available. Corpora can be general or specific. For example, the British National Corpus (BNC) is a general purpose, 100-million-word corpus drawn from spoken and written texts from a range of sources. Another general corpus is the Corpus of Contemporary American English (COCA). This is a 520-million-word corpus drawn from spoken and written American English texts including academic journals.

Subject-specific corpora range from large-scale to small-scale corpora. An example of a large-scale, specific corpus is the Cambridge and Nottingham Business English Corpus (CANBEC). This collection of texts featuring spoken and written British and American English from business situations is used to inform Business English textbooks published by Cambridge. In the field of EAP, the Professional English Research Consortium has produced the Corpus of Professional English (CPE), which is a 140-million-word corpus drawn from research articles.

Not all corpora are accessible. The CANBEC and the Cambridge and Nottingham Corpus of Discourse in English (CANCODE) are only accessible by those associated with Cambridge University Press; and the TOEFL 2000 spoken and written academic-language corpus (TKSWAL) is not freely available to the public. However, there are many resources that are freely available. While the corpus used to generate the Academic Word List (AWL) (Coxhead, 2000) is restricted, the results of the analysis are freely available. The AWL takes the form of word lists ordered in terms of frequency, a very useful resource for EAP practitioners and students, and the list has been widely exploited for pedagogic purposes – see, for example, the University of Nottingham's material on using the AWL (Haywood, online). The many other corpora that are freely available are listed in Chapter 15 on resources for ESP course design.

Corpora can also be specifically designed and built for ESP courses or for research. In these cases the corpus will be small but may be much more useful than the large, institutionally sponsored corpora. Bowker and Pearson (2002) provide guidance on how to design and build such a corpus. An example of a specialist corpus is Staples' (2015) nursing corpus. She collected 102 interactions between nurses and standardised patients (that is, actors playing patients and providing the same response across a number of interactions). From this corpus she analysed the interactions for genre moves and then conducted a lexico-grammatical analysis. This was translated into course objectives and a syllabus (see Chapter 10 for more discussion of her approach).

An example of a business-English corpus is Mike Nelson's, based on his PhD thesis. He analysed this using the Wordsmith concordancing software to identify keywords and frequency lists of spoken and written business English. He compared his corpus with the BNC and noted some important differences in usage (Nelson, 2000). The corpus is not yet available online; however, Nelson's Business English Lexis Site is a valuable resource for EBP practitioners and includes frequency lists and key phrases in business English (Nelson, online).

A current focus in workplace ESP is business English as a lingua franca (BELF). This term refers to the use of English between non-native speakers of English, while the term international business English (IBE) refers to interactions that involve both native and non-native speakers of English. The majority of global business interactions use BELF (Nickerson & Planken, 2016). The Vienna–Oxford International Corpus of English (VOICE) (online), directed by Barbara Seidlhofer, is a million-word corpus of spoken ELF interactions and is available free of charge, while the Wolverhampton Corpus of Business English (WBE) (online) includes both BELF and IBE interactions and contains web-based written texts in English from different countries (this corpus is not available free of charge). For a discussion of this see Fuertes-Olivera (2007).

Word lists

Generating word lists is a common output of corpus analysis – for example, Coxhead's (2000) Academic Word List (AWL). Such lists can be large and general or small and specific. Word lists, particularly those ranked by frequency, can be a good tool to use in teaching and useful for students to refer to. Two recent examples are Yang (2015) and Liu and Han (2015). Yang developed a nursing academic word list (NAWL) based on 252 nursing research articles published online. The result is a 676-word list ranked by frequency. Liu and Han (2015) developed an environmental academic word list which they used to indicate the differences in coverage between the AWL and environmental science. The corpus comprised 200 academic journal articles, 20 each from 10 different areas of environmental science.

Reflection 11.1

Using word lists

Have you used a word list in teaching?

Which word list?

How did you use this?

Corpus analysis

Corpus data is analysed using corpus software tools. These tools can generate word-frequency lists, collocations and keywords. These tools are referred to as concordancers. Software is available for online analysis, such as the Compleat Lexical Tutor (online), which accesses a number of corpora, including COCA and BNC, enables the user to analyse his or her own texts and provides KWIC (Keyword in Context) analysis as well as a phrase extractor that generates word clusters. Another example is Spaceless (online), which provides online analysis of inputted texts.

Concordance programs are also available for use offline. Laurence Anthony has developed a range of corpus tools which are freely available on his webpage: AntConc is a concordancing program accompanied by a series of YouTube videos on how to use it. This program can identify collocates, frequency lists and clusters. Wordsmith, published by Lexical Analysis Software and Oxford University Press, is widely used and comprehensive. It costs £50 for a single licence; however, universities often purchase a site licence for students. Wordsmith can provide concordance analysis, keyword analysis and word lists; and by generating large numbers of examples of word use taken from authentic sources, insights can be drawn that would otherwise be unavailable. An earlier example of this is Thurstun and Candlin's (1998) EAP coursebook, which provides student tasks based on concordance printouts. For example, students might be asked to compare the verb forms of 'analyse' or examine words commonly occurring with analysis. Figure 11.1 shows a segment of concordance lines generated from the British Academic Written English Corpus (BAWE) produced by Coventry University, UK.

Task 11.1

Corpus printouts

1   Looking at the corpus printout in Figure 11.1, what generalisations can you make about the word family 'analyse'?
2   How could you use a concordance with EAP learners?
3   The BAWE has two modes of access: online and offline (requires registration and download). Using either means of access, conduct a search for a common, general academic word. Devise an activity for an EAP class based on the concordance lines produced by your search.

Corpora and materials

The use of corpora to inform published ESP teaching materials is increasing; however, there is still a way to go, with many materials still relying on the

statistics are carefully considered when	**analysing**	the results then the statistics can be
ascertain causes of the illness rather than	**analysing**	social and cultural factors relevant to
argue that 'tests results are matched by	**analyses**	of occupational and scientific attainment
this particular social form can only be	**analysed**	in a wider, macrosocial context. Especially
how'' of interpretation, and subsequently	**analysed**	at a different level. This approach, however
events, the logical question would be: why?	**Analysing**	history, Marx and Engels had discovered
analytically separable; this is so because	**analysing**	their interplay over time is only possible
methodology, to provide a framework with which to	**analyse**	substantive sociological issues). The substantive
time consuming and there is no scope to	**analyse**	expression in vivo as the plants need to
epigenetic modifications in the germ line by	**analysing**	the effects on a somatic nucleus (11).
needed. The answers were then collected and	**analysed**	. Responses were put into the following
used in its raw form. The results were then	**analysed**	in a three way within groups analysis of
immediately after any observations, without	**analysing**	, and to write quickly but in great detail
notes, as the content can be repeated and	**analysed**	fully, detailed content is assured and
Aldert Vrij's study on detecting deceit via	**analyses**	of verbal and nonverbal behaviour, (2004
videotaped and their behaviour and speech	**analysed**	from the tape. To increase validity of
responses were given and content was coded and	**analysed**	according to a set of pre-established criteria

Figure 11.1 Example of concordance lines from British Academic Written English corpus (BAWE)

Source: Coventry University (online).

intuitions of the author. Burton (2012) surveyed ELT coursebook writers and found that a sizeable proportion did not consult corpora, for reasons such as doubting their relevance and not having access to them. Harwood (2014) reports that both coursebook writers and publishers show a reluctance to apply issues in corpus studies to their textbooks.

Mike Nelson (2000) found that there was a mismatch between the corpus and the lexis found in published EBP coursebooks. It is important that ESP coursebook writers reflect the language of the target situation and that this is supported empirically rather than being based on the writer's intuitions. An example of corpus-informed courses are Swales and Feak's series of EAP books (for example, Swales & Feak, 2011). In business English, Koester *et al.* (2012) used the BEC to inform their coursebooks.

Developing an ESP corpus

Developing a corpus of written texts is relatively easy if the discipline is open to sharing texts – for example, an academic department could make a reading list available to the ESP practitioner. However, in some settings this may be more problematic – for example, in a medical setting acquiring authentic patient case notes would not be ethical. In this case data may be collected based on simulated interactions, as is the case with Staples' (2015) study referred to earlier. In these interactions the medical experts would be genuine but the patients could be played by actors.

A further consideration is that of intellectual copyright. If the texts in the corpus are published – for example, in textbooks or journals – then permission from the author or copyright holder needs to be obtained. This is essential if the corpus is to be made publicly available or will result in published research. Permissions can be a slow and expensive business but, increasingly, academic journals have made this process simpler with online applications and the increase in open-access material.

Spoken texts are more difficult to collect for practical reasons, as it is difficult to gain access to target-situation interaction; for example, it would be impossible to get permission to record an important business negotiation.

Task 11.2

Considerations in corpus selection

Think of an ESP situation.

What types of written text would it be useful to include in a corpus?

What types of spoken text?

What criteria would you use to select texts to include in your corpus?

How would you access the texts for your corpus?

To be pedagogically useful, ESP corpora need to be relevant to the needs of the learners. This always needs to be considered when building a corpus. Choosing texts to include in a corpus needs to be based on selection criteria. Figure 11.2 lists some possible criteria for inclusion of texts in a corpus.

After the corpus has been collected and stored electronically, the next step is to document or annotate the corpus. Texts do not occur in isolation and contextual information can be lost when compiling a corpus. One way of dealing with this is to use documentation and annotation. In the large-scale corpora this is probably already done, but in a small, specialised corpus the ESP practitioner will need to do this. Documentation seeks to capture as much contextual information as possible – for example, demographics of the interlocutors, text purpose, genre family and disciplinary norms. Annotation refers to the tagging of grammatical, semantic categories and stylistic patterns (Laurence Anthony (online) has a tagging tool). In annotating a spoken corpus, information may refer to tone and pitch in the recordings (Nesi, 2013).

Learners and corpora

Corpora can be made up of published and unpublished professional texts or of learners' texts. An example of a learner corpus is the Hong Kong University of Science and Technology (HKUST) Corpus of Learner English (Flowerdew, 1996). One important distinction in learner corpora is whether the texts are produced for authentic communication or for practice – for example, writing practice. In this instance students can analyse differences between expert and novice texts (Flowerdew, 1998). Another example might be comparing a student's written article with a published article.

Data-driven learning is the term used to describe learner activities based on student corpus analysis. Students engage directly with corpora to complete language tasks. For example, students may be presented with a page of concordance lines and asked to find collocates of a given word (Timmis, 2015). Collocates are words that commonly occur with other words – for example, some collocates of 'academic' are 'achievement', 'skills', 'community' and 'journal' (Timmis, 2015).

Another interesting approach is for students to compile their own corpora. Charles (2014) conducted a study that involved EAP students at a UK university developing personal corpora in their own disciplinary fields (see Part 3, Course 7). She examined the longer-term of use of these corpora by

---

Size of corpus – number of texts
Mode – electronic/print
Date
Length of texts
Topics
Relevance to target communicative situation
Text genres
Ease of access
Source
Need for permissions/payment
Who makes the selection

Figure 11.2 Criteria for corpus text selection

the students and found this to be a useful activity for improving the academic literacies of international students.

Corpora and course design

The role of corpora in the design of an ESP course needs careful consideration. An ESP course that has a strong focus on corpora will include texts and analyses as part of the structure of the ESP course. For example, a course could be ordered according to frequently occurring text types in the target situation. In business English this might include company reports, emails and negotiations. The next level of organisation would then be based on analyses of the corpus and the findings. A weaker focus may include corpus-informed elements – for example, including activities based on the AWL in an EAP course.

Task 11.3

Designing a course based on corpus analysis

How could an ESP course outline be based on corpora? Develop a course grid that utilises a strong or weak approach to corpus-based course design.

Summary

This chapter has considered the role of corpora in ESP course design. It has discussed ready-made corpora and the steps needed to build a course-specific corpus. Chapter 15 includes a list of available corpora and concordancing software for corpus analysis.

Further reading

For an overview of corpora in ESP see Hilary Nesi's (2013) chapter in Paltridge and Starfield. For an in-depth treatment of corpus linguistics see the *Routledge Handbook of Corpus Linguistics*, edited by O'Keeffe and McCarthy (2010).

References

Anthony, L. (online). AntConc. Accessed 10 September 2016 at www.laurenceanthony.net/software/antconc/.

Bowker, L., & Pearson, J. (2002). *Working with specilized language: A practical guide to using corpora*. London: Routledge.

Burton, G. (2012). Corpora and textbooks: Destined to be strangers forever. *Corpora, 7*(1), 91–108.

Charles, M. (2014). Getting the corpus habit: EAP students' long term use of personal corpora. *English for Specific Purposes, 35*(1), 30–40.

Compleat Lexical Tutor. (online). Accessed 21 April 2017 at http://lextutor.ca/.

Coventry University. (online). British Academic Written English Corpus. Accessed 10 September 2016 at www.coventry.ac.uk/bawe.

Coxhead, A. (2000). A new academic word list. *TESOL Quarterly, 34*(2), 213–38.

Flowerdew, J. (1996). Concordancing in language learning. In M. Pennington (Ed.), *The power of CALL* (pp. 97–113). Houston, TX: Athelstan.

Flowerdew, L. (1998). Integrating 'expert' and 'interlanguage' computer corpora findings on causality: Discoveries for teachers and students. *English for Specific Purposes, 17*, 329–45.

Fuertes-Olivera, P. A. (2007). A corpus view of lexical gender in written business English. *English for Specific Purposes, 26*(2), 219–34.

Harwood, N. (Ed.) (2014). *English language teaching textbooks: Content, consumption and production*. Basingstoke: Palgrave-Macmillan.

Haywood, S. (online). Accessed 15 March 2017 at www.nottingham.ac.uk/alzsh3/acvocab/.

Koester, A., Pitt, A., Handford, M., & Lisboa, M. (2012). *Business advantage*. Cambridge: Cambridge University Press.

Liu, J., & Han, L. (2015). A corpus-based environmental academic word list building and its validity test. *English for Specific Purposes, 39*, 1–11.

Nelson., M. (2000). *A corpus based study of the lexis of business English and business English teaching materials*. Unpublished PhD thesis, University of Manchester.

Nelson, M. (online). Mike Nelson's business English lexis site. Accessed 21 April 2017 at http://users.utu.fi/micnel/business_english_lexis_site.htm.

Nesi, H. (2013). ESP and corpus studies. In B. Paltridge & S. Starfield (Eds.), *The handbook of English for specific purposes* (pp. 407–26). Oxford: Wiley-Blackwell.

Nickerson, C., & Planken, B. (2016). *Introducing business English*. London: Routledge.

O'Keeffe, A., & McCarthy, M. (Eds.). (2010). *Routledge handbook of corpus linguistics*. London: Routledge.

Sinclair, J. (2004) Corpus and texts – basic principles. In M. Wynne (ed.), *Developing linguistic corpora: A guide to good practice*. Accessed 21 August 2017 at http://ota.ox.ac.uk/documents/creating/dlc/

Spaceless. (online). Accessed 15 Febuary 2017 at www.spaceless.com/concordancer. php.

Staples, S. (2015). Examining the linguistic needs of internationally educated nurses: A corpus-based study of lexico-grammatical features in nurse–patient interactions. *English for Specific Purposes, 37*, 122–36.

Swales, J., & Feak, C. B. (2011). *Creating contexts: Writing introductions across genres.* Ann Arbor, MI: University of Michigan Press.

Thurstun, J., & Candlin, C. (1998). *Exploring academic English: Workbook for student essay writing.* Sydney: NCELTR, Macquarie University.

Timmis, I. (2015). *Corpus linguistics for ELT: Research and practice.* London: Routledge.

Vienna–Oxford International Corpus of English (VOICE). (online). Accessed 10 September 2016 at www.univie.ac.at/voice/.

Wolverhampton Business English Corpus. (online). Accessed 10 September 2016 at http://catalog.elra.info/product_info.php?products_id=627.

Yang, M.-N. (2015). A nursing academic word list. *English for Specific Purposes, 37*(0), 27–38.

Chapter 12

Discipline-based methodologies

ESP often adopts teaching methodologies that are commonly used to teach subject areas. In medical training courses, for example, problem-based learning is very common, while case studies are widely used in business. These two approaches to teaching are similar and share epistemology with 'project-based' language teaching. This chapter addresses the various stages of these two approaches and how these can be implemented as follows:

- Problem-based learning

   What is problem-based learning (PBL)?
   Stages of using PBL
   Implementing PBL

- Case-study approach

   What is the case-study approach?
   Stages of using the case-study method
   Implementing the case-study method

What is problem-based learning (PBL)?

PBL is a methodological approach that emerged in the 1970s as an alternative to traditional methods of teaching medicine at the McMaster Medical School in Canada. PBL shifted the focus from the subject being taught to the learners themselves (Maudsley, 1999). While the approach is perhaps most widely applied in medical training, there are examples from other areas, such as business (Bosuwon & Woodrow, 2009), biblical studies (Harding, 2001) and high-school economics (Maxwell *et al.*, 2001). In many respects PBL, as a constructivist approach to teaching and learning, shares values with the collaborative-learning and task-based-learning methodologies prevalent in EFL today. The focus of the PBL approach to learning and teaching is based on the premise that learning occurs during the process of investigating and producing a solution to a problem. Of course, given that it is common in mainstream

Present problem
Define and analyse problem
Identify learning objectives
Research to find solution to problem
Share and synthesise knowledge
Solve problem
Evaluate process

Figure 12.1 Typical stages of PBL

medical training, it is logical to use it in medical-based ESP; and the advantage of this is that the students can become familiar with the methodology they will encounter in their discipline. Typically, students are presented with a medical scenario – for example, a patient presenting with a disease. They then work in groups to research the problem over time and suggest a solution.

Barron (2002) describes two types of problem in PBL in ESP in relation to learners and teachers: weak and strong. In the weak version of PBL the teacher knows the answer to the problem while the students do not. In the strong version of PBL the solution of the problem is entirely student-driven and there is the possibility of a variety of answers and complex solutions.

Stages of PBL sessions

The use of PBL in ESP requires staging over a period of time, typically several lessons. It involves considerable group work out of class. Figure 12.1 shows the typical phases of PBL.

Task 12.1

Staging of PBL

Think about the staging and timing of the stages of PBL presented in Figure 12.1. How would this work for an ESP class?

The role of content in PBL is central. PBL can compensate for an ESP practitioner's lack of subject knowledge because of the student-driven nature of the approach. The solution of the problem in PBL does not depend on the ESP practitioner's expertise. For example, Wood and Head (2004) integrated EAP needs and subject-specific needs into a biomedical English course by getting groups to come up with a disease scenario which they presented orally to other groups. The groups then researched the possible diagnoses, which were presented orally. The groups were then required to decide on the disease based on the presentation and their own research in the field (Wood & Head, 2004). Figure 12.2 presents the steps used in Wood and Head's course.

Bosuwon and Woodrow (2009) suggested a problem-based approach to reading based on business topics identified through a needs analysis. The topic areas were then used to generate problems, which groups of students researched through reading. The pedagogical realisation of this approach is presented in Figure 12.3.

Week 1:   Oral presentation of disease by group 1 (not naming disease)
           Note-taking and questioning by other groups
           Work outside class by other groups to identify the disease
           Production of written reports by other groups.
Week 2:   Written reports given to group 1
           Written reports analysed and evaluated by group 1.
Week 3:   Critique
           Oral feedback on other groups by group 1
           Evaluation of their own performance by group 1.

Figure 12.2   PBL cycle

Source: based on Wood & Head (2004).

Section 1: Warm-up activities

- Students look at a picture concerning business etiquette and then discuss
- Students read an article about business etiquette and then discuss

Section 2: PBL activities

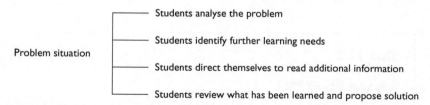

Problem situation

— Students analyse the problem

— Students identify further learning needs

— Students direct themselves to read additional information

— Students review what has been learned and propose solution

Section 3: Evaluation and reflection activities

- Students evaluate all groups' presentations and their own group teamwork
- Students share PBL experiences, reading skills practised and knowledge gained

Figure 12.3   The implementation of PBL in a business-English class

Source: Bosuwon and Woodrow (2009, p. 55).

Table 12.1 Advantages and disadvantages of PBL

Advantages	Disadvantages
Relevant to target-situation needs	Requires a lot of class time
Student-centred	May require collaboration with subject specialists
Demands high level of communication	Teacher is not in control and may not like the unpredictable nature of PBL
Aligns well with current methodological approaches (task-based, communicative)	No focus on formal course
ESP teacher content knowledge not so important	May lose focus on language and vocabulary, with sole focus on content
Students find it motivating	Assessment of students difficult
Promotes sense of identity	Some students will not like lack of teacher focus

The advantages and disadvantages of using PBL

Not every setting can benefit from the application of PBL. Obviously, medicine is an area that lends itself to this approach, since it is common practice in medical training. However, in more traditional ESP settings, PBL may be difficult to implement, as it may not match the expectations of the students, teachers and the institution. Barron (2002) outlines some of the challenges to using PBL in EAP. These mostly relate to collaboration. Collaboration with the subject specialist is often very difficult. The subject specialist may have very different epistemological views and it may be hard to find a common ground. Table 12.1 lists some of the advantages and disadvantages of using PBL as a methodology in ESP teaching. As with all discipline-based methodologies, it is important to maintain a focus on language. This can often be lost because of the content-based nature of the problem. Figure 12.4 presents the typical stages of ESP course design using a PBL approach.

Task 12.2

Applicability of PBL

Do you think a PBL approach would work in a language school? In which branch of ESP?

What would be the advantages?

What would be the disadvantages?

Analyse objectives of ESP course
Generate problem based on context
    In collaboration with discipline experts
Plan stages of PBL activity
Consider timing for each stage
Plan tasks and purposes
    Skills
    Content
    Language
Ensure resources are available
Devise evaluation system to measure efficacy and relevance of course

Figure 12.4 Steps in using PBL in ESP course design

Task 12.3

Designing an ESP course using PBL

Using the typical stages presented in Figure 12.1, devise a unit for an ESP course based on PBL. You will need to decide on:

Type of ESP course
Available time
Articulating the problem
Use of resources
Tasks
Skill focus
Treatment of content
Treatment of language
Step-by-step procedure
Evaluation

What is the case-study approach?

While PBL is a common approach in medical studies, the case-study approach is commonly used in business. The two approaches are similar because the teaching and learning is student-led rather than teacher- or course-led. Both approaches focus on groups finding a solution to a problem. As with PBL, the case-study approach replicates the target situation – in this situation a business problem than needs to be solved. With the case-study method, groups consider a business problem and collaborate to suggest solutions, which requires consideration of the consequences of these solutions. The main difference between PBL and the case-study method lies in the solutions to the problem. In PBL there tends to be just one solution – for example, identification of a disease and treatment. In a case study there may be a number of possible solutions. Case studies are also likely to be more complex and may comprise multiple sources of information and documentation.

Types of case study

A case study is usually a description of a situation or problem in a company. This is typically a written account and may come in different formats. In the Harvard approach to case study a narrative account is provided; in the abbreviated case-study approach a condensed version of the situation is presented. In an open case study participants need to find additional information in order to complete the task, whereas in a closed case study all the information is provided to the participants (Esteban & Cañado, 2004).

According to Daly (2002), there are three main types of case study activity:

1   Suggest a solution to a problem faced by management
2   Evaluate courses of action already taken
3   Conduct an appraisal of whether the situation is proceeding as it should

As with PBL, students work in groups. In the case-study method the class is usually conducted to replicate a business-meeting format.

While the case-study method may be widely used in business studies, it needs some consideration to make it work in the language classroom. Unlike business settings, the participants in a business-English classroom lack language skills, and the ESP practitioner may lack subject knowledge. As with PBL, it is necessary to bear in mind language issues to ensure the success of the activity. The procedure of using the case study follows an introduction, analysis and debriefing structure (Figure 12.5).

```
Introduction of case study
      Ensure case study is understood
      Ensure learners have language to discuss case study
Analysis of case study
      Group discussions
      Research (if open case)
      Presentations, reports
Debriefing
      Feedback on analysis, language, skills and products
```

Figure 12.5   Typical stages of a case study

Table 12.2 Advantages and disadvantages of the case-study method in ESP

Advantages	Disadvantages
Develops communication skills	Cases are usually long and complex
Develops decision-making skills	Students find cases challenging linguistically
Links business theory and practice	Teaching difficult and unpredictable
Full range of grammar and vocabulary	Assessment difficult
Opportunity for sheltered practice	Few published materials, so teachers need to devise materials
Develops skills other than language – for example, leadership qualities	Assessment of students difficult
Promotes independent thinking	Lesson planning can be complicated if case study long and complex.

Read case study several times
Identify main issues/problems
List firm's objectives
Consider firm's options
Draw up criteria to evaluate options
Select best option
Think about how option could be implemented
Draw up a plan of action to implement the option

Figure 12.6 Steps for students to analyse a case study

Source: Daly (2002).

The advantages and disadvantages of using the case-study method

The advantages and disadvantages of using the case-study method are similar to those for PBL. Table 12.2 presents some further advantages and disadvantages of using this approach, which would be most applicable in business settings rather than across the ESP spectrum of disciplines.

Implementation

Daly (2002) describes how the case-study method can be applied in English classrooms. He provides a step-by-step account of how to conduct classes using this method. He divides the case-study procedure into three stages: case-study introduction, case-study class and debriefing. In the introduction class the case is presented and explained to the students together with necessary lexis and language (Figure 12.5). He then provides a step-by-step procedure for students to analyse the case (Figure 12.6). The case-study class takes the form of a meeting with groups discussing the case and giving presentations. In the final class, the debriefing, students are provided with feedback on language, managerial skills and writing.

Task 12.4

Designing an ESP course using the case-study method

Find one or more suitable case studies. These are easily available in business courses or online.

Produce a plan on how this could be included in a business-English course.

Plan a series of sessions that are based on a case study following the recommended stages in Figure 12.5.

Summary

This chapter has considered two discipline-informed methodological approaches to teaching ESP: problem-based learning (PBL), widely used in medical studies, and case-study methodology, widely used in business studies. These two approaches fit in well with task-based learning and communicative-language teaching (see Chapter 5) as they are both learner-centred and promote learner autonomy. Both are based on authentic texts and reflect the target communicative situation of their disciplines, making these approaches both motivating and useful. Chapter 15 provides some resources for using PBL and case-study approaches to ESP.

Further reading

Wood and Head (2004) and Yu and Seepho (2015) describe how PBL can be used with medical students, while Barron (2002) describes a project that applied PBL in an EAP setting. Esteban and Cañado (2004) address the challenges of implementing the case-study approach in a course focusing on foreign trade. Daly's (2002) article is very practical and provides instructions on how to implement a case-study approach in a business-English class.

References

Barron, C. (2002). Problem-solving and EAP: Themes and issues in a collaborative teaching venture. *English for Specific Purposes, 22*(3), 297–314.
Bosuwon, T., & Woodrow, L. (2009). Using a problem-based approach to enhance English reading abilities of Thai undergraduate students. *RELC Journal, 40*(1), 42–64.

Daly, P. (2002). Methodology for using case studies in the business English language classroom. *Internet TESL Journal, 8*(11). Retrieved 15 March 2017 from http://iteslj.org/Techniques/Daly-CaseStudies/.

Esteban, A. A., & Pérez Cañado, M. a. L. (2004). Making the case method work in teaching Business English: A case study. *English for Specific Purposes, 23*(2), 137–61.

Harding, J. E. (2001). Problem-based learning in biblical studies: Reflections from classroom experience. *Teaching Theology and Religion, 4*(2), 89–97.

Maudsley, G. (1999). Roles and responsibilities of the problem based learning tutor in the undergraduate medical curriculum. *British Medical Journal, 318*(7184), 657–61.

Maxwell, N. L., Bellisimo, Y., & Mergendoller, J. (2001). Problem-based learning: Modifying the medical school model for teaching high-school economics. *Social Studies, 92*(2), 73–8.

Wood, A., & Head, M. (2004). "Just what the doctor ordered": The application of problem-based learning to EAP. *English for Specific Purposes, 23*(1), 3–17.

Yu, L., & Seepho, S. (2015). Problem-based learning materials design for a medical English course. *Theory and Practice in Language Studies, 5*(7), 1346–51.

Chapter 13

Specific EAP approaches

Academic literacies and content-based instruction

The role of content is crucial in ESP. In this chapter the focus is on different types of EAP course, with a focus on specificity. EAP courses range from English for general academic purposes (EGAP), such as a pre-sessional English course, to English for specific academic purposes (ESAP) courses, where the main focus is on content. In recent years there has been a move towards more situated and context-informed approaches to EAP, regardless of the type of course (pre-sessional or in-sessional). This means that there is a greater focus on content. This chapter is about how EAP courses can be made more specific. It discusses two main approaches to course design: content-based instruction (CBI) (Snow & Brinton, 1997; 1988), also termed 'content and language integrated learning' (CLIL) (Airey, 2016), and academic literacies (Lea & Street, 1998). The chapter addresses the role of subject specialists in ESP course design. It also considers how specificity can be achieved by utilising a students-as-researchers approach (Johns, 1997), where students investigate the contextual influences on academic language and tasks. The chapter covers the following topics:

- EGAP and ESAP
- CBI and CLIL
- Collaboration with subject specialists
- Academic literacies
- Students as researchers

Reflection 13.1

Reflecting on EAP university learning experiences

Can you recall any problems you had with academic communication when you went to university?

How did you solve these problems?

Did you take any academic-skills classes?

Were these pre-sessional? In-sessional?

What approach was used on this course?

Do you think the course was helpful?

In what ways was it helpful or not helpful?

The role of specificity is a common theme in current EAP research. Often institutions offer both EGAP and ESAP courses. For example, Hyland and Shaw (2016) contrast two EAP courses at Hong Kong University. One is a general EAP course, 'Core University English', which is a compulsory course for all undergraduates. It seeks to form a bridge between secondary-school English and university English. The second type is a specific EAP course, 'English in the Discipline'. This targets students in the second year and involves collaboration with subject specialists. This is discussed in more detail below.

CBI and CLIL

The term 'content and language integrated learning' (CLIL) refers to an approach to course design and teaching that focuses on both content and language: that is, content is taught through the foreign language, thus gaining a 'two for the price of one' effect (Brunton, 2013). 'CLIL' is the term commonly used in Europe that reflects the European Commission's recommendation that all Europeans operate in two languages other than their mother tongue (MT+ 2). While the languages are not specified, it is usual that one of those additional languages is English (Dalton-Puffer, 2011). CLIL is common as an approach to teaching language in secondary-school settings but is somewhat controversial in its perceived efficacy (Brunton, 2013; Broca, 2016). One argument against CLIL is that it advantages those students who have a high level of language proficiency, while those with lower levels struggle to cope with the content (Brunton, 2013). The discussion in this book focuses on ESP settings in tertiary EAP – so to simplify matters I shall use the term 'content-based instruction' (CBI). CBI has a long tradition in the US (Brinton *et al.*, 1989; Snow & Kamhi-Stein, 2002). It is an approach to language teaching that also originated in general English teaching. The basic premise of CBI is that by teaching content learners will be more motivated than by teaching which focuses solely on language. Two types of CBI are commonly referred to: sheltered and adjunct. The sheltered model is content-driven and utilises linguistically sensitive strategies.

The adjunct model, discussed in more detail below, emphasises an equal focus on both language and content in a more equal manner (Met, 1999). An example of this type of course is a foundation course, whereby students need to pass subject courses as well as a language course.

Rather than having a primary focus on skills, grammar or tasks, CBI courses use content as a major organising feature of the course (Richards & Rodgers, 2001). CBI may come in a 'strong' form, whereby the ESP course focuses on teaching the subject through another language, or 'weak' in that it may be more language-driven with a thematic approach to the syllabus (Crandall, 2012). Airey proposes a language–content continuum in terms of learning outcomes. At one end of the continuum is English-based instruction (EMI), focusing on content, while at the other end is EAP, focusing on language. CBI/CLIL rest in the middle with a focus on both language and content. One significant consideration concerning content in CBI is who does the teaching. At the EMI end of the continuum the subject instructors are wholly responsible, while at the EAP end language teachers are wholly responsible. CBI models rely upon collaboration between subject and language specialists. Crandall (2012) outlines three types of CBI model reflecting collaboration. The adjunct model is one whereby language-support classes are provided concurrently with content courses. They typically focus on reading and writing and use the texts and tasks from the content area. The simulated adjunct model uses content and tasks from a subject area, but these are not paired directly. A modified adjunct model reflects a content course paired with a study group, which may be taught by a language instructor or trained peer tutors. These are presented in Figure 13.1.

Adjunct – language classes supporting content courses
    Using texts and discussion in language support
    Develop reading and writing skills required
    (Snow & Brinton, 1988)
Simulated adjunct
    Using same content and tasks from subject to simulate content course
    (Brinton & Jensen, 2002)
Modified adjunct
    Subject course paired with study group taught by peer tutors
    (Snow & Kamhi-Stein, 2002)

Figure 13.1 Types of CBI/CLIL model

Source: Crandall (2012, pp. 150–1).

Collaboration with subject specialists

Central to CBI is the collaboration between EAP practitioners and subject specialists. However, this collaboration is not always easy. Problems can arise because language specialists and subject specialists may have different epistemological and ontological perspectives. Most EAP teachers come from a humanities background, which may be difficult to reconcile with a positivist scientific perspective on knowledge and learning.

Task 13.1

Models of CBI/CLIL

Using Figure 13.1, consider how you could develop a course informed by Crandall's models:

Adjunct
Simulated adjunct
Modified adjunct

Dudley-Evans and St. John (1998) refer to three types of collaboration, reflecting the level of contact between the ESP practitioner and the subject specialist: cooperation, collaboration and team-teaching. Cooperation reflects minimal input from the subject specialist: an example would be the ESP practitioner collecting data about the target situations of the students. The next level, collaboration, reflects a situation where the ESP practitioner and the subject specialist work together more closely – for example, where the ESP practitioner links the ESP class very closely to the subject class. In a team-teaching situation the ESP practitioner and the subject specialist deliver the ESP class together. For further discussion of Dudley-Evans and St. John's perspective and an example of its application, see Esteban and Martos (2002).

Using a content-based approach in a EGAP course

While the advantages of CBI lie in the relevance of the focus on the tasks and language of the target communicative situation, it is possible to utilise a content-based approach in more general terms. Garner and Borg (2005) describe a pre-sessional course implemented at Northumbria University in which they used a textbook on global issues as the starting point, thus providing the course with a topic-based order. To this they applied what they referred to as an ecological approach, which can account for contextual influences. This approach sees language as holistic, dynamic, interactive and situated, with an emphasis on both context and the interactions that create that context. The teaching team selected the topic as they were interested in it, and this was supported by input from the receiving departments. The whole course developed a genuine academic community, focusing on tasks, genres and communicative events. Murray (2016) presents a strong case for decentralising pre-sessional courses by relocating these to the disciplinary departments. Informed by academic literacies, Murray suggests aligning EAP teachers with academic departments. As these teachers become more experienced in the setting they will gain more knowledge of the demands of the subject.

An academic-literacies approach

An academic-literacies approach to EAP is based on a theoretical model of communication in academic settings. It emerged from the expansion of higher education to increase student diversity at South African and UK universities (Lilis & Tuck, 2016). The past 20 years have seen a great increase in the number of people able to access a university education. This means that the student body is a lot more diverse than in previous decades. All students, whether using language as a first or additional language, need to acquire expertise in academic skills. Academic literacies views reading and writing in an academic setting as being socially situated. An academic-literacies approach is based in the conceptualisation of academic skills as being dictated by context-community membership. It rejects the unitary concept of a single 'literacy', which rests on the view that there is a generic set of skills whose acquisition leads to academic success (Lea & Street, 1998; 2006). Central to academic literacies is the notion of the academic community and the roles members of this community fulfil in terms of literacy (Lilis & Tuck, 2016). The academic-literacies approach sees knowledge and literacies as being varied and based on perspectives in the academic or professional field. So the qualities of excellence in writing about chemistry will vary from those of writing about primary-school teaching. In the former the chemist may need to write a report on an experiment, while in the later the student may have to devise a lesson plan.

Academic discourse communities are discussed in Chapter 9 and illustrated in Table 9.1. A discourse community comprises the network of people that contribute to the communicative situation. One suggested network is presented in Figure 13.2. Members in discourse communities do not have equal power. For example, in the case of a PhD students submitting a thesis, the external examiner is the most powerful person because it is this person who decides whether a thesis passes or fails. In an academic course the lecturers and tutors have a great deal of power: they have expectations of competence and excellence in academic tasks. These views may vary between individuals. For example, one lecturer may expect grammatically accurate essays from students, while another may tolerate minor grammatical errors.

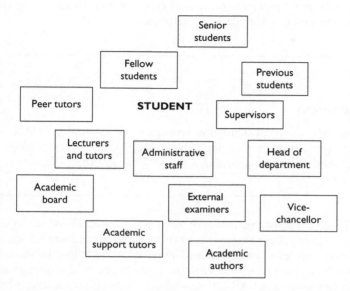

Figure 13.2 Some participants in an academic community

Task 13.2

Collaboration with subject specialists

Think about levels of collaboration with the subject specialist and suggest some ways you could apply each in an EAP course:

Cooperation
Collaboration
Team-teaching

What issues do you think might arise with each level?

How could you avoid or address these issues?

An academic-literacies perspective can be found in a number of other approaches, such as CBI and genre. According to Murray (2016), an academic-literacies approach can be implemented by locating the EAP course and the EAP teacher within the disciplinary setting. This is a somewhat radical departure from traditional pre-sessional courses taught in large-scale university language centres. However, an academic-literacies approach can be applied to more traditional types of EAP by involving the students in the analysis of their academic settings.

Task 13.3

Academic literacies

Think about two different academic settings – for example, TESOL and psychology. Look at the department webpages, course offerings, assessment tasks and course readings. What are the differences between them?

Johns (1997) put forward the notion of 'students as researchers' informed by ethnographic approaches to research. In this approach students ask questions about texts, context, strategies and experts' knowledge. In Part 3, Course 5 Woodrow uses the 'students as researchers' technique in an academic-literacies-informed EAP course within an education faculty. Johns uses this approach to develop a deep understanding on the part of the students about the requirements of their academic tasks. In Woodrow's course the students asked questions of the text and the task and consulted members of the academic community about what constitutes good academic-writing practice in their specific field.

Task 13.4

Students as researchers

Make a list of possible questions EAP students could ask members of the academic discourse community about:

Texts
Contexts
Experts
Self

To facilitate a deep understanding of the communicative setting, Woodrow used a context-analysis framework (Paltridge, 2000). This framework is presented in Figure 13.3 with an example of its application, an analysis of a popular EAP textbook.

What is the text about?	Writing in academic style
What is the purpose of the text?	Instructional manual and practice book for international students
What is the setting of the text?	Textbook, university level, published, English for general academic purposes
What is the tone of the text (formal/informal)?	Formal, instructional
Who is the author of the text?	Expert teacher Western, native English speaker University teacher
Who is the audience of the text?	International students at university, graduate and undergraduate
What is the relationship between the author and the audience?	Author, expert writer Reader, novice writer
What knowledge do the author and the audience share?	Studying at university – English-speaking country Familiarity with issues of study Aspects given about essay writing Metalanguage for talking about language
What are the rules and expectations on how the text might be written?	According to publisher Sales considerations Expectations of reader Exercises
What is the relationship to other texts?	Uses authentic sources Books/journals in own field In general academic field Addresses issue of plagiarism

Figure 13.3 Context-analysis framework

Source: based on analysis of Bailey (2011).

Task 13.5

Context analysis

Pick a text you are familiar with – for example, a journal article, an advertisement or your upcoming applied-linguistics assignment – and conduct a context analysis using the grid below.

What is the text about?	
What is the purpose of the text?	
What is the setting of the text?	
What is the tone of the text (formal/informal)?	
Who is the author of the text?	
Who is the audience of the text?	
What is the relationship between the author and the audience?	
What knowledge do the author and the audience share?	

What are the rules and expectations on how the text might be written?	
What is the relationship to other texts?	

Ethnography plays an important role in recent EAP research. Researchers observe and experience writers' views and practices from the inside in different settings. There is a need for further research in this area in different fields – for example, the transition from school to university. A practical application of this is using expert student writers as tutors to develop the writing skills of novice writers. Both students and teachers are practising members of the academic community and as such have a deep understanding of the setting. An example of an activity that may occur in this approach is that of conferencing, whereby the tutor and student work together on the students' writing, unpacking the demands and execution of the task. This approach originates from composition studies in the US. The focus of composition is on developing undergraduate writing skills at university, often through a mandated first-year course for credit, which all students regardless of their L1 must take (Tardy & Jwa, 2016)

Task 13.6

Peer tutors

Consider how using students as peer tutors could be implemented in an EAP writing course.

What are the major considerations in choosing and training peer tutors?

Summary

This chapter has considered some current perspectives on EAP course design. The main focus of the chapter was how specificity can be reflected in EAP course design. The approaches to course design considered were CBI/CLIL, academic literacies and students-as-researchers.

Further reading

Crandall (2012) has a succinct chapter on CBI and CLIL in Burns and Richards. Hyland and Shaw's (2016) edited book on EAP includes chapters on CBI/CLIL, academic literacies and composition studies. The seminal work on academic literacies is Lea and Street (1998). Johns (1997) provides an excellent guide to implementing the students-as-researchers approach. For a thorough treatment of ethnographic EAP see Paltridge *et al.* (2016).

References

Airey, J. (2016). EAP, EMI or CLIL? In K. Hyland & P. Shaw (Eds.), *The Routledge handbook of English for academic purposes* (pp. 71–83). Oxford: Routledge.

Bailey, S. (2011). *Academic writing: A handbook for international students.* London: Routledge.

Brinton, D. M., & Jensen, L. (2002). *Appropriating the adjunct model: English for acaemic purposes at the university level. Content-based instruction in higher education settings.* Alexandria, VA: TESOL.

Brinton, D. M., Snow, M. A., & Wesche, M. B. (1989). *Content-based second language instruction.* New York: Newbury House.

Broca, A. (2016). CLIL and non-CLIL: Differences from the outset. *ELT Journal, 70*(3), 320–31.

Brunton, A. (2013). CLIL: Some of the reasons why and why not. *System, 41,* 587–97.

Crandall, J. (2012). Content-based language teaching. In A. Burns & J. Richards (Eds.), *The Cambridge guide to pedagogy and practice in language teaching* (pp. 149–60). Cambridge: Cambridge University Press.

Dalton-Puffer, C. (2011). Content-and-language integrated learning: From practice to principles? *Annual Review of Applied Linguistics, 31,* 182–204.

Dudley-Evans, T., & St. John, M. (1998). *Developments in English for specific purposes: A multi-disciplinary approach.* Cambridge: Cambridge University Press.

Esteban, A. A. E., & Martos, M. C. V. (2002). A case study of collaboration among the ESP practitioner, the content teacher and the students. *Revista Alicantina de Estudios Ingleses, 15,* 7–21.

Garner, M., & Borg, E. (2005). An ecological perspective on content-based instruction. *Journal of English for Academic Purposes, 4*(2), 119–34.

Hyland, K. (2016). General and specific EAP. In K. Hyland & P. Shaw (Eds.), (2016) *The Routledge handbook of English for academic purposes.* Oxford: Routledge.

Hyland, K., & Shaw, P. (Eds.) (2016). *The Routledge handbook of English for academic purposes.* Oxford: Routledge.

Johns, A. M. (1997). *Text, role and context.* Cambridge: Cambridge University Press.

Lea, M., & Street, B. (1998). Student writing in higher education: An academic literacies approach. *Studies in Higher Education, 23*(3), 157–72.

Lea, M., & Street, B. (2006). The academic literacies model: Theory and applications. *Theory into Practice, 45*(4), 368–77.

Lilis, T., & Tuck, J. (2016). Academic literacies: A critical lens on writing and reading in the academy. In K. Hyland & P. Shaw (Eds.), *The Routledge handbook of English for academic purposes* (pp. 30–43). Oxford: Routledge.

Met, M. (1999). *Content-based instruction: Defining terms, making decisions*. Retrieved 24 April from http://carla.umn.edu/cobaltt/modules/principles/decisions.html.

Murray, N. (2016). An academic literacies argument for decentralizing EAP provision. *ELT Journal, 70*(4), 435–43.

Paltridge, B. (2000). *Making sense of discourse analysis*. Gold Coast: Antipodean Educational Enterprises.

Paltridge, B., Starfield, S., & Tardy, C. M. (2016). *Ethnographic perspectives on academic writing*. Oxford: Oxford University Press.

Richards, J. C., & Rodgers, T. S. (2001), *Approaches and methods in language teaching* (2nd ed.). Cambridge: Cambridge University Press.

Snow, M. A., & Brinton, D. M. (1988). Content-based instruction: Investigating the effectiveness of the adjunct model. *TESOL Quarterly, 22*(4), 553–74.

Snow, M. A., & Brinton, D. M. (Eds.). (1997). *The content based classroom: Perspectives in integrating language and content*. New York: Longman.

Snow, M. A., & Kamhi-Stein, L. (2002). Teaching and learning academic literacy through project LEAP. In J. Crandall & D. Kaufman (Eds.), *Content-based instruction in higher education settings* (pp. 169–81). Alexandria: TESOL.

Tardy, C. M., & Jwa, S. (2016). Composition studies and EAP. In K. Hyland & P. Shaw (Eds.), *The Routledge handbook of English for academic purposes* (pp. 56–68). Abingdon: Routledge.

Chapter 14

The role of materials

This chapter examines the use of materials in ESP course design, with reference to ESP coursebooks, and covers a range of issues within the topic. First, the term 'materials' is defined and discussed. Of great significance in the debate about ESP materials is the role of the ESP practitioner in terms of being a materials provider and/or designer. While the terms 'textbook' and 'coursebook' are used interchangeably in ESP, I have found it useful to distinguish between them. I refer to textbooks as being about a specific subject, whereas I use 'coursebook' to refer to a publication designed to teach language. The chapter covers the following areas in ESP materials:

- What are ESP materials?
- Authentic materials
- Adapting authentic materials
- ESP practitioner and materials
- ESP coursebooks

What are ESP materials?

According to Tomlinson, materials refer to "anything used by teachers or learners to facilitate the learning of a language" (Tomlinson 2011, 2). This broad definition encompasses a wide range of sources for learning, incorporating technological contributions such as social media and computer-mediated instruction. There is a wealth of literature about the use and development of language-learning materials in EGP (see, for example, Tomlinson, 2008; 2012; 2011). In ESP the role of materials has an added significance in comparison to EGP, since the learners are often concerned with learning both language and disciplinary content.

The most important aspect of ESP materials is that they reflect the target communicative situation. ESP courses usually include authentic materials: that is, texts that are not designed for language-learning purposes but for experts in the ESP field. Examples of authentic texts are subject textbooks, journal articles and online sources. These may be used as is or changed in some way to make texts more accessible for students and/or easier to exploit from a language-learning point of view. This is discussed below.

Principles of SLA in materials

Tomlinson (2011) refers to the principles of second-language acquisition (SLA) in relation to materials. Below are some of the principles he suggests should inform materials development. Tomlinson's work concentrates on EGP; however, these principles could equally be applied to ESP and are certainly useful basic considerations for evaluating ESP materials.

Materials should:

1   Have an impact – that is, the materials have an effect
2   Promote positive affect (confidence) or at the very least not induce negative affect (anxiety)
3   Be perceived as useful by learners
4   Require and facilitate learner self-investment
5   Expose learners to authentic use
6   Draw attention to linguistic features
7   Provide learners opportunity to use target language
8   Account for learner styles

Authentic materials

The notion of authentic materials in ESP is not straightforward. For example, an ESP practitioner may select a magazine article on a topic relevant to the ESP field – for example, education. However, this type of article is written for a lay person rather than a subject specialist and as such would not be relevant to the communicative needs of the ESP student. One issue much discussed concerning the use of authentic materials both in EGP and ESP is whether the texts selected should be used as is or whether the texts should be adapted to meet the linguistic level of the students. Lower-level learners may find authentic ESP texts too complex. How to adapt authentic texts is discussed below.

Reflection 14.1

Experience with authentic materials

What experience have you had with authentic materials?

How did you choose your texts?

Did you change the texts in any way? Why?

How did you exploit the texts (tasks/activities)?

Make a list of authentic materials that could be used in your chosen ESP field.

Types of authentic material

Authentic materials can come from many sources. These can be published – for example, academic journals, subject textbooks, specialist business magazines – or they can be unpublished, such as company reports and dissertations. They can be oral texts, such as business presentations or seminar discussions, or written texts. Texts should be selected systematically based on specific criteria. The most important criterion is that the texts are relevant to, and occur in, the target communicative situation. Authentic texts should be relevant in topic and genre. The intended audience of the text needs consideration and texts should be selected based on exploitability in terms of rhetorical functions, grammar and vocabulary. Table 14.1 presents these criteria and some questions an ESP practitioner needs to ask when deciding whether to use an authentic source.

Newspapers and magazines are easy and accessible sources for authentic materials, but it can be hard to justify using such texts for students other

Table 14.1   Considerations in selecting authentic materials

Criteria	Question to ask
Topic	Is the topic interesting and relevant to the target communicative situation?
Genre	Is the text of a genre students will need to produce or understand?
Audience	Is the text written for an expert or lay audience? Does this match the ESP students' needs?
Register	Is the text written in a register commonly found in the ESP context?
Rhetorical function	What rhetorical functions in the text might be exploited?
Grammar	Does the text display common grammatical structures appropriate to the level of the students?
Vocabulary	Is there a sufficient range of technical and semi-technical vocabulary in the text?

than those involved in the media. Newspaper articles can be interesting and can provoke discussion, but they do not adhere to the criteria outlined in Table 14.1. For example, the genre of newspaper articles is very specific and unlikely to be relevant to ESP students. The texts are usually recounts, the sentences are short and the language uses a great deal of adjectives; the texts are written for a lay rather than an expert audience and the register is unlikely to be useful for students.

Subject textbooks are a popular choice as a source of authentic texts for ESP, particularly in EAP. The content is relevant and instructional and may provide a scaffolding for subject learning (Bondi, 2016). They are also very useful for field-specific vocabulary. However, using such texts for language learning can be problematic and they need to be treated with caution. Subject textbooks are a specific type of genre and are referred to as communicative events in their own right (Bondi, 2016). For Bondi, textbooks tend to be explanatory, with a pedagogic focus. Such a stance would not be appropriate in academic writing by university students – so the generic and rhetorical structure of textbooks is not the same as that required by the target communicative settings.

Another issue when considering using authentic materials is that of copyright. ESP course designers may need permission from the author or publisher to use certain texts in their courses. This is particularly important if the materials constitute a course run for profit.

Adapting authentic materials

Adapting authentic materials should be done in a systematic way. Stoller (2016) suggests a series of materials-adaptation processes which may be applied to authentic texts. These processes range from changes to the text itself to providing additional explanatory help. These are outlined in Figure 14.1.

Adjust materials by simplifying vocabulary or content
Converting texts from one skill to another – for example, reading into listening
Expanding texts, including definitions and extra information
Shortening or reordering texts
Simplifying grammar and vocabulary
Supplementing with additional, more accessible texts

Figure 14.1 Ways of adapting authentic texts

Source: adapted from Stoller (2016).

Task 14.1

Using authentic materials

1   Select an authentic text based on the criteria in Table 14.1.
2   Adapt the text for a group of ESP learners using Stoller's criteria in Figure 14.1

   a   What did you do?
   b   Did you encounter any difficulties?

3   What types of task and activity do you think would be appropriate for your selected text?

While the use of authentic texts, either in their original or modified form, is very important in ESP, authenticity of task is more important (Alexander *et al.*, 2008). This means that the task is realistic and reflects tasks found in the target communicative situation.

The ESP practitioner and materials

One of the reasons ESP teachers are referred to as practitioners is to capture the contribution the teacher may make to the overall ESP course. Frequently, ESP practitioners are responsible for the syllabus and the selection, adaptation and production of materials, along with student assessment. Figure 14.2 captures the levels of an ESP practitioner's freedom in terms of ESP course design and materials. At one end of the scale of teacher control is a purely prescriptive course, where the ESP practitioner has no input into the course design. Such an approach may be useful for novice teachers but is likely to be frustrating for more experienced teachers. At the other end of the scale is no external input to course design. This perspective may be referred to as a process syllabus or a negotiated syllabus (Nation & Macalister, 2010). In this approach the ESP practitioner liaises with the students to provide a tailor-made course. This approach can only be executed by experienced teachers who have extensive knowledge that can be accessed in real time.

In-house materials

ESP practitioners are often involved in materials production. This is one aspect of the job that may be attractive and satisfying to practitioners. The major argument for using practitioner-developed materials is that they can be very needs-specific, However, there are several drawbacks in relying on such materials. First, developing materials is very time-consuming

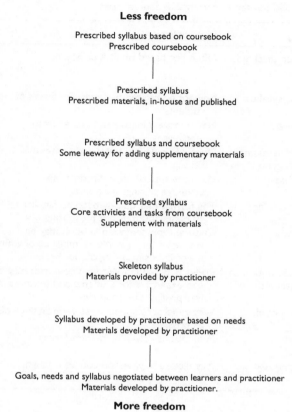

Less freedom

Prescribed syllabus based on coursebook
Prescribed coursebook

Prescribed syllabus
Prescribed materials, in-house and published

Prescribed syllabus and coursebook
Some leeway for adding supplementary materials

Prescribed syllabus
Core activities and tasks from coursebook
Supplement with materials

Skeleton syllabus
Materials provided by practitioner

Syllabus developed by practitioner based on needs
Materials developed by practitioner

Goals, needs and syllabus negotiated between learners and practitioner
Materials developed by practitioner.

More freedom

Figure 14.2 Levels of ESP practitioner freedom in course design and materials

and therefore expensive. In addition, not all teachers are good at developing materials that are effective. Another issue is that there is a tendency to 're-invent the wheel', with teachers repeating the same activities and tasks in terms of materials development.

However, a well-structured programme of in-house materials may be viewed as the best of both worlds. Materials that are systematically developed or a system of materials-sharing means that materials can be tailored to meet the needs and context of the programme at the same time as providing adequate support for new ESP teachers (Esteban, 2002).

ESP coursebooks

There is a large range of published ESP coursebooks available, particularly in the field of business English and EAP. Some are based on corpora – for

Table 14.2 Advantages and disadvantages of using ESP coursebooks

Advantages	Disadvantages
Provides scaffolding for novice teachers, particularly when there is a teacher's book	Often not based on SLA principles
Can serve as a framework or syllabus	May not be related to needs and wants of students
Provides a systematic progression	May remove initiative and power from teachers
Usually provides revision and assessment thus measuring student progress	Does not reflect cultural and contextual setting
Activities usually 'work' in class	May have superficial and reductionist coverage of language points
Teachers not always good at writing materials	The format may quickly become familiar to students and thus not motivating
Saves lesson preparation time	Cultural representation in book may be suspect – for example, dominance of white males in business-English book
Overall it may be the cheapest option to provide students with materials	Books published in Western countries may be too expensive for students and teachers in less prosperous countries
Students usually like to have a book	Very general to appeal to as wide an audience as possible
Students can revise and work from book out of class	Publications driven by market forces
Media such as audio, video and text integrated	May dictate how lesson/course is taught

example, the CANBEC corpus is the basis for several Cambridge ESP coursebooks. Many practitioners shun the use of coursebooks because it is hard to find a book that can address specific ESP students' needs. However, there is an increasing range of coursebooks available for a wide range of disciplines in ESP. Table 14.2 presents some of the advantages and disadvantages of using coursebooks.

Teachers use coursebooks in different ways and for different purposes. Hutchinson (1996) conducted a study that indicated that coursebook use is influenced by teacher training and experience, beliefs, personality and knowledge of subject matter. In Menkabu and Harwood's (2014) study teachers reported a lack of time, the pressure of examinations and a lack of specialist knowledge as reasons for coursebook reliance. Shawer (2010) discusses the coursebook use of EFL teachers and categorises teachers into three types in terms of their use:

1   Curriculum makers – those who rarely use a coursebook and create their own materials

2 Curriculum developers – those who adapt the coursebook to suit learners if they perceive a shortcoming
3 Curriculum transmitters – those who strictly follow the coursebook without making any changes

---

Task 14.2

What type of teacher are you?

What type of teacher are you in terms of materials? 1, 2 or 3? Why?

Choosing an ESP coursebook

Choosing any language-teaching coursebook is difficult. Sometimes students respond well and sometimes they do not. When selecting a suitable coursebook, the ESP practitioner should consider needs, learning objectives, methodological approach, context relevance and the level of student autonomy (Chan, 2009). Chapter 15 includes an adaption of Chan's framework for evaluating business-meeting materials that can be applied to other ESP settings.

Adapting ESP coursebooks

Probably all ESP practitioners adapt coursebooks in some way. By adapting materials, practitioners can better match students' needs. It is also possible to account for local contexts and educational practices by adapting materials. Yakhontova (2001) described the experience of introducing a new coursebook in the Ukrainian context and concluded that there was a need to modify materials to reflect the local environment and to reflect local intellectual traditions that differed from those assumed in the coursebook. McDonough and Shaw (2003) outline three main ways of adapting coursebooks. These are presented in Figure 14.3.

Task 14.3

Adapting ESP materials

Using McDonough and Shaw's methods of coursebook adaptation and an ESP coursebook, decide what adaptations you would make for a specific group of learners.

Why would you make these adaptations?
How would you do this?

Adding
> Extending the material: adding activities to further practise language points
> Adding more exercises
> Introducing a related skill – for example, speaking

Deleting
> Reducing the number of activities – for example, removing speaking activities or reducing the number of exercises focusing on a particular grammar point

Modifying
> Rewriting activities to match learners' needs, match the local context
> Simplifying activities
> Restructuring

Reordering
> Approaching activities in a different sequence

Figure 14.3   ESP coursebook adaptation

Source: based on McDonough and Shaw (2003).

Summary

This chapter has considered the role in ESP of materials. It has discussed authentic materials and the use of coursebooks in ESP and provided guidelines for adapting them. It has provided links to resources in Chapter 15.

Further reading

Most of the further reading listed here refers to EGP, as many of the principles are relevant to ESP. Tomlinson is a must read for those interested in materials. Similarly, the materials development association (MATSDA, online) is a useful resource for those interested in developing materials. Their journal *Folio* has a wealth of articles relevant to materials design and evaluation.

Alexander *et al.* (2008) is an excellent resource for EAP materials development and evaluation. Harwood's (2014) edited volume on English-language coursebooks provides an up-to-date perspective on coursebook content, consumption and production.

References

Alexander, O., Argent, S., & Spencer, J. (2008). *EAP essentials: A teacher's guide to principles and practice*. Reading: Garnet.

Bondi, M. (2016). Textbooks. In K. Hyland & P. Shaw (Eds.), *The Routledge handbook of English for academic purposes* (pp. 323–34). Oxford: Routledge.

Chan, C. S. C. (2009). Forging a link between research and pedagogy: A holistic framework for evaluating business English materials. *English for Specific Purposes, 28*(2), 125–36.

Esteban, A. A. (2002). How useful are ESP textbooks? *ODISEA, 2*, 29–47.

Harwood, N. (Ed.) (2014). *English language teaching textbooks: Content, consumption and production.* Basingstoke: Palgrave-Macmillan.

Hutchinson, E. G. (1996). *What do teachers and learners actually do with textbooks? Teacher and learner use of a fisheries-aased ELT textbook in the Phillipines.* PhD thesis, University of Lancaster.

MATSDA (Materials Development Association). (online). Accessed 25 April at www.matsda.org/folio-issues.html.

McDonough, J., & Shaw, C. (2003) *Materials and methods in ELT: A teacher's guide* (2nd ed.). Oxford: Blackwell.

Menkabu, A., & Harwood, N. (2014). Teachers' concpetualization and use of the textbook on a medical English course. In N. Harwood (Ed.), *English language teaching textbooks: Content consumption and production* (pp. 145–77). Basingstoke: Palgrave Macmillan.

Nation, I. S. P., & Macalister, J. (2010). *Language curriculum design.* Oxford: Routledge.

Shawer, S. (2010). Classroom-level curriculum development: EFL teachers as curriculum-developers, curriculum-makers and curriculum-transmitters. *Teaching and Teacher Education, 26*(2), 173–84.

Stoller, F. (2016). EAP materials and tasks. In K. Hyland & P. Shaw (Eds.), *The Routledge handbook of English for academic purposes* (pp. 577–91). Oxford: Routledge.

Tomlinson, B. (2008). *English language teaching materials.* London: Continuum.

Tomlinson, B. (Ed.) (2011). *Materials development in language teaching* (2nd ed.). Cambridge: Cambridge University Press.

Tomlinson, B. (2012). Materials development for language learning and teaching. *Language Teaching, 45*(2), 143–79.

Yakhontova, T. (2001). Textbooks, contexts and learners. *English for Specific Purposes, 20*(Supp. 1), 397–415.

Chapter 15

Resources

This chapter presents a range of resources ESP practitioners may find useful in ESP course design. The chapter is arranged in the order in which topics are presented in previous chapters.

Needs-analysis data-collection instruments

Below are three examples of needs-analysis instruments. Example 1 presents a questionnaire, Example 2 presents a semi-structured interview and Example 3 looks at questionnaires used to assess English for legal purposes.

Needs-analysis example 1

Example 1 is a questionnaire given to in-service, novice mountain guides about to graduate. The questionnaire was constructed based on data from unstructured interviews with recruitment staff. The needs analysis was also triangulated with non-participant observation of the final examination and language-proficiency data.

Example 1

Needs-analysis questionnaire from Wozniak, S. (2010). Language needs analysis from a perspective of international professional mobility: The case of French mountain guides. *English for Specific Purposes, 29*(4), 243–52 (excerpt from 251–2).

No	Question	Response
1	How old are you?	
2	What is your gender?	
3	What is your mother tongue?	

No	Question	Response
4	What are the foreign languages you use professionally, apart from English? *(German/Spanish/Italian/Russian/Dutch/other)*	
5	Training	
5.1	As a pupil/student, did you attend English (EGP) classes? *(no/at a junior and/or senior high school/private lessons/at a French university/at an English as a native language (ENL) university/at an English as a foreign language (EFL) university/during a work placement/other)*	
5.2	As a pupil/student, did you attend English (tourism and mountaineering English) classes? *(no/at a junior and/or senior high school/private lessons/at a French university/at an ENL university/at an EFL university/during a professional training period/other)*	
5.3	Have you attended English (EGP) classes since you became a mountain guide? *(no/yes, for professional reasons/yes, out of personal interest/other)*	
5.4	Have you attended English (tourism and mountaineering English) classes since you became a mountain guide? *(no/yes, for professional reasons/yes, out of personal interest/other)*	
5.5	Have you spent time in an English-speaking country? *(Where?/For how long?/What for?)*	
6	As a professional, do you use English to interact?	
6.1.1	In France, as a professional, do you interact in English with clients that are native English speakers?	
6.1.2	In France, as a professional, do you interact in English with other guides or professionals that are native English speakers?	
6.1.3	In France, as a professional, do you interact in English with clients that are non-native English speakers?	
6.1.4	In France, as a professional, do you interact in English with other guides or professionals that are non-native English speakers?	
6.1.5	Are there other people with whom you interact in English?	
6.2.1	Abroad, as a professional, do you interact in English with clients that are native English speakers?	
6.2.2	Abroad, as a professional, do you interact in English with other guides or professionals that are native English speakers?	

No	Question	Response
6.2.3	Abroad, as a professional, do you interact in English with clients that are non-native English speakers?	
6.2.4	Abroad, as a professional, do you interact in English with other guides or professionals that are non-native English speakers?	
7	*Language skills*	
7.1	Do you read non-specialised newspapers and magazines in English? (*Time, Newsweek, The Guardian, The New York Times*, etc.)	
7.2	Do you read specialised magazines? (*Climbing, Rock and Ice, Alpinist*, etc.)	
7.3	Do you read professional documents in English? What are they?	
7.4	Do you write texts in English like email, posts on internet forums, letters, articles, etc. pertaining to your profession?	
7.5	Do you take part in general interest conversations in English with English native speakers? (*greeting a guest/organising an expedition or a trip abroad – accommodation and transport, etc.*)	
7.6	Do you take part in general interest conversations in English with English non-native speakers? (*greeting a guest/organising an expedition or a tri abroad – accommodation and transport, etc.*)	
7.7	Do you take part in professional conversations in English with English native speakers?	
7.8	Do you take part in professional conversations in English with English non-native speakers?	
7.9	Generally speaking, do you think that being able to interact in English is useless or unnecessary in your profession?	
7.10	Do you think that mountain guides should be able to interact in basic English?	
7.11	Do you think that mountain guides should be able to interact in good English, to make themselves understood by all in all circumstances?	
7.12	Do you think mountain guides should be fluent in English?	
7.13	Do you think mountain guides should be proficient in mountaineering English?	

No	Question	Response
7.14	More specifically, do you think that mountain guides should be able to: – understand/send an emergency message? – understand the description of/describe the characteristics of a medical emergency? – give safety instructions? – explain a decision made in a complex situation? – describe the equipment used? – interact with their clients in EGP (describe the mountain environment, their job etc.)? – take part in written or oral discussions dealing with professional topics? – know about stakes for the profession in foreign contexts? – be able to deal with cultural differences (foreign clients' expectations, etc.)?	
7.15	Considering your own experience, do you think that it would be useful to offer a training course in English at Ecole Nationale de Ski et d'Alpinisme (ENSA)?	
7.16	Considering your own experience, do you think that it would be useful to offer a training course in English as part of the guides' continuous education?	

Needs-analysis example 2

Example 2 is a set of semi-structured interview questions to assess the needs of engineers at a semi-conductor manufacturing company in Taiwan (TSMC). The needs analysis was triangulated with questionnaire data from an online survey: www.surveymonkey.com/r/?sm=GTZBlkCm%2fjBVF0Fm WqBaEw%3d%3d (accessed 15 March 2017).

Example 2

Semi-structured interview questions for English for engineers from: Spence, P., & Liu, G.-Z. (2013). Engineering English and the high-tech industry: A case study of an English needs analysis of process integration engineers at a semiconductor manufacturing company in Taiwan. *English for Specific Purposes*, 32(2), 97–109 (excerpt from 107–8).

A1 Background

1 Have you ever talked to a foreigner in English other than your teacher? If yes, how did you feel?

– Did you feel you could communicate effectively?
– What problems did you encounter?
– What success do you feel you had in communicating?

A2 Consequences and strategies for coping with insufficient language skills

2   To what extent is a lack of English language skills a barrier [for you] at TSMC?
3   What are the potential consequences of this language barrier? (e.g. reduced profits, delays, reprimands etc.)
4   What are some coping strategies for this language barrier? (problems remain unresolved, using an interpreter, etc.)
5   Can you give an example of problems caused by insufficient English language skills at TSMC?
6   Can you think of an example of benefits brought by sufficient English language skills at TSMC?

A3 Coping at work

7   What kind of tasks do you have to perform in English at TSMC?
8   Does TSMC support your English studies financially or in some other way?
9   With whom do you most often communicate in English while at work?

Needs-analysis example 3

Example 3 is an example of needs-analysis questionnaires given to stakeholders used to assess the needs of law students. One questionnaire was given to law lecturers and one to lawyers, so providing triangulation of perceived needs.

Example 3

Needs analysis questionnaires to assess English for legal purposes taken from: Deutch, Y. (2003). Needs analysis for academic legal English courses in Israel: A model of setting priorities. *Journal of English for Academic Purposes,* 2(2), 125–46 (excerpt from 142–4).

Law Lecturers' Questionnaire

1 How important is English for law students during their law studies?

| 1 very important | 2 important | 3 not very important | 4 not important |

2 How important is English for legal research?

| 1 very important | 2 important | 3 not very important | 4 not important |

3 What kind of courses do you teach at law school?

| 1 required courses | 2 elective courses | 3 seminars |

4 In which of the above kinds do you require the biggest amount of reading in English?

| 1 required courses | 2 elective courses | 3 seminars |

5 What percentage of the reading for your courses is in English?

| 1 30% and above | 2 between 10–30% | 3 below 10% |

6 Rank the following skills in English by the order of their importance for law students. (Mark 1 as the most important and 4 as the least important.)

   reading _____

   writing _____

   listening _____

   speaking _____

7 Rank the following genres of legal material by their order of importance for the English reading requirements in your courses. (Mark 1 as the most important and 5 as the least important.)

   court decisions   _____

   legal articles   _____

   books   _____

   legislation   _____

   legal documents   _____

8 Does the required reading in your course come from

   American law _____

   English law _____

   Other laws _____

Rank them by order of importance. (Mark 1 as the most important and 3 as the least important.)

Lawyers' Questionnaire

1 Where did you acquire your knowledge of English?

1 Only Israeli high school and university studies	2 Long stay or studies abroad as well

2 How important is English for the practice of law in Israel?

1 very important	2 important	3 not very important	4 not important

3 What are the major areas of your legal practice?

_____

4 In which of the above areas do you need English most?

_____

5 Are you able to read English or American material for comparative or interpretive purposes?

1 definitely	2 yes	3 with difficulty	4 no

6 Are you able to draft legal documents, such as wills or contracts, in English?

1 definitely	2 yes	3 with difficulty	4 no

7 If you are required to read a legal document in English, do you rely on yourself or do you seek help?

1 I rely on myself	2 I usually rely on myself	3 I usually seek help	4 I seek help

8 If you need to read legal material (other than documents) in English, such as books and articles, do you rely on yourself or do you seek help?

1 I rely on myself	2 I usually rely on myself	3 I usually seek help	4 I seek help

9 Rank the following genres of legal material in English by their order of importance for the English reading requirements in your courses. (Mark 1 as the most important and 5 as the least important.)

court decisions   _____

legal articles   _____

books   _____

legislation   _____

legal documents _____

10 If you are required to draft a legal document in English, do you rely on yourself or do you seek help?			
1 I rely on myself	2 I usually rely on myself	3 I usually seek help	4 I seek help

11 Rank the following skills in English by the order of their importance for law students. (Mark 1 as the most important and 4 as the least important).

    reading   _____

    writing   _____

    listening   _____

    speaking   _____

12 When did you acquire your skill of drafting legal documents in Hebrew?		
1 1st year law school	2 2nd and 3rd year law school	3 in practice

13 Do you actually use English in your legal practice?			
1 a lot	2 moderately	3 I don't really use	4 not at all

Resources for vocabulary in ESP course design

This section presents some resources that can be used to help with vocabulary in ESP course design. It includes word lists, resources to exploit these and a list of subject-specific dictionaries that can be very useful for both students and ESP practitioners. Included in this section is a list of links to corpora and concordancing software. Some of these are available free of charge.

Word lists

Word lists can be useful in course design. They can be used as the basis for vocabulary exercises in class and they can also be exploited by the students. Some word lists are accompanied by websites with tasks and exercises in electronic form.

Academic word list

In EAP a very useful instrument is the Academic Word List (Coxhead, online). This is freely available for download. The list contains 570 word families excluding the most frequent 2000 words. Discussion about the development of the list can be found in Coxhead (2000). The whole list can be found at: www.victoria. ac.nz/lals/resources/academicwordlist/ (accessed 9 September 2015).

Resources using AWL

The University of Nottingham has a site that exploits the AWL for use by teachers and students. The site includes activities such as gap making, highlighting and generating concordance lines of user input texts. Available at: www.nottingham. ac.uk/alzsh3/acvocab/ (accessed 8 February 2017).

Compleat lexical tutor

Tom Cobb's Compleat Lexical Tutor is a very useful source for vocabulary. It includes concordancers, lists tests and exercises: www.lextutor.ca/ (accessed 8 March 2017).

General Service List (GSL)

This is the original GSL list, developed by West (1953), and available at: www.lextutor.ca/freq/lists_download/ (accessed 8 March 2017).

There are two new versions of this list. The first is by Brown *et al.* (2014): www.newgeneralservicelist.org/ (accessed 8 January 2017). The site also includes a diagnostic test based on the list. The second is by Brezina and Gablasove (2015), which can be accessed as part of a published research article: http://applij. oxfordjournals.org/content/early/2013/08/25/applin.amt018/suppl/DC1 (accessed 26 August 2015).

Academic phrasebank

The academic phrasebank developed by the University of Manchester and updated in 2015 is useful because it lists common academic phrases rather than single lexical items: www.click2go.umip.com/i/academic_phrasebank/appe.html (accessed 9 September 2015).

Engineering word lists

Ward, J. (1999). A basic engineering list for less proficient engineering undergraduates. *English for Specific Purposes*, *28*(3), 170–82.

This list ranks terms according to frequency in the fields of chemical, electrical, civil, industrial and mechanical engineering.

Todd, R. W. (2017). An opaque engineering word list: Which words should a teacher focus on. *English for Specific Purposes*, *45*, 31–9.

This list includes 186 key words.

Medical word lists

Wang, J., Liang, S. I., & Ge, G. (2008). Establishment of a medical academic word list. *English for Specific Purposes*, *27*(4), 442–58.

This article includes a word list of medical academic words.
Yang, M.-N. (2015). A nursing academic word list. *English for Specific Purposes*, *37*(0), 27–38.

This article includes a word list of nursing academic words.

Webpages

Charles Kelly and Lawrence Kelly have a website that focuses on vocabulary. Although this is mostly for EFL students, the site includes a business word list and words commonly found in a range of ESP fields. The site features vocabulary games and tests on the lists: www.manythings.org/vocabulary/lists/e/ (accessed 10 December 2016).

Paul Nation's web page has a vast array of resources available about vocabulary. The site includes links to vocabulary lists, levels and tests: www.victoria. ac.nz/lals/about/staff/paul-nation (accessed 10 December 2016).

Dictionaries

There is a large number of published and online specialist dictionaries, which can be useful for course designers, teachers and students. Some examples of these are listed below.

Academic English

Oxford dictionary of academic English (2015)
This comes in different versions, including apps for mobiles and iPads. It is based on the Oxford Corpus of Academic English and includes word lists, collocations, grammar and writing advice. It is linked to the Oxford EAP series of coursebooks.

Medical English

Medline
Medline publishes a medical dictionary that includes pronunciation, meaning and grammatical information. It has an interesting link to how medical words are formed: https://medlineplus.gov/mplusdictionary.html (accessed 8 February 2017).

Medical Dictionary Online
The Medical Dictionary Online includes a glossary of medical terms: www. online-medical-dictionary.org/ (accessed 8 March 2017).

A dictionary of nursing (2008)
Oxford University Press publish this dictionary authored by Martin and McFerran. It is now in its 6th edition. Limited entries available free online: www.oxfordreference.com/view/10.1093/acref/9780199211777.001.0001/acref-9780199211777 (accessed 13 February 2017).

McGraw-Hill nurses' dictionary (2015)
The 4th edition of this dictionary, authored by Panda. New York: McGraw-Hill.

Ballière's nurses' dictionary for nurses and healthcare workers (2014) This dictionary, authored by Weller, is in its 26th edition and published by Tindall Elsevier.

Business English
All three of the dictionaries listed below are designed for learners of English.

Cambridge business English dictionary (2011)
There is also an interactive website available: http://dictionary.cambridge.org/dictionary/
business-english/ (accessed 8 February 2017).

Longman business English dictionary (2007)
Harlow: Pearson.

Oxford business English dictionary for learners of English (2005)
Oxford: Oxford University Press. Includes CD ROM.
The following two sites are online business dictionaries which are not specifically
designed for learners of English.

Business Dictionary
www.businessdictionary.com/ (accessed 8 February 2017).

Babylon Business Dictionary
www.babylon.com/define/22/Business-Dictionary.html (accessed 9 September 2015).
This site provides access to word lists from a range of business dictionary sources.

Legal English

The Law Dictionary
This online resource includes *Black's law dictionary*, published by Oxford University Press (limited free online dictionary available): http://thelawdictionary.org/
(accessed 8 February 2017). This resource is also available for mobiles.

The Free Dictionary
This online law dictionary includes pronunciation, synonyms and related words:
http://legal-dictionary.thefreedictionary.com/ (accessed 8 February 2017).

Aviation English

Crocker, D. (2007). *Dictionary of aviation English*. 2nd edition. London: Bloomsbury.
Crane, D. (2012). *Dictionary of aeronautical terms*. 5th edition. Newcastle, WA:
Aviation Supplies and Academics.
Kumar, B., Deremer, D., & Marshall, D. (2005). *An illustrated dictionary of aviation*.
New York: McGraw-Hill.
Further online resources are available at: www.asa2fly.com (accessed 10 September
2016).

Engineering English

Oxford has a series of engineering dictionaries in specific fields:

Atkins, T., & Escudier, M. (2013). *Oxford dictionary of mechanical
engineering*.

Gorse, C., & Johnston, D. (2012). *Oxford dictionary of construction, surveying and civil engineering.*

Schaschke, C. (2014). *Oxford dictionary of chemical engineering.*

Engineering Dictionary

This online dictionary includes lists of other technical dictionaries: www.engineering-dictionary.org/ (accessed 9 September 2015).

Maritime English

Maritime terms

The seafarer's word: A maritime dictionary. Ranger Hope: www.splashmaritime.com.au/Marops/Dictionary.pdf (accessed 19 January 2017).

Marine terminology

Online Nautical Dictionary: www.termisti.refer.org/nauterm/dicten.htm#en (accessed 19 January 2017).

Military English

Bowyer, R. (2004). *Campaign: Dictionary of military terms.* London: Macmillan. This dictionary accompanies Macmillan's coursebook series of the same name.

DOD *dictionary of military and associated terms* (2016)

The US Department of Defense publishes an extensive dictionary of terms. This publication is regularly updated: www.dtic.mil/doctrine/new_pubs/dictionary.pdf (accessed 19 January 2017).

ESP corpora

Links to corpora

Bank of English
www.titania.bham.ac.uk/docs/svenguide.html (accessed 10 September 2016).

British Academic Spoken English Corpus (BASE)
www.coventry.ac.uk/base (accessed 10 September 2016).

British Academic Written English Corpus (BAWE)
www.coventry.ac.uk/bawe (accessed 10 September 2016).

British National Corpus (BNC)
www.natcorp.ox.ac.uk/ (accessed 10 September 2016).

Corpus of Contemporary American English
http://corpus.byu.edu/coca/ (accessed 10 September 2016).

International Corpus of English
http://ice-corpora.net/ice/index.htm (accessed 10 September 2016).

PERC Corpus, Professional Research Consortium (CPE)
https://scn.jkn21.com/~percinfo/ (accessed 10 September 2016).

Michigan Corpus of Academic Spoken English (MICASE)
http://quod.lib.umich.edu/cgi/c/corpus/corpus?page= home;c=micase;cc=micase
(accessed 10 September 2016).

Wolverhampton Business English Corpus
http://catalog.elra.info/product_info.php?products_id=627 (accessed 10 September 2016).

The Oxford Corpus
www.oxforddictionaries.com/words/the-oxford-english-corpus (accessed 10 September 2016).

Vienna–Oxford International Corpus of English (VOICE)
www.univie.ac.at/voice/ (accessed 10 September 2016).

The University Catholique de Louvrain (UCL) Centre for English Corpus Linguistics provides details and links to corpora around the world, including bilingual and leaner corpora: www.uclouvain.be/en-cecl-lcworld.html (accessed 10 September 2016).

Concordancers

AntConc
Laurence Anthony's page for concordancing. This includes software for download: www.laurenceanthony.net/software/antconc/ (accessed 10 September 2016).

Compleat Lexical Tutor
www.lextutor.ca/ (accessed 10 September 2016)

Mike Nelson's Business English Lexis Site
http://users.utu.fi/micnel/business_english_lexis_site.htm (accessed 10 September 2016).

Spaceless
www.spaceless.com/concordancer.php (accessed 15 February 2017).

Wordsmith
www.lexically.net/wordsmith/index.html (accessed 15 February 2017).

Sense-based General Service List
http://crs2.kmutt.ac.th/sense-based_GSL/ (accessed 15 February 2017).

Business Letter Corpus KWIC Concordancer
www.someya-net.com/concordancer/ (accessed 10 September 2016).

Choosing and evaluating ESP materials

Table 15.1 provides a checklist that can be used by course designers to evaluate ESP materials.

Sources of authentic materials

A common source of authentic materials is discipline-based texts, such as company reports, journal articles and subject textbooks. In addition to these there are several resources freely available online. Some examples are listed below.

Table 15.1 Checklist for evaluating ESP materials

Area	✓	Comments
Needs analysis		
Does the material suit the learners' needs in terms of work experience and types of target communicative situations?		
Are the activities suitable for the target learners' levels and interests?		
Learning objectives		
What is/are the main learning objective(s)? – general language knowledge, specialist language knowledge, general communication skills, professional communication skills or a combination of these?		
If grammar and vocabulary items are presented, are they relevant to target communicative situations?		
Methodological approach		
What is the main methodological approach?		
Is it suitable for the target learners?		
Do the exercises and activities help learners to practise the language and strategies required in the target communicative situations?		
Do the exercises and activities reflect real-life communication?		
Naturalness of the language models		
How natural are the language models?		
Does the material contain authentic written text?		
Does the material contain authentic spoken text?		
Does the material cover the features of spoken grammar relevant to the target communicative situations?		
Contextualisation of the language		
Does the material provide contextualised examples?		
Does the material use a discourse approach to teaching ESP language?		
Learner autonomy		
Are learners expected to take a degree of responsibility for their own learning?		
Does the material include any advice/help to learners on learning strategies?		
Are self- and peer-evaluation tasks included? Is help given to the learners on what to look for?		

Source: based on Chan (2009, p. 132).

TED Talks
This site has a wide range of videoed talks by influential people: www.ted.com/talks (accessed 15 February 2017).

Yale online courses
This site has free introductory courses on a range of subjects delivered by experts: http://oyc.yale.edu/ (accessed 15 February 2017).

MIT online courses
This site provides free-of-charge materials from MIT courses in a wide range of subjects: https://ocw.mit.edu/courses/ (accessed 15 February 2017).

Open University online courses
This site offers short courses free of charge on a range of subjects: www.open.edu/openlearn/free-courses (accessed 15 February 2017).

Podcasts

BBC
This site provides access to podcasts on a range of topics often with a UK focus: www.bbc.co.uk/podcasts (accessed 15 February 2017).

This American Life
This site provides access to podcasts on a range of topics with a US focus: www.thisamericanlife.org/ (accessed 15 February 2017).

Medical podcasts

On the wards
This site targets medical students and junior doctors and includes published blogs: www.onthewards.org/?gclid=Cj0KEQjwg8i_BRCT9dHt5ZSGi90BEiQAItdjpAjV KDFXDM5JSrpqiNOzS5xjiJwqol4P2m7xZNhizfsaAvCv8P8HAQ (accessed 15 February 2017).

Science podcasts

Radio Lab
This site provides access to podcasts on a range of topics, often with a scientific focus: www.radiolab.org/ (accessed 15 February 2017).

Some resources for technology in ESP

Links for free blog-writing software

Blogspot
www.blogger.com/ (accessed 15 February 2017).

Wordpress
wordpress.com/ (accessed 15 February 2017).

Examples of ESP blogs

Teaching EAP
This blog features discussion about major issues in EAP.

Ding, A. King, J., & Jones, M.: https://teachingeap.wordpress.com/about/ (accessed 15 February 2017).

Using English for Academic Purposes
Andy Gillet's EAP page: www.uefap.net/blog/ (accessed 15 February 2017).

Evan Frendo's English for the Workplace
This blog discusses a wide range of topics, usually with a business-English focus: http://englishfortheworkplace.blogspot.co.uk/ (accessed 15 February 2017).

Oxford's English Language Teaching Global Blog
This blog addresses a range of topics in general EBP, often related to coursebooks and their use: http://oupeltglobalblog.com/category/business-english-for-specific-purposes/ (accessed 15 February 2017).

Example of a classroom blog
For an example of a classroom blog, see Marisol's (University of Valladolid, Spain) blog for Spanish speakers: http://classroomblogenglish.blogspot.co.uk/ (accessed 15 February 2017).

E-readers

Kindle
www.amazon.co.uk/gp/digital/fiona/kcp-landing-page (accessed 15 February 2017).

Garnet publications
www.garneteducation.com/ebooks.html (accessed 15 February 2017).

Bookari
https://play.google.com/store/apps/details?id=com.mantano.reader.android.lite (accessed 15 February 2017).

iBooks
www.apple.com/uk/ibooks/ (accessed 15 February 2016).

Learning Management Systems (LMS)

Blackboard
http://uki.blackboard.com/sites/international/globalmaster/ (accessed 15 February 2017).

Moodle (free)
https://moodle.org/ (accessed 15 February 2017).

Text-matching software

Turnitin
http://turnitin.com/ (accessed 15 February 2017).

Some sources of language tests

Cambridge tests

General: KET, PET, FCE, CAE, CPE
www.cambridgeenglish.org/exams/ (accessed 15 February 2017).

IELTS
International Testing Service information and practice: www.ielts.org/test_takers_
   information.aspx (accessed 15 February 2017).

Online IELTS practice
www.cambridge.org/gb/cambridgeenglish/official-exam-preparation-materials/
   product/online (accessed 15 February 2017).

Business: BEC preliminary, vantage and higher
www.cambridgeenglish.org/exams/academic-and-professional-english/ (accessed 15
   February 2017).

BULATS
Business Language Testing Service (Cambridge) www.bulats.org/ (accessed 15 February 2017).

Common European Framework of Reference (CEFR)
Internationally recognised classification of language levels: www.coe.int/t/dg4/
   linguistic/cadre1_en.asp (accessed 15 February 2017).

Diagnostic English Language Needs Assessment (DELNA)
Diagnostic in-sessional EAP assessment: www.delna.auckland.ac.nz/en.html (accessed
   15 February 2017).

Dialang
Diagnostic online language tests: www.lancaster.ac.uk/researchenterprise/dialang/about.
   htm (accessed 15 February 2017).

Measuring the academic skills of university students (MASUS)
MASUS is a diagnostic procedure for in-sessional EAP: https://sydney.edu.au/stuserv/
   documents/learning_centre/MASUS.pdf (accessed 8 March 2017).

Occupational English Test
OET is a test of English for healthcare professionals: www.occupationalenglishtest.
   org/test-information/ (accessed 15 February 2017).

Oxford English language tests
These tests are designed to be EGP placement tests: www.oxfordenglishtesting.com/
   (accessed 15 February 2017).

Test of English for Educational Purposes (TEEP)
This site features practice tests and answers: www.reading.ac.uk/ISLI/TEEP–english-language-test/islc-teep-practice-tests.aspx (accessed 8 March 2017).

TOEFL
Advice for teachers on TOEFL related matters: www.ets.org/toefl/teachers_advisors (accessed 8 March 2017).
TOEFL iBT: www.ets.org/toefl/ibt/about (accessed 15 February 2017).

TOEIC
Information and links for the Test of English for International Communication: www.ets.org/toeic (accessed 15 February 2017).

Test of Legal English (TOLES)
Information about exams and practice papers: www.toleslegal.com/# (accessed 15 February 2017).

Academic journals for ESP

The following is a list of academic journals that focus on research in ESP.

Annual Review of Applied Linguistics (ARAL) (Cambridge)
This is a general applied linguistics journal that sometimes features ESP studies: www.cambridge.org/core/journals/annual-review-of-applied-linguistics (accessed 15 February 2017).

Applied Linguistics (Oxford)
This is a general and applied linguistics journal that sometimes features ESP: https://academic.oup.com/applij (accessed 8 March 2017).

Asian ESP journal (TESOL Asia)
This is an online journal that focuses on all areas of ESP in the Asian region: http://asian-esp-journal.com/ (accessed 15 February 2017).

English for Specific Purposes (Elsevier)
This is the leading journal in the field of ESP: www.journals.elsevier.com/english-for-specific-purposes/ (accessed 15 February 2017).

English Today(Cambridge)
This is a general applied-linguistics journal that sometimes features ESP studies: www.cambridge.org/core/journals/english-today (accessed 15 February 2017).

ESP Today (University of Belgrade and the Serbian Association for the Study of English)
This is an online open access journal focusing on ESP at a tertiary level: www.esptodayjournal.org/ (accessed 15 February 2017).

ESP World
This is an online publication with two issues per year: www.esp-world.info/ (accessed 15 February 2017).

IATEFL ESP SIG (International Association of Teaching English as Foreign Language ESP Special Interest Group)
This is the journal of the major ESP organisation in the UK:
  http://espsig.iatefl.org/?page_id=1172 (accessed 15 February 2017).

Institute of Electrical and Electronics Engineers (IEEE) Transactions on Professional Communication (IEEE)
This is a journal aimed at the business community: http://ieeexplore.ieee.org/xpl/RecentIssue.jsp?punumber=47 (accessed 15 February 2017).

International House Journal
This is a pedagogy-focused EGP journal: http://ihjournal.com/ (accessed 15 February 2017).

International Journal of Legal English (Bond University and Chinese University of Politics and Law)
Legal-English journal: http://international-journal-legal-english.com/ (accessed 15 February 2017).

IBERICA
Journal of AELFE (Asociación Europea de Lenguas para Fines Específicos: The European Association of Language) www.aelfe.org/?l=en&s=revista (accessed 15 February 2017).

Journal of Applied Linguistics and Professional Practice (Equinox)
Includes articles about English for professional purposes: https://journals.equinoxpub.com/index.php/JALPP (accessed 15 February 2017).

Journal of English for Academic Purposes (Elsevier)
Focuses on EAP issues: www.journals.elsevier.com/journal-of-english-for-academic-purposes/ (accessed 15 February 2017).

Journal of Second Language Writing (Elsevier)
This journal often features articles about EAP writing: www.journals.elsevier.com/journal-of-second-language-writing/ (accessed 15 February 2017).

Language Teaching (Cambridge)
While this is a general applied-linguistics journal, it often features ESP studies. The 'State of the art' articles are particularly useful for course designers: www.cambridge.org/core/journals/language-teaching (accessed 15 February 2017).

TESOL Quarterly
This is a general applied linguistics journal that sometimes features ESP studies: www.tesol.org/read-and-publish/journals/tesol-quarterly (accessed 15 February 2017).

Taiwan International ESP Journal (Taiwan ESP Association)
ESP journal with a Taiwanese focus: http://tespaj.tespa.org.tw/index.php/TESPJ/index (accessed 15 February 2017).

World Englishes (Wiley)
Has a focus on studies of global English: http://onlinelibrary.wiley.com/journal/10.1111/(ISSN)1467-971X (accessed 15 February 2017).

Websites useful for course design

Using English
This is an EGP site but has quite a lot on ESP. It includes articles, materials and activities – for example, the first post of 2016 talks about first lessons in teaching EAP: www.usingenglish.com/articles/first-lessons-for-academic-writing-classes.html (accessed 10 September 2016).

One Stop English
One Stop English has a lot of ESP materials and business materials: www.onestopenglish.com/esp/ (accessed 10 September 2016).

Using English for Academic Purposes
This website on EAP writing by Andy Gillet is a useful resource. It includes sections on functions and genre: www.uefap.com/writing/writfram.htm (accessed 15 February 2017).

The EAP Foundation
This website includes sections on all four skills in EAP and a useful newsletter, which deals with particular issues in EAP – for example, note-taking: www.eapfoundation.com/ (accessed 15 February 2017).

ESP organisations

BALEAP (The British Association of Lecturers in EAP)
The organisation holds conferences and webinars. On the site there are EAP resources and past conference papers online, details about upcoming scholarships and jobs in EAP: www.baleap.org/ (accessed 15 February 2017).

BESIG (Business English Special Interest Group)
This special-interest group operates under IATEFL. It holds an annual conference, hosts webinars, blogs and a Facebook page: www.besig.org/events/default.aspx (accessed 15 February 2017).

IATEFL (International Association of Teachers of English as a Foreign Language)
This is a UK organisation for teachers of English. The organisation holds annual conferences and workshops: www.iatefl.org/ (accessed 15 February 2017).

TESOL English for Specific Purposes Special Interest Section (ESPIS)
This special-interest group operates under TESOL. It has an EAP strand and an EOP strand. The organisation publishes an online newsletter. Back issues are available: www.tesol.org/connect/interest-sections/english-for-specific-purposes (accessed 15 February 2017).

TESOL (Teaching English to Speakers of Other Languages)
Asia-Pacific LSP (Language for Specific Purposes) and Professional Communication Association – Taiwan ESP Association (TESPA). The organisation publishes a twice-yearly journal and hosts an annual conference: www.tespa.org.tw/ (accessed 15 February 2017).

Sources for problem-based learning (PBL)

Stanford sample problems
Examples of problems in PBL in different subjects: http://ldt.stanford.edu/~jeepark/jeepark+portfolio/PBL/example2.htm (accessed 15 February 2017).

Buck Institute of Education
Range of articles and sample problems in a range of subjects: www.bie.org/pbl/reso.html (accessed 15 February 2017).

The Hull–York Medical School (HYMS)
There is a downloadable PDF booklet for teachers explaining PBL and how to implement it: www.hyms.ac.uk/docs/default-source/hyms-downloads/pbl-guide-written-by-students-for-students.pdf?sfvrsn=8
(accessed 15 February 2017).

Sources for case studies

Business case studies in range of subjects
http://businesscasestudies.co.uk/case-studies/by-topic/#axzz4XQVuem1V (accessed 15 February 2017).

***Times* 100 free case studies**
www.deanstalk.net/deanstalk/2008/07/the-times-100-f.html (accessed 15 February 2017).

Harvard Business School
Website for case-study teaching with tips for teaching. The site also offers publications to purchase: https://cb.hbsp.harvard.edu/cbmp/pages/content/casemethodteaching (accessed 15 February 2017).

Open-access teaching resources
This includes free case studies: https://library.ryerson.ca/copyright/resources/teaching-resources/general-resources/free-or-open-access-business-case-studies/ (accessed 15 February 2017).

The Case Centre
www.thecasecentre.org/educators/casemethod/resources/freecasesoverview (accessed 15 February 2017).

Asian case studies, NTU Singapore
Nanyang Technological University, Singapore provides free case studies with an Asian focus: https://asiacase.ntu.edu.sg/abcc.web/main.aspx (accessed 15 February 2017).

Business case studies for teaching
The case studies are designed for international students. Offers US$25 licence for teachers to make multiple copies: www.kurucz.ca/cases/ (accessed 15 February 2017).

Examples of authentic ESP courses

Introduction

This part presents a range of ESP courses, generously shared by their authors, reflecting different settings, approaches and fields. Each of the courses outlines needs analysis, an approach to course design, course outlines and sample classroom tasks. After each course, a reader task is presented which highlights an aspect of the course in question. The courses are linked to topics in Part 1 and Part 2 of this book and are summarised below.

Course 1: *Language in the workplace* by Catherine Nickerson

This is an excellent example of a business-English course utilising a project-based approach. It reflects a discipline-based methodology, as discussed in Chapter 12. The context is an undergraduate business-English course in a university setting in the UAE. There was no formal needs analysis but the course is research-driven. This research is presented in Nickerson's article (2015). The course is interesting because it provides a perspective on how ESP courses can be made relevant and specific even when there are time restrictions, institutional constrains and varying levels of English proficiency.

Course 2: *English for cross-cultural nursing* by Susan Bosher

Course 2, by Susan Bosher, is about English for nursing. The course targets immigrant and international nursing students and professional needs for subject knowledge and terminology, and it addresses the cultural issues of patient–nurse interaction. This course has been researched and developed over several years; and Bosher has produced two student coursebooks. The students have found this course useful in preparing them for the study and practice of nursing. This well documented course explains the journey from needs analysis to course content very well. The needs analysis identified 10 language-related tasks which stakeholders indicated as being problematic. The course uses a varied range of assessment tasks from informal journals to formal tests.

Course 3: *English for lawyers* by Jill Northcott

While this course is offered through Edinburgh University, it is a short course targeting European commercial lawyers and is not connected to EAP skills. This is a good example of using a course framework as a starting point and then fine-tuning the course to meet specific needs of small groups. The size of the group is limited to eight, and all the participants are experienced in the field. The course rests on authentic spoken and written sources and is task-based; however, the course content and tasks are determined by participant needs. This data is collected through individual student interviews on the first day of the course.

Course 4: *Airport English* by Joan Cutting

This course is based on a European project to provide employment opportunities for young Europeans in airports. The courses target four trades in an airport setting: security guards, ground handlers, catering staff and bus drivers. The course is based on observational data and uses a grammatical and functional approach to develop a multimedia course that provides models of interactions for learners.

Course 5: *English in academic settings* by Lindy Woodrow

This is a specific EAP course using an academic-literacies perspective and a students-as-researchers approach. The course emerged from a research project that identified the academic needs of international students in an education faculty at an Australian university. The course is presented as a regular elective on a Master's degree course. Because of this, the course focuses both on theoretical perspectives of academic communication and on the necessary academic skills students need to complete their Master's degree.

Course 6: *Writing for publication* by Brian Paltridge

This is an EAP course that targets academic publication. This is an essential aspect of being a successful academic, which is often the goal of students studying for doctoral degrees. The course adopts a genre approach and focuses on the process of writing an academic-journal article, from selecting the most appropriate journal to submit an article to through to dealing with reviewers' feedback. The course presented here includes some excellent examples of class materials and activities.

Course 7: *Writing in your field with corpora* by Maggie Charles

Specificity is always an issue in ESP, and Maggie Charles demonstrates how EAP can be made more specific to individuals through using corpora.

The students are introduced to how to establish a personal corpus and how to use corpus software tools. This approach can have a long-lasting effect, with students using their corpora long after the EAP course is finished. Charles includes an evaluation questionnaire which is given to students one year after the completion of the EAP course.

Course 8: *Programme for business-English majors* by Zuocheng Zhang

This course differs from the others in this book because it is a degree programme that includes several units or areas of study. It was introduced at the University of International Business and Economics (UIBE) in China to address the perceived need for international communication in the field of business. The programme adopts a text-based and content-based approach, with a focus on language and business subjects. The units of study in this programme are taught by lecturers who have expertise both in language and business. Zhang exemplifies this programme by describing one unit of study: *Business marketing writing in English* in terms of approach and content.

Language in the workplace

Catherine Nickerson

Language in the workplace is a research-based communication course for senior Emirati business students at a Middle-Eastern business school. It is a credit-bearing course.

Rationale for the ESP course

The course attempts to address two areas that have been identified as needs at both a federal level within the country and through observation:

1   There is a need for undergraduate students to become more actively engaged in research relevant to their professional specialisation.
2   There is a need to develop the English business-communication skills of students who have a wide variation in language proficiency. This is because of their educational background. Many students have attended international English-medium schools, whereas other have attended Arabic-medium government schools.

The course provides the development of disciplinary knowledge and skills in business communication on five important focus areas: cultural literacy, language and genre, audience awareness, social capital and sustainability and persuasion. We labelled this the *CLASP* model. These five areas were identified in the scholarly literature on business communication (e.g. Fraser *et al.*, 2005) and through our own observations over a period of several years in the country interacting with our students and alumni (Nickerson, 2015). The model components are described below:

1   Cultural literacy: this reflects how knowledge of culture impacts on communication
2   Language and genre: this refers to the understanding of and ability to use the various communicative genres within organisational settings
3   Audience awareness: this refers to responsiveness to audience and how this determines the form and content of communication

4   Social capital and sustainability: this refers to the ability to net-
    work, build goodwill and create positive, enduring relationships in
    organisational settings
5   Persuasion: this refers to ability to communicate effectively to achieve
    objectives (Nickerson, 2015).

Participants

Language in the workplace is one of two compulsory courses in business
communication that all students follow in the business school. This is an
advanced course (at a 400 level). The students are senior Emirati business
students in their penultimate year of study in a bachelor's programme. All
the students speak and use English as an additional language and many of
them have attained near-native proficiency. All of them speak Arabic as a
first language. They are taught in groups of between 25 to 35 students, and
we generally have around seven groups in process each semester.

Length of the course

The course lasts for 16 weeks and comprises three hours per week.

Needs analysis

A formal needs analysis was not completed to design the course. However, federal government in the UAE, and therefore our university, has a
clear mandate to provide students with relevant materials. In our case this
meant providing them with a research-based course that would complement
their existing knowledge of business-communication skills (dealt with in
a previous course at the 200 level) as well as allowing the participants to
explore a number of areas that would be relevant to their careers as business
professionals working in the multicultural society of the UAE.

Approach to course design

The course uses a project-based methodology, as described by Stoller (2006),
in that it combines language work and content work, or relevance to the
business context in the UAE, and includes reflection.

Students are taught using a combination of a lecture-type format, introducing them to the theoretical concepts and research methods that they will
be using for their projects, and a series of tasks that are completed during the classroom sessions – for example, prepared reading, presentations
and discussions. They work in small project groups of between two and
four students; for assessment purposes students complete their examinations
individually.

Course aims

The following are the major course aims:

1   *Ability to communicate effectively in the business environment –*
    students will be required to demonstrate competence in professional
    communications, both written and oral.
2   *Ability to think critically, solve problems and be creative –*
    students will be required to demonstrate the ability to make informed
    choices regarding strategies for handling all forms of professional
    communications, including those of a complex or sensitive nature.
3   *Compete successfully in a global business environment –*
    students will gain an understanding of culturally determined differ-
    ences in communication and learn how to operate within multicultural
    work settings to ensure harmonious and efficient communication among
    different cultural groups.

These course aims are directly related to three of the six Major Learning Outcomes that are in place at the university (Language, International
technology, Critical thinking, Quantitative reasoning, Global awareness and
Leadership).

Syllabus list

Table C1.1 presents the syllabus list of projects, with a list of possible
readings for each session. Typically, a project is based on three or four set
readings, and the students are required to select their own literature on the
same project. Students complete four or five projects. The first project is a
practice project and is not evaluated.

Assessment

As this is a course for credit, assessment is very important. Most of the
assessment is based on the students' project work. This means assessment
criteria need to be very clear and each component assigned marks which
will contribute to the course's overall grade.

Projects

Students need to complete four or five research projects related to *Language
in the workplace* (e.g. one practice project and four evaluated projects).
Students work in teams, and each project consists of several assigned background readings, together with one or more project options. Each project is
marked out of 15 with a total of 60 marks.

Table C1.1 Syllabus list for *Language in the workplace*

Week	Project title topic	Assigned materials (provided by faculty on Blackboard (BB))	Project description	Additional information
1	Introduction and academic conventions	Barrett, chapter 6 (or 8) – 'Realizing the value of cultural literacy' Canwall Case		Materials posted on BB
2	Giving presentations	Barrett, chapter 1 Canwall Case	Case analysis	
3–4	Intercultural communication	Barrett, chapter 5 www.geert-hofstede.com Goby (2009) Jameson (2007)	Case analysis	Not evaluated
5–8	Impact of English as a business lingua franca in the UAE	Charles & Marschan-Piekkari (2002) Ehrenreich (2010) Hoeken et al. (2007) Nickerson (2009)	Survey of language use OR Attitudes to language use	Evaluated
9–12	Web-based communication: The ZU site	Askehave & Ellerup-Nielsen (2005) Chaudhri & Wang (2007) Hynes & Janson (2007) Rogers et al. (2011)	Benchmarking survey OR Attitudes to ZU site	Evaluated
13–16	CSR communication	Barrett, chapter 10 Planken et al. (2010) Planken et al. (2007) Rettab et al. (2009) Visser (2007)	Survey of CSR communication in UAE OR Attitudes to CSR communication in UAE	Evaluated
17–19	Women and leadership language	Web-based materials, as listed below (Tannen, Baxter, Cameron & Holmes) Barrett, chapter 1 – 'Pathos, ethos, logos'	Literature survey + Attitudes to leadership language	Evaluated

---

Case study: Engaging with stakeholders. The creation of a CSR campaign
The communication department at the Joyful Corporation has been tasked with developing the corporation's annual breast-cancer-awareness campaign. The department has been tasked with engaging with as many groups of stakeholders as possible during the campaign as part of the corporation's wider corporate social responsibility (CSR) policy.

Questions:

1   Create an appropriate CSR campaign in two versions. Version 1 should be for employees as internal stakeholders. Version 2 should be for customers as external stakeholders. In version 2 you may also need to decide who your customers are, i.e. young/old, Emirati/expat, men/women, etc.
2   Compare the two different versions of your campaign; make sure that you include details on the different communication strategies and media that you will use in each of your different versions. Decide which version would be easiest to implement as a short-term option.
3   Write a 500-word report in which you present the recommendations on your CSR campaign to management.

Figure C1.1   Sample student project for *Language in the workplace*

Project 1 is a practice project and is not evaluated. Projects 2 to 4/5 are evaluated based on three equally weighted components:

1   the completion of background reading assignments (5 marks)
2   a project presentation (5 marks)
3   a project report (5 marks)

Tests

In addition to projects which are group assessments, the students sit two tests during the course. These are multiple choice tests worth 15 marks each:

1   mid-term assessment (15 marks)
2   final assessment (15 marks)

Special issues and constraints encountered

During the development of this course special issues needed to be considered. Course scheduling is often difficult because of the irregular nature of the Islamic year. This means that university semesters can vary in length from year to year. We therefore use a flexible format so that we can put in either four or five projects, depending on how many teaching days we have. A further consideration in our course design relates to gender. Because many of our students are Emirati females, we need to work with projects that they can carry out within their own community if they choose to do so. For example, collecting data at a shopping mall or public place would be acceptable for some of our female students but not all, and we need to make sure that we offer viable alternatives. A further issue is the varying levels of the students' language proficiency. This is the result of their educational background and family experience. We need to accommodate this in our classroom sessions and in the assignments we ask our students to complete.

Course materials

The course materials comprise PowerPoint slide packs for all lecture sessions. These are provided on Blackboard (BB) LMS. Also on BB are the sets of required readings for each topic and selected readings – these vary each semester and are regularly updated. The materials are selected and circulated on BB by faculty; they are NOT required in advance. The following are examples.

Language in the workplace sample materials

Figure C1.1 is an example of a project task given to students. The task was designed based on the following student-learning outcomes:

1 Analyse business situations critically and apply communication strategies for creative problem-solving independently and in teams (Question 1)
2 Use appropriate communication strategies to deal effectively with internal and external stakeholders, and to critically assess and report on business issues professionally (Questions 2 & 3)

Examples of selected course readings

Askehave, I., & Ellerup Nielsen, A. (2005). Digital genres: A challenge to traditional genre theory. *Information Technology and People, 18*(2), 120–41.
Barrett, D. (2008). *Leadership communication* (2nd edition) (primarily chapters 1, 4, 5, 6 & 10). Boston: McGraw-Hill.
Charles, C., & Marschan-Piekkari, R. (2002). Language training for enhanced communication. *Business Communication Quarterly, 65,* 9–29.
Chaudhri, V., & Wang, J. (2007). Communicating corporate social responsibility on the Internet: A case study of the top 100 IT companies in India. *Management Communication Quarterly, 21*(2), 232–47.
Ehrenreich, S. (2010). English as a business lingua franca in a German multinational corporation: Meeting the challenge. *Journal of Business Communication, 47*(4), 409–31.

Course 1: reader task

Using a project-based approach

Why would a course designer or stakeholder decide to have a course for credit?

What are the reasons for adopting a project-based approach to ESP course design?

Think of an ESP course that you are familiar with. How could this incorporate a project-based approach?

Design a project task for a group of ESP students.

> What type of project will it be?
> What are the instructions for the students?
> How long will the students have for their projects?
> What input sources will be available?
> How will the project be assessed?

Gerritsen, M., Nickerson, C., Hooft, A. v., Meurs, F. v., & Korzilius, H. (2010). English in product advertisements in non-English-speaking countries in Western Europe: Product image and comprehension of the text. *Journal of Global Marketing, 23*(4), 349–65.

Goby, V. P. (2009). Primacy of personal over cultural attributes. Demonstrating receptiveness as a key to effective cross-national interactions. *Canadian Social Science, 5*(3), 91–104.

Hoeken, H., Starren, M., Nickerson, C., Crijns, R., & van den Brandt, C. (2007). Is it necessary to adapt advertising appeals for national audiences in Western Europe? *Journal of Marketing Communications, 13*(1), 19–38.

Jameson, D. A. (2007). Reconceptualizing cultural identity and its role in intercultural business communication. *Journal of Business Communication, 44*(3), 199–235.

Nickerson, C. (2009). The challenge of the multilingual workplace. In L. Louhiala-Salminen & A. Kankaanranta (Eds.), *The ascent of international business communication* (pp. 193–204). Helsinki: Helsinki School of Economics.

Planken, B., Sahu, S., & Nickerson, C. (2010). Corporate social responsibility communication in the Indian context. *Journal of Indian Business Research, 2*(1), 10–22.

Planken, B., Waller, R., & Nickerson, C. (2007). Reading stories and signs on the internet: Analyzing CSR discourse on the BP website. In G. Garzone, G. Poncini, & P. Catenaccio (Eds.), *Multimodality in corporate communication. Web genres and discursive identity* (pp. 93–110). Milan: Franco Angeli.

Rettab, B., Ben, Brik A., & Mellahi, K. (2009). Study of management perceptions of the impact of corporate social responsibility on organisational performance in emerging economies: The case of Dubai. *Journal of Business Ethics, 89,* 371–90.

Visser, R. (2007). Revisiting Carroll's CSR pyramid: An African perspective. In A. Crane & D. Matten (Eds.), *Corporate social responsibility* (pp. 195–212). London: Sage.

References

Fraser, L., Harich, K., Norby, J., Brzovic, K., Rizkallah, T., & Loewy, D. (2005). Diagnostic and value-added assessment of writing. *Business Communication Quarterly, 68*(3), 290–305.

Hynes, G. E., & Janson, M. (2007). Using semiotic analysis to determine effectiveness of internet marketing. *Proceedings of the 2007 Association for Business Communication Annual Convention.* Retrieved from https://rtvf173.pbworks.com/f/Semiotic_Analysis_Internet_Marketing.pdf.

Nickerson, C. (2015). Unity in diversity: The view from the (UAE) classroom. *Language Teaching, 48*(2), 235–49. doi: http://dx.doi.org/10.1017/S0261444812000237.

Rogers, P. S., Gunesekera, M., & Yang, M. L. (2011). Language options for managing Dana Corporation's philosophy and policy document. *Journal of Business Communication, 48*(3), 256–99.

Stoller, F. (2006). Establishing a theoretical foundation for project-based learning in second and foreign-language contexts. In G. H. Beckett & P. C. Miller (Eds.), *Project-based second and foreign language education: Past, present, and future* (pp. 19–40). Greenwich, CT: Information Age Publishing.

English for cross-cultural nursing

Susan Bosher

This course is designed to prepare immigrant and international students at a US university for the academic and discipline-specific language skills and cultural content needed to succeed in a baccalaureate-degree nursing programme.

Rationale for the ESP course

The goal of the course is to increase students' success in the nursing programme, thereby increasing diversity in the nursing profession and improving healthcare provided to culturally and linguistically diverse populations.

Participants

The participants on this course are pre-sessional nursing immigrant and international students.

Length of course

The course lasts for three and a half months (a 15-week semester). The course meets three times per week for one hour and five minutes each time.

Needs analysis

The objective needs of the students were defined as the language-related tasks and activities they needed to be able to perform as well as the cultural content they needed to be able to integrate into their work in order to be successful in the nursing programme. Nursing students, faculty and administrators were consulted. The data was collected through observations, interviews, document analysis and questionnaires. Observations of a first-year course's lectures, labs and clinicals were conducted; course syllabi and assignments were analysed as well as examples of students' written responses to those assignments. Faculty were also interviewed about the various tasks and assignments, as well as about their perceptions of second-language students' challenges in the nursing programme and their own challenges working with second-language students. A questionnaire was then constructed about the tasks, activities and cultural content identified in the target-situation analysis. Faculty were asked to rate each item on a five-point scale of difficulty. The means of these ratings were then compared with students' ratings of the same items to determine the ten most difficult language-related skills and tasks that should be covered in the course, as perceived by both students and faculty. Second-language students were also interviewed about their experiences in the nursing programme to provide rich, qualitative data to corroborate the results of the questionnaire and to identify constraints on the learning situation. Interviews were transcribed and analysed for themes.

Results of needs analysis

Nine of the ten most difficult language-related tasks identified by both faculty and students in the needs analysis were incorporated into the course. The tenth task concerned a mental-health assignment that students completed during their second year in the programme. The analysis revealed the following as the most difficult tasks:

1 Taking multiple-choice tests
2 Integrating culturally sensitive content, such as sexuality and mental health, into practice
3 Using reading strategies effectively
4 Asking questions in class
5 Editing papers for grammatical errors
6 Organising and presenting ideas clearly and effectively in academic papers
7 Preparing effectively for clinicals
8 Asking personal questions of clients
9 Managing time effectively.

Methodological approach

The course uses authentic nursing content to work on academic and discipline-specific language skills and cultural content. For example, students read chapters from nursing textbooks and articles from nursing journals, and work on reading strategies and skills, such as reading charts and graphs, and expand their academic and nursing-specific vocabulary, including medical terminology and abbreviations. They write papers on various nursing-related topics, and work on developing, organising and documenting their ideas, as well as editing for errors. They listen to lectures on various healthcare topics delivered by nursing faculty, and practise their note-taking skills and multiple-choice test-taking strategies. They also work

on communication skills that are specific to and essential for the clinical setting, including therapeutic communication, interviewing and assertiveness
skills, as well as documentation skills, change-of-shift reports and telephone
reports.

Course aims

The following are the course aims:

Reading skills

1   Apply reading strategies and skills to chapters from nursing textbooks
    and journal articles.
2   Understand, define and use medical and nursing terminology and
    abbreviations.

Writing skills

1   Write coherent, well-organised and well-developed papers on various
    nursing/healthcare topics, demonstrating an awareness of and ability to
    self-edit the most frequently made errors in writing.
2   Research a nursing/medical topic using online nursing databases, includ-
    ing the Cumulative Index to Nursing and Allied Health Literature
    (CINAHL).
3   Integrate appropriate information from outside sources, demonstrat-
    ing effective paraphrasing, quoting and documenting, for both in-text
    citations and reference lists, using the system of documentation of the
    American Psychological Association (APA).
4   Demonstrate understanding of basic principles of documentation.

Listening and note-taking skills

1   Demonstrate effective note-taking skills while listening to lectures by
    nursing faculty.
2   Demonstrate effective note-taking skills while listening to taped change-
    of-shift and telephone reports.

Oral communication skills

1   Demonstrate understanding and effective use of therapeutic communi-
    cation skills, interviewing techniques, assertiveness skills and avoidance
    of blocks to therapeutic communication.
2   Present effectively and with confidence in front of the class.
3   Participate actively in class and group discussions.

Background knowledge and cultural issues

1 Demonstrate an understanding of the profession of nursing and reflect on their personal reasons for wanting to become a nurse.
2 Demonstrate an understanding of cultural influences on nursing and healthcare, including their own culture.
3 Demonstrate an ability to think critically about cultural issues in nursing and healthcare, including nursing research.
4 Demonstrate background knowledge and increased comfort level talking about culturally sensitive topics, such as mental illness and sexuality.

Study skills

1 Demonstrate effective multiple-choice test-taking strategies.

Syllabus list

Table C2.1 presents the syllabus list for *English for cross-cultural nursing*. The syllabus is organised according to topics in nursing, skills and language-learning strategies.

Assessment

Students are assessed using a variety of means: tests, quizzes, academic papers, reflective journals, oral presentations and an exercise folder.

Tests

Two tests are given, one on medical/nursing terminology and the other on therapeutic communication and interviewing skills.

Quizzes

Quizzes are based on readings and lectures about various nursing-related topics, such as the history of nursing, cultural perspectives on mental health and illness, culture and pain management, sexuality in nursing and the basic principles of change-of-shift reports and documentation of patient care.

Papers

Students write three papers about various nursing-related topics which require them to access and use a variety of outside sources appropriately.

Table C2.1 Syllabus list for *English for cross-cultural nursing*

Topic	Practical skills
Reading skills for nursing	
Pre-reading strategies	Activating prior knowledge about a topic
	Previewing a reading for organisational features
Reading skills and	Skimming for an overview of a reading
strategies	Predicting content
	Scanning for specific information
	Underlining main points
	Writing marginal notes
	Predicting test questions
Vocabulary strategies	Using contextual clues
and skills	Understanding general versus specialised definitions
	Understanding parts of speech
	Checking definitions
Thinking critically about nursing	
Critical reading skills	Making inferences
	Analysing and synthesising information
	Applying and evaluating information
Critical thinking kills	Evaluating sources of information
	Understanding different perspectives on a topic
	Understanding the author's perspective and purpose
Reading and	Understanding and using information from figures to
interpreting figures	support ideas
Writing about culture in nursing	
Research skills	Locating appropriate books and articles on nursing and
	healthcare topics, using online library catalogues and
	nursing-journal databases
	Evaluating information from websites
Writing skills	Integrating information from outside sources through
	paraphrasing and quoting
	Documenting outside sources through in-text citations and
	reference list
	Referring to outside sources through introductory sentences
	and phrases
	Choosing verbs to reflect author's stance towards ideas
	Summarising an article
	Developing a critique of an article
	Maintaining an objective voice
Developing note-taking skills for nursing	
Effective listening	Strategies for overcoming barriers to listening
skills	
Understanding note-	Guided notes/outline
taking systems	Think-link
	Cornell system

Table C2.1 continued

Topic	Practical skills
Note-taking strategies and skills	Listening for signal words and phrases Recognising repetition and redundancy Using telegraphic language Using symbols and abbreviations Recognising stress and intonation

Understanding quantitative and qualitative research in nursing

Reading quantitative research	Understanding the organisation of a quantitative-research article Reading and interpreting tables Understanding quantitative-research terminology
Reading qualitative research	Understanding the results of qualitative data analysis Understanding qualitative-research terminology

Documentation skills for the clinical setting

Telephone reports
Telephone orders
Progress notes

Change-of-shift reports for the clinical setting

Listening for nursing terminology
Listening for nursing abbreviations
Listening for care-plan instructions and details

Therapeutic communication skills for the clinical setting

Empathy, attending to client, 'I' statements, reflection, verbal reassurance, nonverbal reassurance, caring touch, silence

Blocks to therapeutic communication	Giving advice, expressing disapproval, judging the client, false reassurance

Interviewing skills for the clinical setting

Open-ended questions, focused questions, probes, paraphrases, requests for clarification, testing discrepancies, summarising, closing

Pitfalls to effective interviewing	Asking multiple questions, overusing closed questions, asking 'why' questions

Assertiveness skills for the clinical setting

Asking personal health-related questions
Responding assertively, using the describe, express, specify, consequences (DESC) and describe, express/indicate, specify, consequences (DISC) formats

Paper 1 is on the profession of nursing, specifically the responsibilities, challenges and rewards of nursing, as well as students' reasons for wanting to become a nurse.
Paper 2 is a summary and critique of a nursing-journal research article.
Paper 3 is about cultural influences on nursing practice, including the student's own healthcare beliefs and practices that may influence their practice as a nurse.

Journals

Three journal assignments give the students the opportunity to reflect on culturally sensitive topics in nursing.

Journal 1 is on mental health and illness.
Journal 2 is on sexuality in nursing.
Journal 3 is on cultural differences in assertiveness.

Oral presentations

Two oral presentations give the students the opportunity to work on their confidence and skills presenting orally in front of a group.

Oral presentation 1 is about the summary and critique of a nursing research article that students completed for Paper 2.
Oral presentation 2 is based on lessons from nursing from Gordon (2010).

Exercise folder

Students keep an exercise folder of the answers to assigned activities and discussion questions in the two textbooks. Students correct their own work during the class and turn it in twice per semester. Credit is given for the effort they have put into their work, as determined by the degree of completion and thoroughness of responses, not the percentage of correct answers.

Special issues and constraints encountered

The course is not a required course for entry into the nursing programme, though immigrant and international students are often encouraged to take it. It is a regular English-department course that counts as a four-credit course towards graduation and is offered every other year. It does count as a writing-intensive course, of which the students need to take four to graduate, but does not fulfil any distribution requirements, and nursing students have very little if any room for elective courses. All students who have taken the course who have applied to the nursing programme have been accepted and have successfully completed the programme. No doubt the usefulness of the programme and its impact on the success of immigrant and international students in the baccalaureate-degree nursing programme could be greatly expanded if it were made a requirement for some students.

Course materials

Bosher, S. D. (2008). *English for nursing, academic skills.* Ann Arbor, MI: University of Michigan Press.
Bosher, S. D. (2014). *Talk like a nurse: Communication skills workbook.* New York: Kaplan Nursing.

These two books, one addressing academic reading, writing and listening skills for nursing, the other oral and written communication skills for the clinical setting, were written using materials developed and piloted in the *English for cross-cultural nursing* course.

Gordon, S. (2010). *When chicken soup isn't enough: Stories of nurses standing up for themselves, their patients and their profession.* Ithaca, NY: Cornell University Press.

Further reading about the development of the course

Bosher, S. D. (2006). ESL meets nursing: Developing an English for nursing course. In M. A. Snow & L. Kamhi-Stein (Eds.), *Developing a new course for adult learners* (pp. 63–98). Washington, DC: TESOL.
Bosher, S. D. (2010). English for nursing: Developing discipline-specific materials. In N. Harwood (Ed.), *English teaching materials: Theory and practice* (pp. 346–72). Cambridge: Cambridge University Press.

English for cross-cultural nursing sample materials

Multiple-choice test analysis

Directions. If you would like to improve your grade on Reading Test #1 and more importantly learn from your mistakes, complete this assignment. It requires you to analyse how you studied for the test, as well as how you read and understood the test items. (Complete and thoughtful answers to this assignment *could* increase your grade on Test #1 by 50%.)

1   First, describe how you prepared for the test. How long did you study? When did you study? What did you do when you studied? Describe your process of studying. What reading/study strategies did you use to learn the material? Also, were there other factors in your life that affected your ability to prepare well for the test? Be honest and specific in your discussion.

2   For each test item you got wrong, reread the item, and answer the following questions:

   a   Write down the specific Learning Outcome (see p. 1 of Reading #1) that this item relates to.
   b   Why did you select the answer that you did? Write down your thought process here, as if you were retaking the test.
   c   The correct answer has been circled for you on the test. Locate in Reading #1 the correct answer or the information in the reading from which you can infer the correct answer. Write the page number AND paragraph number AND copy portions of the relevant text (with line numbers). (The point here is to see the connection between the test item and the information in the reading, so whatever you need to copy to show me that you have seen the connection is enough.)
   d   Reread the test item and the correct answer. Does the correct answer make sense to you now? Why or why not?

3   Was this exercise useful? Why or why not?
4   What will you do differently the next time you prepare for a test?

Example of item analysis

Item X   Which of the following is not a characteristic of transracial nursing?

a   Racism in nursing can be overcome through education alone.
b   Racial categories tend to equate race with culture.
c   Nurses need to know how political, economic and social factors influence healthcare.
d   The nursing profession needs to become more culturally and racially diverse.

Item analysis of item X

a   This item relates to Learning Outcome X.
b   I selected distractor b) because I thought I remembered from the reading that there were shortcomings with the transracial approach to nursing. (When I reread the discussion on _____ in Reading #1, I realised I had confused transcultural and transracial and that, in fact, there are short-comings with the *transcultural*, not the transracial approach.) Anyway, when I read the four choices, I was looking for the option that sounded negative because I was thinking of shortcomings. Since I remembered from the reading that racial categories are problematic because they simplify and limit people based on false categories, rather than describe

who people are based on culture, I chose that one. (The other choices –
a, c, and d – all sounded positive and I agree with them, so I didn't
choose any of them.)

c The correct answer is a) because "education <u>alone</u> is not likely to overcome racism in nursing" (p. ____, par. ____, lines ____). The author
talks about the importance of nurses becoming politically active: "social
action by nurses is need[ed] to address racism" (p. ____, par. ____, lines
____).

d Yes, I see my mistake now. First, I confused the terms transcultural and
transracial, so my strategy for selecting the key took me in the wrong
direction. Also, I didn't realise the importance of the word "alone".
Education is important, but is it enough? No.

Course 2: reader task

Assessment tasks

1 Course 2 includes the following assessment tasks:

> Tests
> Quizzes
> Papers
> Reflective journals
> Oral presentations
> Exercise folder

2 Why do you think the course contains so many assessment tasks?
3 Think about how these types of assessment task could be used in
an ESP course you are familiar with.

English for lawyers

Jill Northcott

English for lawyers is a commercial legal English course which has been offered once every summer at the University of Edinburgh for over 20 years. It offers a safe space for lawyers to develop their English skills with others from similar professional backgrounds.

Rationale for the ESP course

The course has primarily targeted European commercial lawyers who need to develop their English for use either with clients from other jurisdictions and language backgrounds or colleagues from other law firms. The types of course participant, however, can vary a lot from year to year, depending on a variety of external factors. Most recently, there have been early-career lawyers keen to move to cross-border firms or those responding to possible changes in the structure of their firms, requiring greater use of English. All have clear, well-defined purposes for attending and there may be several very different agendas in any one group.

Participants

The participants for this course are experienced law professionals with at least two years' experience. The group size is limited to eight.

Length of course

This is a short, two-week intensive course with 20 hours a week class-contact time. We have experimented with longer and shorter courses but two weeks seems to be the longest period lawyers can be away from the office.

Needs analysis

Ongoing needs analysis is essential because the course runs infrequently. Small changes are made to the course content each year based on the last year's participant feedback. Adjustments are also made according to the legal background of the current year's participants. This may affect the selection of law topics for focus. University-law-school academics, legal practitioners and the participants themselves are the major source of information on needs.

Information is collected through an ad hoc needs analysis on the first morning of the course. This involves individual interviews with all the students. This allows the participants to reflect on how they can best use the course to develop language skills for their own specific professional purposes, and the course tutors to reflect on how to adapt materials and their teaching methods and focus to meet the needs of the group.

There is strong emphasis on developing language skills for professional legal contexts – meetings, negotiations, giving presentations, advising clients, writing letters and dealing with contracts. Only participants with a minimum of two years' practical experience can attend, to ensure relevance of these core areas of language skills' development and ability for flexible adaptation of tasks by the participants themselves.

Approach to course design

This course is an intensive, short-term course with a small number of specialised participants. The course uses a needs-driven approach with a focus on productive skills – speaking and writing. Materials design uses a task-based approach, utilising a deep-end strategy that focuses on task completion, plus a focus on language-performance feedback. This leads to further opportunities to accomplish related tasks in order to maximise language use and opportunities for improvement.

Course aims

The broad course aims enable the participants to:

1   Extend and activate legal vocabulary in English
2   Increase fluency and confidence in using English in professional contexts
3   Prioritise language-learning needs with a view to continued English-language development after the course

A variety of topics are covered by the course, including aspects of the UK legal system, company law, contract law and property acquisition.

The course activities include:

1   Role-plays of meetings and negotiations
2   Giving short presentations on legal topics
3   Reading and discussion of legal texts, including case reports
4   Vocabulary-building exercises

Table C3.1 *English for lawyers* – week one, sample timetable

Session	Monday	Tuesday	Wednesday	Thursday	Friday
Session A 09.15 – 10.45	Assessment and individual interviews	Reading, discussion and vocabulary development: Aspects of the UK legal system	Reading, vocabulary development and information exchange: Types of business organisation in the UK	Video listening and discussion: *The property acquisition* (A lawyer–client interview)	Role-play: A lawyer–client interview
Session B 11:15 – 12:45	Reading, discussion and vocabulary development The legal profession	Reading skills and vocabulary development: Case report task and law library visit	Court visit	Writing skills: Professional letter writing	Language review: Individual tutorials
Session C 14:00 – 15.40	City bus tour	Reading, discussion and vocabulary development: Aspects of the UK legal system	Individual study/free (self-access/law library)	Speaking-skills development: Giving explanations, opinions and advice	Individual study/free (self-access/law library)

The course includes guest speakers from the University's school of law and local law firms, and there are opportunities for individual work – for example, in preparing and giving a short talk. Participants are also expected to do a certain amount of self-study.

Syllabus list

The syllabus varies as this is a needs-specific course. However, Table C3.1 shows a sample timetable of a week one.

Assessment

We interview the lawyers and set a diagnostic legal writing task at the beginning of the course. They receive feedback on this and regular feedback throughout the two weeks. The course culminates in a conference when everyone gives a short presentation on a legal topic with feedback from their peers and the course tutor. Tasks are staged within the course to develop presentation skills – including an oral summary of a legal case report. There are opportunities for extra writing tasks to be completed outside class and support for individualised grammar and legal-vocabulary development.

Special issues and constraints encountered

Finding guest speakers from the School of Law and local law firms can be challenging. These speakers play a very important role in the course as the tutors on the course are not necessarily dual-qualified tutors in law and ESP. When recruiting tutors for this course we prioritise employing those with strong ESP-teaching backgrounds. Specialist legal input is provided by speakers on areas such as drafting commercial contracts.

Course materials

In-house materials are produced for the course. Two examples are provided below.

Course 3 *English for lawyers* sample materials

The licence agreement: language of negotiating

QUESTIONING

"Statements generate resistance. Questions generate answers."

Fisher, R., & Ury, W. (2012). *Getting to yes: Negotiating an agreement without giving in*. London: Random House.

1   Closed questions

These can be used:

a   to check precisely where the other side stands on a particular issue;
b   to close down the discussion and force agreement on the other side.

2   **Open-ended questions**

These can be used to gather information.

3   **Reflective questions**

These can help to establish whether you have accurately understood what the other side has been saying and what they are feeling.

4   **Process control questions**

These will help you to control the negotiating process.

What type of question are the following? Mark them 1 (a or b), 2, 3 or 4. If there are any questions which do not clearly fall into one of these categories, explain the function of the question.

- How do you feel about our proposals on (delivery)? Should we turn to discuss these now?
- How would you feel if we were to say that we would be willing to meet you half way on (the price), if at the same time you were willing to allow us to . . . ?
- I have no authority from my client on this point, but what if X?
- If we said we were willing to . . . how would you feel about that?
- Perhaps you can explain why your client feels particularly strongly that he should do X?
- Please correct me if I am wrong, but I get the impression from what you have said that your client is still upset with my client for (leaving him and going to live with the correspondent) and that he consequently feels that in justice (he should have the lion's share of the family assets). Am I right?
- Shall we move on to consider . . . ?
- So what do you think the next step should be?
- So on the basis that our client does X and Y, your client will be happy to pay £Z?
- Would you like to consider (issue A) at the same time as we consider (issue B)?
- You surely do not expect my client to be able to find the kind of money we have been discussing in two weeks?
- You would agree that my client has moved a considerable way towards meeting your demands?

The licence agreement: discussion

Background:

Michael, from Europe, has had several meetings with Andrew Andrews, a computer-software developer. As a result of the meetings, Andrews has agreed to grant Michael a licence for Michael to use, promote and develop Andrews' software abroad on terms broadly similar to this licence given to Digitron. Michael has therefore consulted a local solicitor about the licence agreement, and wishes to have various points clarified.

Task

Study the Digitron licence, then discuss **one** of the following questions:

a   If you were Michael, what would you want to discuss with the local solicitor? Make a list of the questions you would ask.
b   If you were the local solicitor consulted by Michael but in your own jurisdiction, what points would you wish to raise? Make a list.

Course 3: reader task

Tailored ESP

Think of a small group of ESP learners from a narrow field of ESP.

1   How does small class size impact on ESP course design?
2   What is the ESP field?
3   Who are the learners?
4   What skills do they need?
5   How can these skills be incorporated in the ESP course?

Airport English

Joan Cutting

Airport English is an ESP course that is aimed at airport workers such as security guards and catering staff. By providing language training this project has provided work opportunities for young and unemployed local people.

Rationale

At the beginning of the twenty-first century, airports in Europe had unfilled airport ground-staff job vacancies. Those applying for the jobs did not have the required level of English-language proficiency. In particular, there was a large unemployed under-qualified young immigrant population living near Charles de Gaulle Airport. ELSY (**EL**aboration d'un **SY**llabus multimédia aéroportuaire pour les jeunes sans emploi et peu qualifiés) sponsored a project to address these issues.

The course design has three main aims:

1   Prepare training in specialist English language for airport jobs
2   Provide employment opportunities for young Europeans (wage-earners and unemployed people)
3   Answer firms' training needs as well as public-sector needs

Participants

The course participants are people applying for jobs as security guards, ground handlers, catering staff and bus drivers in the airport. For the *Airport English* course, the participants can work independently with multimedia course materials, or they can join classes to supplement the materials with interactional activities such as role-plays. The number of participants per class depends on the capacity of the training institution where it is held and the needs of the learners.

Length of course

The course length varies depending upon needs, training institution and the learners.

Needs analysis

For the initial needs analysis, data was collected from typical communicative situations and exchanges that occurred in the daily life of the four trades mentioned above: security guards, ground handlers, catering staff and bus drivers. In the needs-analysis process, ground staff, managers and trainers were consulted. In addition, native-English-speaker linguists and language teachers involved in the project visited UK and French airports to observe the four trades at work and interview the managers, trainers and workers about the daily routines and the language used. The resulting field notes contained descriptions of situations and functions, snippets of overheard verbal interactions and typical longer exchanges provided by ground-staff managers and trainers.

The next phase in the course-design process was building the dialogues, analysing them and building the exercises based on the dialogue analysis. Linguistic analysis of the dialogues had to show the most frequent forms and functions, i.e. to show what grammar had to be taught. Each trade database was divided into eight 'scenarios' (functional-situational speech events) and these were divided into seven 'exchanges' (notional and situational sequences or adjacency pairs with insert sequences). Excel was used to code each line for verb forms (e.g. present simple, present continuous, clausal ellipsis with past participle), functions (e.g. suggest, order, offer) and overt stance and mood indicators (e.g. irritated, worried, positive politeness). Excel advanced searches were carried out to calculate the number of lines with each of the verb forms and functions and to calculate the percentage of each out of all the lines.

Approach to course design

The approach used in this course was a traditional, grammar-translation, form-focused one, and it used the following activities to achieve its aims:

1 Semi-authentic dialogues with a video-recording, to memorise, prompted by photos
2 Vocabulary to translate
3 Controlled written exercises, teaching and reinforcing grammar and vocabulary, such as substitution drills, gap-filling exercises and matching exercises

Course aims

The course comprised generated models of communicative situations that trade staff could use. The following were the course's aims:

1 Familiarise learners with basic vocabulary of the trade
2 Enable learners to use very simple grammatical structures related to their daily routines
3 Help the learners to remember typical linguistic exchanges and moves in typical scenarios of their trades

Syllabus list

Table C4.1 presents the broad syllabus list that emerged from the needs analysis. The actual syllabus may vary according to the learners' needs and abilities.

Assessment

Student assessment is in the form of exercises similar to course tasks:

1 Vocabulary to translate
2 Controlled written exercises based on grammar and vocabulary: substitution drills, gap-filling exercises, matching exercises
3 Role-plays

There is no official feedback mechanism from managers, trainers, teachers or learners.

Special issues and constraints encountered

The methodology of online materials when used alone did not enable learners to interact spontaneously in real-life situations. Opportunities to practise these had to be provided for the groups of learners with a teacher.

Course materials

The learning materials contained simple, videoed, semi-authentic dialogues to serve as models for pseudo-beginners to emulate, with the features of effective service encounters, such as clarity, informativeness and politeness. The materials also contained online controlled practice exercises based on the syllabus in Table C4.1.

Table C4.1 Syllabus list for Airport English

Situations				Vocabulary typical of each trade and verb forms	Functions	Attitude (examples)
Security guard	Ground handler	Catering staff	Bus driver			
At the check-in desk	Plane arriving at stand	Greeting customers	The connecting passenger shuttle bus	PC (present continuous)	Inform 1 (inform about self: "I/we do this")	Irritated ("But why?")
In the queue for a security check	Requests for handling services	Taking orders at the fast-food counter	Passenger bus from the departure lounge to the aircraft for boarding	PS (present simple)	Question 1 (question about self: "Do I/we do this?")	Worried ("Oh no")
At the archway metal detector	Handling freight and baggage	Taking an order at the restaurant	Passenger bus from the aircraft to the boarding lounge	PASTS (past simple)	Inform 2 (inform about interlocutor: "You do this")	Positive politeness ("please")
Body search	Problems during turnaround	Explanations concerning	Crew shuttle bus from airport hotel to aircraft	PP (present perfect) orders	Question 2 (question about interlocutor: "Do you do this?")	
Bag search – random	Boarding and departure	Drinks	Crew shuttle bus from aircraft to hotel	going to (future)	Inform 3 (inform about third party, event, situation: "They/she do(es) this")	
Bag search and confiscation of dangerous items (1) and (2)	Pushback	The service		will (future)	Question 3 (question about third party, event, situation: "Do(es) they/she do this?")	

(Continued)

Table C4.1 continued

Situations	Security guard	Ground handler	Catering staff	Bus driver	Vocabulary typical of each trade and verb forms	Functions	Attitude (examples)
Dealing with various security problems			Paying		aux (other auxiliary verb)	Suggest ("You could do this"), request ("Could you do this?")	
Emergency evacuation			Understanding complaints Refusing politely		imp (imperative) -ed (clausal ellipsis with past participle)	Order ("Do this", "You must") Offer (state own action: "I'll do this")	
			Farewells		-ing (clausal ellipsis with present participle) - zero (clausal ellipsis – no verb form).	Offer goods ("Would you like this?") Apologise ("I'm sorry") Confirm (echo, short affirmative response: "OK", "confirm") Complain (protest: "But why?"), Greeting/farewell and please/thanks	

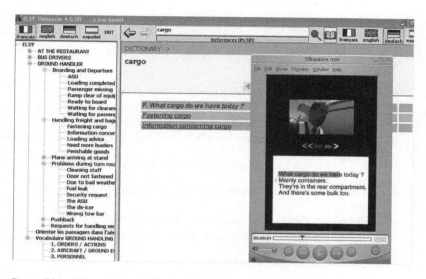

Figure C4.1 Example from online materials

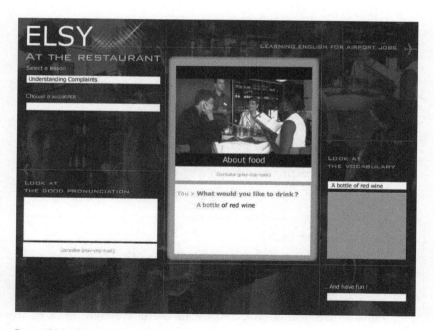

Figure C4.2 Example from online materials

Course 4 Airport English sample materials

1 Dialogues to memorise

Security guards

SG I'll just have to give you a search. Step forward a bit.
P Why?
SG This is just a random check.
P Look, I've been waiting here for 30 minutes. Can we just skip this?

[P waves her arms around. SG remains still]

SG I'm sorry. This is part of international regulations. It'll take a
minute.
P I'm sorry. I'm not going to stand here and miss my flight.
SG OK. I'll have to call a police officer, I'm afraid.

[SG reaches for his walkie-talkie]

2 Vocabulary to translate

Ground handlers

- Bats
- Ramp jacket
- Headset
- Load sheet

3 Grammar exercises

- Substitution drills
- Gap-filling exercises
- Matching exercises
- Memorised dialogue prompted by photos

Course 4: reader task

Vocational ESP

Think of a group of vocational ESP learners.

1 How would you collect data about the interaction needs of this
group?
2 Make a list of language functions this group might need.

3   Make a list of possible verb forms the students would need to express these functions.
4   What types of multimedia could be utilised in such a course and how could they be used?

For an account of the research informing this course design see Cutting, J. (2012). English for airport ground staff. *English for Specific Purposes*, *31*(1), 3–13.

English in academic settings

Lindy Woodrow

English in academic settings (EAS) is a credit-bearing EAP elective course for graduate students in education and language-related subjects.

Rationale for the ESP course

Postgraduate education is now available to a larger range of people than in previous decades, with students coming from culturally, linguistically and socio-economically diverse backgrounds. In particular, there has been an increase in international students from non-English-speaking backgrounds studying at English-speaking universities. Because of these different backgrounds there is often a mismatch between students and academic staff regarding the requirements and expectations of academic study. *English in academic settings* was introduced to enable students to understand academic expectations and fully participate in the academic community. It is informed by an academic literacies theoretical perspective and utilises Johns' 'students as researchers' approach (1997). *English in academic settings* is a narrow-focused, specific EAP course which emerged from a research project into how best to improve the academic skills of postgraduate students of education at an Australian university. For a discussion about the distinction between English for general academic purposes (EGAP) and English for specific academic purposes (ESAP), see Chapter 3.

EAS is specific in that it focuses on the individual academic needs of the students in terms of reading and course assignments.

Participants

English in academic settings is a regular elective course available to postgraduate non-English-speaking background students. It is worth six credit points, which is equal to one eighth of the total number of credit points required for a taught coursework master's degree. On average, there are 30 students per course, and these are drawn from education, TESOL, applied linguistics, translation and communication studies. The course is offered each semester to match the graduate intake. Students enrol on this course in their first semester.

Length of course

The course lasts a semester, which is 13 weeks. Each week students have two hours of class time. The first hour is a large group lecture-type format focusing on theoretical and practical aspects of academic communication, and the second hour is in a small group format focusing on practical tasks and discussion. The course is supported by online resources.

Needs analysis

Needs analysis was based on a research project investigating perceived language problems and the trialling of possible solutions. Students, academic staff and the academic board of the university were consulted during the needs-analysis process using questionnaires and interviews. Published research and practice in EAP was also consulted. The data collected in the research phase of the project revealed that academic writing was most needed, and that the course needed to be as specific as possible.

Stage one of the needs-analysis process identified weaknesses in academic skills as reported by academic staff and students. Stage two of the project involved trialling a range of EAP options, such as one-to-one consultations, voluntary weekly classes and short-term, one-off workshops targeting specific skills – for example, referencing and web-based resources. These options were evaluated and it was found that the students who were struggling with their academic coursework found attending voluntary sessions an added burden. So, it was decided in stage three of the project to put into place a course for credit focusing on academic skills, particularly academic writing.

The course needed to be approved by the university at a faculty and academic-board level. The academic board deemed that as the course was at a graduate level and was for credit it could not be exclusively skill-based and needed to reflect higher intellectual engagement. So, the theoretical underpinnings of academic writing were included in the course.

Approach to course design

The course design was informed by several different theoretical perspectives; however, the main theorising was that of academic literacies (Lea & Street, 1999) and students as researchers (Johns, 1997). In the academic-literacies perspective, academic writing is seen as being informed by the academic discourse community in which it is located. Thus an expert writer has skills and understandings shared by others in the same field but which differ from those of others in different disciplines. They also refer to the power balance within that community and how students need to be aware of this and the extent to which this is open to negotiation. The second perspective adopted was that of the student as a researcher, put forward by Ann Johns (1997). By using this framework students research the requirements and expectation of academic tasks as determined by academics and the institution. They do this by analysing texts and interviewing academic staff who have the responsibility for assessment.

Course aims

The broad course aims are that, by the end of the course, students should:

1   Have an understanding of the theoretical underpinnings of academic communication
2   Have a good understanding of expectations of academic work
3   Have a good understanding of the conventions and practices of academic writing
4   Improve their personal academic writing skills

Syllabus list

Table C5.1 presents the basic syllabus list, which corresponds to the 13-week course. The topic is addressed through lectures and seminars about theory and research in academic writing. Students are required to read about the topic out of class, as is the case for other academic modules. They have discussion sessions and out-of-class tasks to complete. A reserve collection of materials is available electronically through the Blackboard LMS.

Assessment

The module is quite heavy with assessment tasks. All the tasks involve a formative component that facilitates a deeper understanding of the nature of academic communication. These tasks are outlined below. For Assessment Task 1 and Assessment Task 2, students are only required to complete the task; there is no grading system. Assessment Task 3 and 4 are the formal, summative-assessment components of the course. The assessment criteria reflect general postgraduate attributes and are reported to the university examining board.

Assessment task 1

Journal entries

Students submit journal entries on a regular basis. The lecturer or tutor provides feedback on issues identified in journals. The aim of this assignment is to establish a dialogue between the lecturer and student to help the student adapt to the new academic environment as quickly as possible. The journals are confidential and are viewed by the lecturer only. The journals may be written in an informal first person style and students may write about any issue related to academic communication, although the following topics are suggested for guidance.

Journal 1: Reflections on academic life.
Journal 2: Reflections on sources and academic reading.
Journal 3: Reflections on plagiarism and using reading in writing.
Journal 4: Reflections on the expectations of academic writing for your assignments.
Journal 5: Reflections on what you have learned about academic writing this semester.

Assessment task 2

Out-of-class tasks

Small homework tasks are set each week to help with academic writing. Students are expected to complete a minimum of five of these. Some of the tasks involve completing exercises which are available on the LMS – for example,

Table C5.1   Syllabus list for *English in academic settings*

Topic	Practical skills
Nature of academic communication	Audience and purpose
	Using library and electronic sources, databases
Academic reading	Selecting resources, evaluating sources
Referencing	Using references to support argument, citing appropriately, generating reference lists, referencing styles
Plagiarism	Levels of plagiarism, avoiding plagiarism, paraphrasing
Expectations of academic writing	Interpreting assignment tasks, interpreting assessment criteria, stages of writing process
Cultural issues of writing	Organisation of writing, deductive and inductive reasoning in academic writing
Grammar and academic writing	Role of grammar, most important grammar errors, least important grammar errors
Academic vocabulary	Using academic word list (AWL)
Academic discourse communities	Identifying academic discourse community and hierarchical structure
	Developing an argument
Genre	Text analysis of specific relevant genres, move structure within texts
Students as researchers	Context analysis
	Interviewing and emails
Drafting and editing	Peer review
	Editing and drafting skills

the plagiarism exercise. Homework tasks are assigned and responded to each week online.

List of out-of-class tasks

List of academic journals in your field
A writing diary for one week
Paraphrasing exercise
An annotated list of sources for an assignment
Assignment introduction
Plagiarism exercise
Referencing exercise
Academic-style exercise
Grammar exercise
Organisation of text

Assessment task 3

Academic assignment

Students are required to submit an assignment they are working on for one of their other units that is due at the end of the semester. They are expected to choose this assignment early in their *EAS* course because they will be working on this during tutorials. This essay should **NOT** have been marked by their unit-of-study lecturer. Their assignment is assessed per issues covered during the *EAS* course.

Assessment criteria

Relevance of writing
Text structure
Retrieval of information from sources
Academic style
Accuracy of referencing
Grammar
Vocabulary

Assessment task 4

Research project

Students are required to analyse a specific assignment task in terms of audience, purpose, discourse-community expectations, assumed knowledge, structure of text and typical language features of the text. The assignment should be one that **has not been assessed** by their unit tutor or lecturer.

Students need to analyse the assessment task and their assignment, and they need to interview the lecturer who set the assignment about his/her expectations. The analysis of the task and interviewing of the lecturer can be done as a group but the assignment analysis and subsequent production of the research project should be individual.

Assessment criteria

In-depth analysis of issues of academic communication
Organisation of writing
Academic style
Referencing conventions
Presentation
Grammar
Vocabulary

Course evaluation is conducted through an online questionnaire given to the students, as well as lecturer feedback.

Special issues and constraints

The course is well attended, with 30 or more students each semester. As detailed above, for Assessment task 4, students are required to interview at least one of their lecturers. In the first offering of the course, students completed this requirement individually; however, academics complained of large numbers of students wanting to interview them – so the task was reformulated to be done in groups based on the selection of the text under investigation.

The course used a range of authentic past assignments as models for analysis. Students wanted to keep these, but as there was a risk of plagiarism for some of the assignments this was not allowed. The problem was addressed by providing three examples of model assignments. Assignments that were sufficiently different from students' own assignments were made available online. The university has now introduced the use of Turnitin text-matching software, so this is no longer an issue, as assignments can be compared to all previously submitted texts.

Course materials

The course materials were designed to meet the needs of the students working on particular assignments. The students work in subject groups. For example, one group, as part of their Master of Education degree, may be enrolled on a course in a second-language-acquisition unit of study. In class they will work with others enrolled on the same course, sharing ideas and problems. All the materials were designed to be as specific as possible, involving authentic tasks.

English in academic settings sample materials

Academic reading

Considerations in choosing academic readings
Bring one of the readings you need to do for one of your academic courses to class.

1   In subject groups discuss the following:

   What are the main considerations in choosing your readings?

2   Previewing readings

   How do you preview readings?
   Why did you choose this reading?
   Is it a primary or secondary source?
   What type of text is your reading?
   Is the article recent?
   What are the major claims of your text?
   What is your view of these claims?

3   Reading a research article

   What are your strategies for reading a research article according to the following aims?
   Get general idea
   Get specific information
   Make critical analysis

Course 5: reader task

Academic literacies and students as researchers

Think of a group of specific EAP learners, for example accounting graduates.

1   How could you design a course for these learners based on an academic-literacies approach?
2   How do you think you can train learners to be researchers?
3   Design a task to facilitate the 'students as researchers' approach.

Further reading

Johns, A. M. (1997). *Text, role and context*. Cambridge: Cambridge University Press.

Lea, M., & Street, B. (1999). Writing as academic literacies: Understanding textual practices in higher education. In C. Candlin & K. Hyland (Eds.), *Writing: Texts, processes and practices* (pp. 62–81). London: Longman.

Woodrow, L. (2006). English in academic settings: A postgraduate course for students from non-English-speaking backgrounds. In M. A. Snow & L. Kamhi-Stein (Eds.), *Developing a new course for adult learners* (pp. 197–217). Alexandria: Teachers of English to speakers of other languages (TESOL).

Writing for publication

Brian Paltridge

The *Writing for publication* course is aimed at research students who hope to publish their research. It is a course offered to final-year doctoral students at an Australian university.

Rationale for the ESP course

There is increased pressure on doctoral students to publish during their candidature. This is especially the case for students who wish to obtain an academic appointment once they have completed their studies in what is now an extremely competitive job market. If they wish to gain an academic appointment, doctoral students need to establish themselves in their field as well as meet tenure track requirements that have been set by their employing institutions. Being able to publish in academic journals is an essential part of this.

Participants

The students on this course are doctoral students in their final year of study, both native speakers and non-English-speaking background students.

Length of course

The course lasts for 12 weeks and there is one session of two hours per week.

Needs analysis

Needs are analysed based on students' experience in writing for publication and their learning needs in relation to this. They complete a pre-course questionnaire and participate in a class discussion in the first session of the course.

Table C6.1 Syllabus list for *Writing for publication*

Session	Topic
1	Writing for academic journals
2	Targeting academic journals
3	The shape of journal articles
4	Writing workshop I: The introduction
5	Writing the literature review
6	Writing the methods section
7	Writing the results section
8	Writing workshop II: The introduction
9	Writing the discussion section
10	Writing abstracts, titles of journal articles
11	Writing workshop III: First full draft
12	Responding to reviewers' reports

Approach to course design

The course is genre-based and task-based. There is a strong focus on students carrying out their own analysis of published research articles in the course, as well as peer review of each other's written work (see the sample materials).

Course aims

The aim of the course is to mentor doctoral students in the writing-for-publication process so they can publish in international peer-reviewed journals. The course leader is a well-published senior academic who has extensive experience in the publishing process. The course focuses on the skills, strategies and understandings that will enable the doctoral students to do this.

Syllabus list

Table C6.1 presents the syllabus list for the course. Each session is a two-hour block and focuses on a particular topic in writing for publication. The sessions progress from choosing an academic journal through each section of a typical journal article and follows to dealing with article reviews.

Assessment

There is no formal assessment of the students because the course is voluntary and not for credit. The students complete a course evaluation questionnaire at the end of each course.

Course materials

The materials used in the course are a textbook and instructor materials (see sample materials). This book emerged in part through workshops offered in a number of universities: Paltridge, B., & Starfield, S. (2016). *Getting published in academic journals*. Ann Arbor, MI: University of Michigan Press.

Writing for publication sample materials

Sample student task 1: targeting academic journals

Decide on the journals that you are especially interested in publishing in and complete the chart below for three of them as far as you can. When you have done this, look at the journals on the internet to see to what extent your article might fit into these journals. Then decide which of these journals is the best place for you to submit your article to.

	Journal 1	Journal 2	Journal 3
Name of the journal			
Is the journal peer-reviewed?			
What is the academic reputation of the journal?			
Who is the publisher of the journal?			
What is the journal's quality of production?			
How many articles does the journal publish each year?			
How accessible is the journal?			
What is the word or page limit for the journal?			
Who is the audience for the journal?			
Do key people in your field publish in the journal?			

Sample student task 2: writing a (successful) abstract

There are four parts of an abstract which are obligatory (purpose, design/methodology/approach, findings and originality/value); the other three (research limitations/implications, practical implications and social implications) may be omitted if they are not applicable to your paper.

Purpose

What is the reason(s) for writing the paper or the aims of the research?

Design/methodology/approach

How are the objectives achieved? Include the main method(s) used for the research. What is the approach to the topic and what is the theoretical or subject scope of the paper?

Findings

What was found in the course of the work? This will refer to analysis, discussion or results.

Research limitations/implications (if applicable)

If research is reported on in the paper, this section must be completed and should include suggestions for future research and any identified limitations in the research process.

Practical implications (if applicable)

What outcomes and implications for practice, applications and consequences are identified? How will the research impact upon the business or enterprise? What changes to practice should be made as a result of this research? What is the commercial or economic impact? Not all papers will have practical implications.

Social implications (if applicable)

What will be the impact on society of this research? How will it influence public attitudes? How will it influence (corporate) social responsibility or environmental issues? How could it inform public or industry policy? How might it affect quality of life? Not all papers will have social implications.

Originality/value

What is new in the paper? State the value of the paper and to whom.

An example

Referees' comments on submissions to peer-reviewed journals: When is a suggestion not a suggestion?

Abstract

This paper examines the ways in which reviewers ask for changes to be made to submissions to peer-reviewed journal articles (**Purpose**). Ninety-seven reviewers' reports were examined. Forty-one of the reviewers also completed a questionnaire (**Design/methodology/approach**). The study found that requests for changes were largely made as *directions, suggestions, clarification requests* and *recommendations*. While a good number of these changes were requested directly, a large number of them were not (**Findings**). For authors who are new to the peer-review process, indirect requests of the kind revealed in the study can be difficult to decode. Very often these indirect requests are directions to make very specific changes to a submission and need, it is argued, to be read as such (**Practical implications**). The findings are especially relevant to beginning researchers as they provide insights into how they can respond to reviewers' reports and, thereby, increase their chances of publication (**Originality/value**).

(Paltridge, 2015: 106)

Sample student task 3

Use the notes provided above to draft an abstract for a paper you are currently working on. Your abstract should be no more than 250 words. Write concisely. The abstract should reflect only what appears in the actual paper.

Sample student task 4: reviewing each other's writing

Working with another member of your group, exchange a section of an article you have been working on. Use this worksheet to make notes on the piece of writing to provide feedback on what the other person wrote. When you have completed the worksheet, discuss your notes with each other.

Title:	
Author:	
Summary of the argument:	
What I learned:	
Strengths of the writing:	

Clarity of the arguments:	
Organisation and structure:	
Evidence provided to support claims:	
Suggestions for improvement:	
Reviewed by:	
Date:	

Course 6: reader task

Using peer review

An important aspect of the writing-for-publication course is the notion of peer review. Students share their writing with others for feedback. Think about a specific ESP course.

How could you include peer review?
How would you set this up?
How would a typical session using peer review be organised?

Reference

Paltridge, B. (2015). Referees' comments on submissions to peer-reviewed journals: When is a suggestion not a suggestion? *Studies in Higher Education, 40*(1), 106–22.

Writing in your field with corpora

Maggie Charles

This EAP course is part of the third term of a three-term course in academic writing at a UK university. It is open access and non-assessed. There are five to seven parallel multidisciplinary and multinational classes with about 10–16 students in each. The classes are held in computer labs with a machine for each student, though students often work on their own computers.

Rationale for the ESP course

Graduate-student writing is highly specialised in terms of lexis and grammar and is geared specifically to the requirements and conventions of the discipline within which it is produced. This makes it extremely difficult for those outside the discipline to respond adequately to the demands of such specialist writers. The ability to tailor course material individually to students' needs was therefore one motivation for the development of this course. Further, after two terms of academic writing – the first focusing on lexico-grammatical issues and the second on the genres of thesis and dissertation – students are ready for a new approach which will equip them to become independent learners and provide them with a resource to improve their academic writing over the long term.

Participants

The course is designed for international graduate students in a wide range of disciplines.

There are roughly equal percentages of natural-science and social-science students and about 10–20 per cent arts/humanities students. Typically, about 50 per cent are doctoral level; about 40 per cent are Master's level; and about 10 per cent are other academic levels, including postdocs and undergraduates.

Participants come from a wide range of countries and language backgrounds. Most have advanced-level English. The university requires a minimum score of 7/7.5 on IELTS or 100/110 on TESOL iBT.

Length of course

The course provides one two-hour session per week for six weeks. The first two sessions introduce students to corpus work and how to build their own corpus. Sessions three to six each consist of one hour spent analysing and discussing texts, focusing on a specific discoursal issue; in the second hour students investigate the issue in their own corpora and discuss their results with other students.

Needs analysis

A needs analysis was conducted with students and academics within several fields and with the teaching staff at the Language Centre. Data was collected using interviews, questionnaires, analysis of past student written work and published research and practice. Data was also collected over several years from students who attended term one and term two of the academic writing course. A corpora of Oxford theses was developed and analysed.

Approach to course design

The highly specialised nature of the student writing and their ongoing need for 'lexico-grammatical fine-tuning' led to the adoption of Lee and Swales' (2006) approach of individual student corpus-building.

Research on data-driven learning, notably by Johns (1991a; 1991b; 2002) emphasises 'the learner as researcher' approach to examining corpora, which was held to be particularly appropriate for graduate students.

Given the huge diversity of the students' writing, it was considered that focusing on individual lexico-grammatical issues would not adequately address the disparate needs of all students. Accordingly, the multidisciplinary nature of the class was harnessed by getting students to share their corpus data and explain the characteristics of their own disciplinary discourse. This promoted greater cognitive involvement and provided opportunities for oral practice.

The software chosen, AntConc (Anthony 2014a; 2014b), provides several tools with different affordances for language learning. Each session therefore offered a demonstration of a different tool and practice in using it to investigate disciplinary discourse.

The course design thus consists of three interlinked strands:

1   Aspects of disciplinary discourse
2   Lexico-grammatical issues
3   Corpus tools and practice

Table C7.1   Syllabus list for *Writing in your field with corpora*

Aspect of disciplinary discourse	Lexico-grammatical issue	Corpus work
Week 1: Solving language problems	Language patterns, collocations	Concordancing
Week 2: Referring to the literature	Noun patterns, collocations	Corpus construction
Week 3: Investigating self-reference	First person forms (*I, we*)	Using the Clusters tool
Week 4: Making and countering arguments	Linking adverbs	Using Word List
Week 5: Making and modifying claims	Reporting clauses, reporting verbs	Using the Collocates tool
Week 6: Defending your research against criticism	Subordination, coordination	Context Searching

Course aims

The course aims are:

1   Explore disciplinary discourse
2   Individualise academic-writing instruction
3   Foster autonomy
4   Provide a resource for students' future long-term use.

Syllabus list

Table C7.1 presents the week-by-week syllabus list for the course.

Assessment

For each session, students complete a search sheet, which they fill in with their corpus data, making generalisations or comments on what the data mean for their own writing (see sample materials). These search sheets are collected and commented on by the teacher.

The students' corpora are monitored by the teacher on a weekly basis. In terms of course evaluation, students complete a feedback questionnaire at the end of the course (see sample materials). Also, one year after the end of each course, students are sent an online questionnaire which asks if they have used their corpus in the intervening 12 months and elicits details of use.

Special issues encountered

Initial issues encountered with this course include attendance. As this is an open-access course, irregular attendance, particularly in the first two weeks, was an issue. For example, students who joined the class in week two did not know what a corpus was, and the teacher had to go over the week one material with them as a separate group, while the other students got on with corpus-building. Similarly, those who missed week two had to be shown how to build a corpus, while the rest of the class carried out tasks on their own. This meant that in the first two weeks the teacher was not always available to respond quickly to individual problems that arose when the regular attendees carried out their corpus searches. This issue primarily affected weeks one and two, and the provision of the material online is expected to improve the situation.

Another issue is that of sharing information. Students sometimes became so absorbed in their own corpus investigations that it was difficult to get them to share their discoveries. This was dealt with by giving them a time limit for the individual tasks, stopping the whole class and focusing on discussion together.

It is worth mentioning that technical issues were minimal. AntConc is very robust and easy for students to download on to their own computers and use at home. The AntFileConverter (Anthony, 2014b), which is a batch converter of pdf files to plain-text format, is now able to convert successfully almost all files.

Course materials

The course materials were designed and produced in-house. Some examples of these are provided below.

Writing in your field with corpora sample materials

Academic writing: making and countering arguments

Making good arguments is fundamental to academic writing as it is one of the major ways of persuading readers to accept your research findings. It may involve not only putting forward and supporting your own view but also arguing against the views of other writers by putting forward a counter-argument.

Task 1: identifying an argument and a counter-argument

1 Read the following extract from a thesis. It presents the argument of other researchers and the counter-argument of the writer.
2 Underline the words and phrases which are used to construct the argument and counter-argument.
3 What function does each of your underlined words/phrases perform in developing the argument or counter-argument?
4 Discuss your ideas with another student.

Extract from a thesis on physiology

Laboratory-based animal feeding studies provided basic information about the transfer of macronutrients from diet to body tissues (DeNiro & Epstein 1978; DeNiro & Epstein 1981; Tieszen et al. 1983; Ambrose & Norr 1993; Tieszen & Fagre 1993). The conclusions from these investigations determined the basic principles that underlie the current theories of palaeodietary reconstruction. However, such conclusions only provide information about the general, first-order relationship between diet and the body. Therefore it is of questionable validity to use the results of animal feeding studies as a basis for some of the more complicated second-order suppositions about human diet. The applicability of the interpretations to specific dietary situations has not been justified.

Making and countering arguments

An argument is often constructed by a chain of signals. These often include contrast markers – for example, the linking adverbs *however, yet, nevertheless* or the coordinator *but* – and result/consequence markers – for example, the linking adverbs *thus, therefore, hence*. Addition markers (e.g. *in addition, moreover, furthermore*) are often used to add further information in support of the argument.

For Tasks 2, 3, 4 and 5, see the search sheets.

Homework

- Add articles to your corpus until you have 40. BRING YOUR CORPUS with you next time.
- Finish the tasks. Take new search sheets, if necessary.
- Write a short argument in your field (about 100–200 words) using some of the vocabulary and language patterns you have found in your corpus.

Search sheet: Tasks 2, 3, 4 and 5

NAME and GROUP ....

Number of files in your corpus .... Field ....

This is the number of TOKENS given at the top of the word list window.

Task 2: finding the number of words in your corpus

1 Load your corpus
2 Select Word List at the top of the window
3 Press start

4   At the top of the window you will see two measures:

Total number of word **tokens** is the **number of words** in the corpus
Total number of word **types** is the number of **different words** in the corpus

5   How many words are there in your corpus?
6   Compare your corpus size with that of another student

Task 3: signalling a counter-argument – linking adverbs of contrast

The default setting of Word List is to list words that are upper-case (beginning with a capital letter) and words that are lower-case (not capitalised) together. However, in Tasks 3–5 we want to find out whether words are used at the beginning of a sentence or not, so we want to list capitalised and non-capitalised words separately – for example, *however, However*.

To change this, go to: **Tool Preferences** at the top of the window

On the left select **WORD LIST**

UNCHECK Treat all data as lower case

Press **APPLY** at the bottom right of the window

Now make a NEW WORD LIST

1   Type in the search term *however*. Under **Hit Location** press **SEARCH ONLY** on the right
2   **Click on the numbers in the box on the right** to show each instance in turn
3   In the table note down how many instances of the linking adverb are sentence-initial and not sentence-initial

Table C7.2 Sample materials, p. 4

Adverb	Freq: Sentence-initial	Freq: Not sentence-initial	Comment
however			
nevertheless			
nonetheless			

Table C7.3 Sample materials, p. 5

Adverb	Freq: Sentence-initial	Freq: Not sentence-initial	Comment
thus			
therefore			
hence			

4   Make similar searches on the other adverbs: *nevertheless* and *nonetheless*

5   For each linking adverb, add to your table the number of sentence-initial and not sentence-initial hits

6   Your table now gives you a clear picture of how these linking adverbs are used in your field. Make generalisations from your data in the 'Comment' column

7   Compare your results with those of another student. Are they similar or different?

Task 4: signalling the conclusion or claim at the end of an argument

1   Now use Word List to examine the following linking adverbs of result/consequence and make a similar table of comparison, using questions 1–7 of Task 3: *thus, therefore* and *hence.*

2   Compare your results with those of another student.

Task 5: signalling an additional point – linking adverbs of addition

1   Now use Word List to examine the following linking adverbs of addition and make a similar table of comparison, using questions 1–7 of Task 3: *in addition* (see 2 below), *besides* (see 3 below), *furthermore* and *moreover.*

2   For *in addition* search just *addition.* Click on *addition* to get the concordance. Then sort by 1L and 1R. Count only instances of *in addition*; **do not** include instances of *in addition to.* Note the totals of *in addition* that are sentence-initial and not sentence-initial.

3   For *Besides,* **search only** the sentence-initial form. Click on *Besides* to get the concordance, which will show both capitalised and non-capitalised forms. **Count only capitalised forms which are followed by a comma:** *Besides,* because *besides* also functions as a preposition e.g. *besides the present study.* We can only be certain that it is a linking adverb of addition **if it is sentence-initial and has a comma after it.**

4   Compare your results with those of another student.

Table C7.4 Sample materials, p. 6

Adverb	Freq: Sentence-initial	Freq: Not sentence-initial	Comment
In addition			
besides			
furthermore			
moreover			

CORPUS WORK TRINITY TERM 2015: EVALUATION QUESTIONNAIRE

Name _____   Class: _____

A.   **Questions 1–10 ask for your opinions about using concordances with your own corpus. For each statement, please circle the number which corresponds to your own opinion.**

		strongly disagree	somewhat disagree	neither agree nor disagree	somewhat agree	strongly agree
1.	It was easy to build my own corpus.	1	2	3	4	5
2.	It is easy to use the Antconc software.	1	2	3	4	5
3.	It is easy to find answers to my own queries using my own corpus and Antconc.	1	2	3	4	5
4.	Using my corpus helps me improve my writing.	1	2	3	4	5
5.	I would like to use corpora in an English course in the future.	1	2	3	4	5
6.	I intend to use my corpus for help with my English in the future.	1	2	3	4	5
7.	I would recommend other international students to build their own corpus to help with their English.	1	2	3	4	5
8.	Working with the concordances was interesting.	1	2	3	4	5
9.	Analysing the concordance lines was difficult because of the language.	1	2	3	4	5
10.	Analysing the concordance lines took too much time because there was a lot of data.	1	2	3	4	5

B. Please answer these questions.

11. How often do you use your corpus outside class? *(Choose ONE option)*
Several times a day _____ About once a day _____ About 5 times a week _____ About once a week _____
About once a month _____ Seldom _____ Never _____ Other *(specify)* _____

12. Do you intend to use your corpus in the future? *(Choose ONE option)*
Definitely yes _____ Probably yes_____ Undecided_____ Probably not_____ Definitely not_____

13. What do you use your corpus for?
Composing written work _____ Revising written work _____ Both _____ Other *(specify)* _____

14. How useful did you find the two types of classwork? *(Choose ONE option)*
a) Work on the extracts was more useful than work on my corpus.
b) Work on my corpus was more useful than work on the extracts.
c) Work on the extracts and work on my corpus were equally useful.

15. In a future class, what corpus would you prefer to work with? *(Choose ONE option)*
a) my own corpus
b) a ready-made corpus (e.g. British National Corpus, natsci corpus, socsci corpus)

16. Please complete this sentence: *The* **advantages** *of working with my own corpus are…*

17. Please complete this sentence: *The* **disadvantages** *of working with my own corpus are…*

PLEASE TURN OVER

Figure C7.1   Student course-evaluation sheet

18. **Did you have any problems in building your own corpus? If so, what were they and how did you overcome them?**

19. **Did you have any problems in using the AntConc software? If so, what were they and how did you overcome them?**

YOUR CORPUS

20. **How many files/papers are in your corpus?**

21. **How many words are in your corpus?**
    (Make a Wordlist. The number of words is the number of TOKENS)

22. **Do you intend to add files to your corpus in the future? Yes _____ No _____**
    Why or why not?

23. **Have you cleaned your corpus? Yes, completely _____ Yes, partly _____ No, not at all _____**

24. **Do you intend to clean it more in the future? Yes _____ No _____**
    Why or why not?

25. **Please give an example of a successful search you made for yourself (i.e. NOT a class task).**

26. **Please give an example of an unsuccessful search you made for yourself (i.e. NOT a class task).**

27. **Please list the journals or other sources in your corpus.**

ANY OTHER COMMENTS?

Thank you for your help. The information will be used to improve courses for future students. The data will be collated and it may be referred to in anonymous form in published work. Please sign if you agree to these uses of your data.

Signature _____ Date _____

Figure C7.1   continued

Course 7: reader task

Using corpora in EAP

How do you think you could apply a corpus approach in an EAP course design?

1   How would you include published corpora use?

   Which corpora would you use?
   How would you exploit these?

2   How could you develop a strand in your course that includes students developing their own corpora?

   Think of tasks which exploit these personal corpora.

Further reading

Anthony, L. (2014a). AntConc. (Version 3.4.4). [computer software].

Anthony, L. (2014b). AntFileConverter (Version 1.2). [computer software]. Retrieved 14 March 2017 from www.laurenceanthony.net/.

Charles, M. (2012). "Proper vocabulary and juicy collocations": EAP students evaluate do-it-yourself corpus-building. *English for Specific Purposes, 31,* 93–102.

Charles, M. (2014). Getting the corpus habit: EAP students' long-term use of personal corpora. *English for Specific Purposes, 35,* 30–40.

Charles, M. (2015). Same task, different corpus: The role of personal corpora in EAP classes. In A. Leńko-Szymańska & A. Boulton (Eds.), *Multiple affordances of language corpora for data-driven learning* (pp. 129–54). Amsterdam: John Benjamins.

Johns, T. (1991a). From printout to handout: Grammar and vocabulary teaching in the context of data-driven learning. In T. Johns & P. King (Eds.), *Classroom concordancing* (pp. 27–37). Birmingham: ELR University of Birmingham.

Johns, T. (1991b). Should you be persuaded: Two samples of data-driven learning materials. In T. Johns & P. King (Eds.), *Classroom concordancing* (pp. 1–16). Birmingham: ELR University of Birmingham.

Johns, T. (2002). Data-driven learning: The perpetual challenge. In B. Ketteman & G. Marko (Eds.), *Teaching and learning by doing corpus analysis* (pp. 107–117). Amsterdam: Rodopi.

Lee, D., & Swales, J. (2006). A corpus-based EAP course for NNS doctoral students: Moving from available specialized corpora to self-compiled corpora. *English for Specific Purposes, 25*(1), 56–75.

Programme for business-English majors

Zuocheng Zhang

This is a degree course in English for business purposes (EBP) for undergraduate students majoring in business English at the School of International Studies, University of International Business and Economics (UIBE) in China. This course is fully accredited by the Ministry of Education in China.

Rationale for the ESP course

This programme has evolved over the past 60 years in response to the social and economic needs of China, in particular the drive for globalisation, where business English serves as the lingua franca for international business. It is also driven by the reform in English as a foreign-language education in the traditional English literature and linguistics faculties at Chinese universities – for example, to address the unsatisfactory development of critical and creative thinking in English-major students. It is argued that business English better responds to Chinese English language students' needs in the age of globalisation and has the potential to promote critical and creative thinking through a close integration of business subject matter and language in the process of English-language learning (Zhang, 2007; Zhang & Wang, 2011).

Participants

The programme admits students who have completed high school and achieved an excellent mark in China's national university-entrance examinations or alternative qualifying assessment, such as the university's own special admissions examinations. Each year the university enrols approximately 60 business-English-major students. There is also a number of international students from Asia and Africa taking the programme at UIBE.

Length of the course

The programme is a four-year, full-time undergraduate degree programme.

Needs analysis

Needs analysis was based on the target international business context in which business-English-major graduates are likely to perform. The areas of focus included identifying the essential knowledge, capabilities and skills they were expected to possess, and sequencing such knowledge, capabilities and skills in a coherent four-year programme.

A wide range of stakeholders were consulted in the needs analysis process:

International business practitioners
Senior business executives
Business administrators
Academics in the business disciplines
Academics in English literature and linguistics
Researchers and practitioners in business discourse and communication
Business-English students

Data was collected using focus-group interviews. The needs analysis was further informed by the literature in research and practice in business discourse, business communication and English for specific purposes. In addition to this, a review of earlier programmes at the university and other universities preparing English-as-a-foreign-language students for international business was conducted.

Approach to course design

The programme was informed by the concept of professional expertise developed by Vijay Bhatia (2004). Professional expertise encompasses three essential components: disciplinary knowledge, discursive competence and professional practices in the context of which discursive competence is executed. The programme includes the parallel teaching of knowledge in the business disciplines, business practices and the English language, with the knowledge in each area sequentially offered through the four years, and the integration of such knowledge in a series of academic and business genres such as essays, business letters and business reports, which are also sequentially offered to students.

The approach to the course can be classified as content-based instruction (CBI) (see Chapter 13), in the sense that the subject matter covered in teaching derives from the business disciplines, practices and discourse. Content and language are integrated, with attention given to both business subject matter and business language.

The delivery of the course is eclectic in the sense that there is no prescriptive approach to teaching in the study areas. The programme reflects the teaching methodology of business disciplines and professional practices, including case study and simulation. The classroom teaching is conducted by staff with expertise in business disciplinary knowledge, business practices and business discourse and communication.

Course aims

According to the Academic Division (Academic Division of UIBE, 2007), the programme aims to cultivate graduates who:

1   Have sound English knowledge and skills
2   Have mastery of fundamental theories and knowledge of international business
3   Have high humanistic qualities
4   Are adept at intercultural communication
5   Are able to meet the needs of economic globalisation
6   Are competitive internationally

Syllabus list

Table C8.1 presents the syllabus list for the programme.

Assessment

Students are assessed at two milestone points – the end of year one and the end of year four – by sitting the Test of English Majors 4 and 8 respectively.

Table C8.1   Syllabus list for *Programme for business-English majors*

Study areas which are delivered in various units of study	Knowledge and practical skills in the study areas
Economics Management International business law	Disciplinary knowledge and thinking
Practices in international business	Practical knowledge of the field such as trading procedures and business ethics
Practices in intercultural discourse and communication	Knowledge and skills of initiating, maintaining and sustaining business relations in intercultural settings such as sensitivity to diversity and adaptivity
English-language skills	Listening, speaking, reading, writing and translating in English
Humanities	Chinese language, literature and culture English language, literature and culture
Business genres	Business-letter writing Business-report writing
Practicum	Internship in international companies and organisations
Graduation thesis	Report on research projects about business disciplines, practices, discourses and communication

This test covers the five language skills – listening, speaking, reading, writing and translating – and knowledge of English vocabulary, grammar, literature and culture. A national Test of Business English Majors 4 and 8 is now being developed to assess the students' mastery of the various components of the programme. Some piloting has been conducted. In addition, the programme is assessed with reference to employability of graduates and the efficiency of running the programme.

Special issues and constraints encountered

One of the challenges of this programme is the need for multidisciplinary expertise of teaching staff. As the programmes requires specialists in all the major areas of professional expertise, getting qualified teachers for the business disciplines, business practices and business discourse and communication is a challenge. For language- and literature-background teachers, handling the integration of language and business in academic and business genres is demanding.

A further challenge is scoping and sequencing. As the business world keeps changing, it is an ongoing process to map the knowledge, capabilities and skills that are required of international business professionals and hence the scoping issue for teaching and training purposes. Organising the content to enable meaningful learning (cumulative) in a coherent manner over the four years requires careful planning and ongoing adjustment.

Course materials

The course relies on a range of commercially and locally available textbooks – for example, *shangwuyingyutingshuo*, published by Higher Education Press (China) and *Market Leader*, published by Cambridge University Press. In addition, in-house materials are developed by study-area coordinators.

Business marketing writing in English

This unit of study is part of the study area of business genres. It lasts for a semester, with 36 teaching hours in total (two hours in each of the 18 weeks in the semester). There are multiple approaches to teaching the unit, which may be summarised as a type of text-based approach and content and language integrated-learning approach. The former approach prioritises the learning of textual features through exemplary business texts, including their generic organisational patterns, syntactic and lexical features and a range of business procedural and rhetorical matters. The latter approach gives dual attention to business subject matter and business language, even though language may be treated in an incidental manner. A version of this latter approach is summarised in Zhang (2016).

The unit of study has the goal of producing a business plan for a start-up company by the end of the semester and was delivered by a former business professional who was also a native speaker of English. The teaching progresses in a piecemeal fashion in the sense that each week focuses on a component of the business plan and students are guided to produce a text reflecting that component, including vision, mission, objectives and values; advertising; a marketing plan that includes the four Ps (product, price, place and promotion); analysis such as SWOT (strengths, weaknesses, opportunities and threats) analysis; an executive and company summary; and an operation and financial plan. For example, the missions, visions and values of the company are dealt with in the first few weeks, and students learn to write the missions, visions and values of their own company. This is followed by the teaching of the marketing plan. The different texts reflecting the components are each reviewed and commented on by the lecturer and finally put together as a business plan.

The lecturer gravitates towards teaching business concepts and cultivating business mindsets. He typically organises his lectures in terms of business concepts and asks his students to consider the relevant business operations instead of beginning with an exemplary text. When he comments on language use in his lectures, his focus is not on accuracy itself but the appropriateness of the language for its rhetorical purpose. For example, when his student wrote that she "had some English skills and could do some translation", the lecturer commented that the first "some" should be replaced with "good" or "excellent" to project a positive image of the writer. He has taught several language lessons but only when he has identified some weaknesses related to language in his students. He constantly reminds his students of the importance of building their personality and injecting it into their writing. He does not impose a set of external marking criteria. Instead, he introduces peer pressure in the business world as his marking criterion, bringing home to his students that business writing is not done to please the lecturer but to compete with one's peers and excel. He marks the way his students have applied the concepts and skills he has introduced in the unit of study and language but not the thinking underlying the students' text, because business thinking is changing and reflects his students' effort to inject their personality.

The way this lecturer has delivered the unit of study has been well received. His students are appreciative of the connections they are guided to see between marketing and their personal and student life, not least the importance of personality-building and projection in writing; and their business-plan writing has been commended by practising international business professionals as professional and business-like.

Course 8: reader task

Approaches to ESP: writing-course design

Consider writing in one type of ESP

1   How do you think a text-based approach can be used in the design of an ESP writing course?
2   How do you think a content-based approach can be used in the design of an ESP writing course?
3   To what extent will discipline-specific methodologies play a role in the delivery of such a course?

Produce an ESP course outline reflecting these three aspects.

References

Academic Division of UIBE. (2007). *Undergraduate programmes*. Beijing: University of International Business and Economics.

Bhatia, V. K. (2004). *Worlds of written discourse: A genre-based view*. London: Continuum.

Zhang, Z. C. (2007). Towards an integrated approach to teaching Business English: A Chinese experience. *English for Specific Purposes, 26*, 399–410.

Zhang, Z. C. (2016). "Somewhere in the middle is the optimal balance": A subject specialist negotiating business and language in teaching business writing. *ESP Today, 4*, 145–64.

Zhang, Z. C., & Wang, L. F. (2011). Curriculum development for Business English students in China: The case of UIBE. *Asian ESP Journal, 7*, 10–27.

Appendix

This section suggests key articles in ESP that could be used for oral or poster presentations. The articles are either published in ESP journals or edited works. They have been selected because they reflect important issues in ESP course design, and they are organised in line with the chapters in this book. The presentation tasks could be used on a course on ESP, as an additional seminar series on a TESOL training course, as professional-development sessions in a language-teaching institution or for individual self-study. In the latter case, a poster presentation could lead to online discussion.

The rationale for these tasks is that engaging with the literature is a useful way of finding out about research and practice in ESP. Reading and thinking in depth about a given study or course in ESP, and then formulating this into another format including critique, is useful both for presenters and listeners. In a group, each participant can present an article that reflects issues covered in a particular chapter in this book. The tasks can be done singly or in pairs.

Seminar/poster task

Select an article from the designated chapter listed below and plan a presentation or poster to present to your seminar group. Microsoft PowerPoint can be used to facilitate communication. As well as describing the content of the article to your seminar group, reflect upon the issues referred to in the corresponding chapter and refer to sources outside the text. You can find these in the reference list of the corresponding chapter.

The following are some typical questions that could be addressed in the presentation/poster:

1   What area of ESP is the article about?
2   Does the article deal with needs analysis?

    a   If so what methods are used?

3 Describe the suggested ESP course in terms of

    a   Students
    b   Discipline area
    c   Theorising
    d   Approach to course design
    e   Course components

4 What is your view about this course? Can you suggest any improvements? Would this course be appropriate in your setting?

The following link includes instructions for generating a poster using MS PowerPoint: www.liverpool.ac.uk/media/livacuk/computingservices/printing/ Creating,a,Poster,in,Powerpoint,2010.pdf

Articles and book chapters for presentation

Chapter 1: overview of English for specific purposes (ESP)

History of ESP

Johns, A. M. (2013). The history of English for specific purposes research. In B. Paltridge & S. Starfield (Eds.), *The handbook of English for specific purposes* (pp. 5–30). Oxford: Wiley Blackwell.

ELF

Nickerson, C. (2005). English as a lingua franca in international business contexts. *English for Specific Purposes, 24*(4), 367–80.

Chapter 2: needs analysis and ESP course design

Bosher, S., & Smalkoski, K. (2002). From needs analysis to curriculum development: Developing a course for health-care communication for immigrant workers in the USA. *English for Specific Purposes, 21*(1), 59–79.

Cowling, J. D. (2007). Needs analysis: Planning a syllabus for a series of intensive workplace courses at a leading Japanese company. *English for Specific Purposes, 26*(4), 426–42.

Wozniak, S. (2010). Language needs analysis from a perspective of international professional mobility: The case of French mountain guides. *English for Specific Purposes, 29*(4), 243–52.

Chapter 3: language and skills in English for specific purposes

Functions and course design

Aldohon, H. I. (2014). English for specific purposes (ESP) for Jordanian tourist police in their workplace: Needs and problems. *International Education Studies, 7*(11), 56–67.

Focus on meaning

Kwan, N., & Dunworth, K. (2016). English as a lingua franca communication between domestic helpers and employers in Hong Kong: A study of pragmatic strategies. *English for Specific Purposes, 43,* 13–24.

BELF

Kankaanranta, A., & Louhiala-Salminen, L. (2010). "English? – Oh, it's just work!": A study of BELF users' perceptions. *English for Specific Purposes, 29*(3), 204–9.

Chapter 4: vocabulary and English for specific purposes

Charles, M. (2012). "Proper vocabulary and juicy collocations": EAP students evaluate do-it-yourself corpus building. *English for Specific Purposes, 31*(2), 93–102.

Palmero, N. C. (2002). A cognitive experience in ESP: Teaching vocabulary to telecommunications engineering students. *ESP World, 1*(2). Retrieved from www.esp-world.info/Articles_2/ESP_2.html.

Wang, J., Liang, S. I., & Ge, G. (2008). Establishment of a medical academic word list. *English for Specific Purposes, 27*(4), 442–58.

Chapter 5: teaching English for specific purposes

ELT and subject teacher's practices

Atai, M. R., & Fathi-Majd, M. (2014). Exploring the practices and cognitions of Iranian ELT instructors and subject teachers in teaching EAP reading comprehension. *English for Specific Purposes, 33,* 27–38.

ESP practitioner roles

Palmero, N. C. (2003). The ESP teacher as a materials designer: A practical example. *Estudios de linguistica inglesa aplicada, 4,* 189–200.

Subject knowledge

Wu, H., & Badger, R. G. (2009). In a strange and uncharted land: ESP teachers' strategies for dealing with unpredicted problems in subject knowledge during class. *English for Specific Purposes, 28*(1), 19–32.

ESP practitioner and subject specialist collaboration

Esteban, A. A. E., & Martos, M. C. V. (2002). A case study of collaboration among the ESP practitioner, the content teacher and the students. *Revista Alicantina de Estudios Ingleses, 15,* 7–21.

Chapter 6: learning English for specific purposes

Transfer

Green, A. (2015). Teaching for transfer: Hugging and bridging revisited. *English for Specific Purposes, 37*(1), 1–12.

Medical ESP

Dias, J. (1999). Developing an ESP course around naturally occurring video-taped medical consultations. *The Internet TESL Journal, 5*(3), available at: http://iteslj.org/Lessons/Dias-MedicalVideos/index.html.

Hoekje, B. J. (2007). Medical discourse and ESP courses for international medical graduates (IMGs). *English for Specific Purposes, 26*(3), 327–43.

EBP

Evans, S. (2012). Designing email tasks for the Business English classroom: Implications from a study of Hong Kong's key industries. *English for Specific Purposes, 31*(3), 202–12.

Legal English

Northcott, J., & Brown, G. (2006). Legal translator training: Partnership between teachers of English for legal purposes and legal specialists. *English for Specific Purposes, 25*(3), 358–75.

Aviation English

Wang, A. (2007). Teaching aviation English in the Chinese context: Developing ESP theory in a non-English speaking country. *English for Specific Purposes, 26*(1), 121–8.

Chapter 7: technology and English for specific purposes

Emails

Gimenez, J. (2014). Multi-communication and the business English class: Research meets pedagogy. *English for Specific Purposes, 35*, 1–16. doi: http://dx.doi.org/10.1016/j.esp.2013.11.002.

Wikis

Kuteeva, M. (2011). Wikis and academic writing: Changing the writer–reader relationship. *English for Specific Purposes, 30*(1), 44–57.

Blogs

Shih, R.-C. (2012). Integrating blog and face-to-face instruction inot an ESP course: English for hospitality and tourism. *The Turkish Online Journal of Educational Technology, 11*(4), 204–9.

Social networking

Zafar, S. A. (2015). The role of social networking websites in assisting blended learning: Class discussion and peer assessment in an ESP classroom. *English for Specific Purposes World, 16*(special issue 1), 1–8.

Chapter 8: assessment of English for specific purposes

English for medical purposes

Elder, C., McNamara, T., Woodward-Kron, R., Manias, E., McColl, G., Pill, J., & O' Hagan, S. (2013) Developing and validating language proficiency standards for non-native English speaking health professionals. *Papers in Language Testing and Assessment, 2*, 114–18. Retrieved 14 March 2017 from www.occupationalenglishtest.org/resources/uploads/2015/07/Elder-C-et-al-2013-Developing-and-validating.pdf?x59645.

EOP

Friginal, E. (2013). Evaluation of oral performance in outsourced call centres: An exploratory case study. *English for Specific Purposes, 32*(1), 25–35.

Aviation

Knoch, U. (2014). Using subject specialists to validate an ESP rating scale: The case of the International Civil Aviation Organization (ICAO) rating scale. *English for Specific Purposes, 33*, 77–86.

Chapter 9: genre

EFL

Badger, R., & White, G. (2000). A process genre approach to teaching writing. *ELT Journal, 54*(2), 153–60.

Business English

dos Santos, V. B. M. P. (2002). Genre analysis of business letters of negotiation. *English for Specific Purposes, 21*(2), 167–99.

EAP

Flowerdew, L. (2016). A genre inspired and lexico-grammatical approach for help-ing post graduate students craft research grant proposals. *English for Specific Purposes, 42*(1), 1–12.

EOP

Parkinson, J., Demecheleer, M., & Mackay, J. (2017). Writing like a builder: Acquir-ing a professional genre in a pedagogical setting. *English for Specific Purposes, 46*(1), 29–44.

Chapter 10: discourse analysis

Planken, B. (2005). Managing rapport in lingua franca sales negotiations: A compar-ison of professional and aspiring negotiators. *English for Specific Purposes, 24*(4), 381–400.
Staples, S. (2015). Examining the linguistic needs of internationally educated nurses: A corpus-based study of lexico-grammatical features in nurse–patient interactions. *English for Specific Purposes, 37*, 122–36.
Sullivan, P., & Girginer, H. (2002). The use of discourse analysis to enhance ESP teacher knowledge: An example using aviation English. *English for Specific Purposes, 21*(4), 397–404.

Chapter 11: corpora

EAP

Lee, D., & Swales, J. (2006). A corpus based EAP course for NNS doctoral students: Moving from available specialised corpora to self-compiled corpora. *English for Specific Purposes, 25*(1), 56–71.
Lee, J. J., & Subtirelu, N. C. (2015). Metadiscourse in the classroom: A comparative analysis of EAP lessons and university lectures. *English for Specific Purposes, 37*, 52–62.

EOP

Yang, W. (2012). Analysing and teaching keywords in hotel brochure texts. *LSP Journal, 3*(1), 32–50.

Chapter 12: discipline-based methodologies

Problem-based learning

Wood, A., & Head, M. (2004). "Just what the doctor ordered": The application of problem-based learning to EAP. *English for Specific Purposes, 23*(1), 3–17.

Yu, L., & Seepho, S. (2015). Problem-based learning materials design for a medical English course. *Theory and Practice in Language Studies, 5*(7), 1346–51.

Case studies

Daly, P. (2002). Methodology for using case studies in the business English language classroom. *Internet TESL Journal, 8*(11). Retrieved from http://iteslj.org/Techniques/Daly-CaseStudies/.

Esteban, A. A., & Pérez Cañado, M. a. L. (2004). Making the case method work in teaching Business English: a case study. *English for Specific Purposes, 23*(2), 137–61.

Chapter 13: specific EAP approaches

CBI/CLIL

Arnó-Macià, E., & Mancho-Barés, G. (2015). The role of content and language in content and language integrated learning (CLIL) at university: Challenges and implications for ESP. *English for Specific Purposes, 37,* 63–73.

Garner, M., & Borg, E. (2005). An ecological perspective on content-based instruction. *Journal of English for Academic Purposes, 4*(2), 119–34.

Academic literacies

Murray, N. (2016). An academic literacies argument for decentralizing EAP provision. *ELT Journal, 70*(4), 435–43.

Wingate, U. (2012). Using acaemic literacies and genre-based models for academic writing instruction: A literacy journey. *Journal of English for Academic Purposes, 11*(1), 26–37.

Chapter 14: the role of materials

Bremner, S. (2010). Collaborative writing: Bridging the gap between the textbook and the workplace. English for Specific Purposes, *29*(2), 121–32.

Edwards, N. (2000). Language for business: Effective needs assessment, syllabus design and materials preparation in a practical ESP case study. *English for Specific Purposes, 19*(3), 291–6.

Esteban, A. A. (2002). How useful are ESP textbooks? *ODISEA, 2,* 29–47.

Yakhontova, T. (2001). Textbooks, contexts and learners. *English for Specific Purposes, 20*(Supp. 1), 397–415.

Glossary

Academic literacies A focus on literacy as pluralistic, informed by the context of the communicative situations. For example, the academic demands of participating in the academic community differ greatly for those in education.

Academic Word List (AWL) A series of lists of common academic words ordered by frequency. The list was developed by Averil Coxhead based on a corpus of academic English.

Blog A blog is like an electronic diary. Bloggers can record their experiences, include visuals and interact with others about specific topics online. There are many online blogs available for ESP. For some links to these, see Chapter 15 on resources. Students can also be encouraged to write blogs. The software to facilitate this is freely available on line.

Business English as a lingua franca (BELF) English as a lingua franca (ELF) is the term used to describe communication in English between non-native speakers and is used by many more non-native speakers to communicate with each other than native speakers. Because English is the international language of communication in business the term BELF is used.

Case study The case-study method is a teaching methodology commonly used in business courses. It is a student-centred approach that uses authentic cases to suggest solutions to business problems. It requires group work, research, reading and presenting.

Common core A model proposed by Bloor and Bloor (1986) that captures the extent to which language is specific to given communicative settings.

Common European Framework of Reference for Languages (CEFR) This framework was developed by the Council of Europe and can be used to design tasks and assessment reflecting six levels (A1, A2, B1, B2, C1, C2). The levels range from beginner to high-advanced.

Communicative competence This comprises three sub-competences, according to Canale and Swain (1980): *grammatical competence*, which refers to knowledge of grammar, vocabulary, semantics and phonology; *socio-linguistic competence*, which refers to knowledge of language use; *discoursal competence*, which refers to knowledge of coherence and cohesion; and *strategic competence*, which refers to verbal and nonverbal communication strategies.

Concordance Concordancing software is used to analyse corpus data. A concordance output provides a list of occurrences of a word or grammatical item taken from a corpus. This software – for example, AntConc and Wordsmith – can generate word lists, collocations and linguistic tagging.

Content-based instruction (CBI) This approach to course design focuses on teaching content using the foreign language. In a strong form of CBI there is more focus on content. In a weak form of CBI there is more of a focus on language.

Content and language integrated learning (CLIL) This term is widely used to refer to CBI models of courses. It is more likely to be used in Europe, whereas CBI has a strong tradition in the US.

Conversation analysis This refers to a type of discourse analysis that focuses on the intricacies of spoken language. The analysis looks at turn-taking, discourse markers, openings and closings.

Corpus A corpus refers to a collection of texts which can be analysed using computer software. An analysis of a corpus can focus on vocabulary, grammar or structure and can provide insights into the textual needs of ESP students.

Critical ESP Critical ESP considers the political nature of communication in ESP. It considers the power balance within ESP networks and highlights the rights of students and the extent to which they can influence decisions made within the target communicative situation.

DELNA This is the Diagnostic English Language Needs Assessment, the procedure mandated by the University of Auckland, New Zealand, as a means of identifying problems with academic skills. These are then partnered with EAP courses targeting particular academic skills.

Discourse analysis Discourse analysis involves the analysis of texts – spoken or written – in terms of structure, language and vocabulary. In current approaches to ESP course design, discourse analysis of texts from the target communicative situation play an important role.

English for academic purposes (EAP) This comes in various guises and refers to courses that aim to prepare or help university students with the English necessary for study. These courses are often termed 'pre-sessional' or 'in-sessional'. Pre-sessional courses prepare students for future study, while in-sessional courses help students while they study.

English for business purposes (EBP) This refers to English used for commerce. It also covers the study area of business English – for example, accounting and business administration. English is used as a lingua franca to conduct business across linguistic boundaries.

English for educational purposes English for educational purposes refers to EAP taught in schools, typically secondary schools preparing students for tertiary study.

English for general academic purposes (EGAP) This term describes EAP that is general in subject area, focuses on content and contains no specialist terms. This is the basis of most published EAP coursebooks.

English as a lingua franca (ELF) ELF refers to the English used by non-native speakers to communicate. ELF is used by a far greater number of speakers than English as a native language.

English for nursing English for nursing has two main areas: technical and social. The technical side rests on being able to understand and communicate about medical treatment and procedures. Nurses also need to be able to communicate with patients, using everyday language.

English for occupational purposes (EOP) This branch of ESP focuses on work-related English. There are a number of branches of EOP related to particular jobs, such as English for engineers and English for careworkers.

English for specific academic purposes (ESAP) This refers to EAP that is specific in content area – for example, English to study chemistry. Students studying such courses will all have a similar discipline background.

ESP practitioner This term is preferred in ESP as it captures the range of roles an ESP teacher has – for example, needs analyser, course designer, assessor.

Ethnography This is a methodological approach to course design that involves participation in the discourse community – for example, students writing ethnographic research from within the community.

Foundation courses A foundation course is a type of EAP course that combines subject study and English study. Foundation courses are typically pre-sessional and undergraduate. They address entry needs in terms of subject and language.

Functions Functions of language attempt to account for the communicative acts language is used for – for example, requesting and inviting.

Genre Genre analysis of texts plays an important role in ESP course design. A genre is basically a type of text, and by analysing regular features of a range of text types or genres this can inform course design. Genre analysis has been greatly enhanced by developments in corpus analysis.

In-sessional EAP This term refers to EAP courses that are provided concurrently with academic courses at English-medium universities. The courses are usually more specific than pre-sessional courses.

Lexical patterning This refers to words that occur together. Multi-word units are words linked together in a idiomatic way: collocations, lexical bundles and word groups commonly occur together.

MASUS   The MASUS (Measuring the Academic Skills of University Students) procedure is a diagnostic technique used at the University of Sydney to identify academic shortcomings. It can be tailored to specific subject areas and assessed by expert or non-expert markers. The shortcomings are paired with academic skills courses offered by the university's Learning Centre.

Needs analysis   Needs analysis is the initial stage in ESP course design. Data is collected from the major stakeholders and the target communicative situation is analysed. Based on these findings, a course can then be drawn up that identifies what learners need to learn in order to operate in the target communicative situation.

Present-situation analysis   This term refers to the needs analysis that is conducted to discover learners' learning and classroom needs. This is contrasted with target-situation needs.

Pre-sessional EAP   This refers to EAP training provided to students prior to enrolling on their academic courses at English-medium universities. These courses are usually EGAP and may include a formal high-stakes assessment, such as IELTS.

Problem-based learning (PBL)   PBL is a methodological approach to teaching that focuses on problem solving. The approach is common in medical studies. It involves presenting a problem which the students need to research and propose a solution for in groups. A typical example in medicine is the presentation of a disease which students have to identify and then suggest how it should be treated.

Process/product approaches to writing   Traditionally the teaching of writing adopted a product approach. This means the emphasis was on identifying the nature of a written text and focusing on reproducing it as a product. A process approach to writing focuses on *how* a text is written. Usually, writers go through stages in writing from planning to drafting and finally editing a text.

Rights analysis   This is a critical perspective on needs analysis that bears in mind the balance of power of stakeholders, as put forward by Benesch (1996).

Systemic functional linguistics/grammar   An approach to describing language in terms of field (what's going on), tenor (who's involved) and mode (channel of communication). Genre plays an important role in this description.

Target-situation analysis   This is a term used in needs analysis to refer to data collected in relation to the target communicative situation. The target communicative situation is the end goal of the learning and reflects authentic situated interaction.

Threshold level   This refers to a minimum level of language competence required before ESP courses can start (originally put forward by van Ek, 1980).

Vocabulary learning strategies (VLS)   These are techniques for learning and planning the learning of vocabulary. They are classed as language-learning strategies (LLS). For a list of these see Schmitt (1997).

Vocabulary types   ESP vocabulary is often classified according to its specificity. Technical vocabulary refers to those specialist words understood by experts; semi-technical words may be understood by a general audience but are likely to have specialist meaning in the field; and general vocabulary refers to everyday words necessary for any form of communication.

References

Benesch, S. (1996). Needs analysis and curriculum development in EAP: An example of a critical approach. *TESOL Quarterly, 30*(4), 723–38. doi:10.2307/3587931.

Bloor, T., & Bloor, M. (1986). *Languages for specific purposes*. Dublin: Trinity College.

Canale, M., & Swain, M. (1980). Theoretical bases of communicative approaches to second language teaching and testing. *Applied Linguistics, 1*(1), 1–47.

Schmitt, N. (1997). Vocabulary learning strategies. In Schmitt, N. & McCarthy, M. (Eds.), *Vocabulary: Description, Acquisition, and Pedagogy*. Cambridge: Cambridge University Press.

van Ek, J. A. (1980). *Threshold level of English: Council of Europe Modern Languages Project*. Strasbourg: Council of Europe.

Index